# SUBSTANCE UNDER PRESSURE

# SUBSTANCE

# UNDER PRESSURE

*Artistic Coherence and
Evolving Form in the Novels
of Doris Lessing*

## Betsy Draine

The University of Wisconsin Press

Published 1983

The University of Wisconsin Press
114 North Murray Street
Madison, Wisconsin 53715

The University of Wisconsin Press, Ltd.
1 Gower Street
London WC1E 6HA, England

First printing

Printed in the United States of America

ISBN 0-299-09230-5

Library of Congress Cataloging in Publication Data
Draine, Betsy, 1945–
Substance under pressure.
Bibliography: pp. 207–215.
Includes index.
1. Lessing, Doris May, 1919–      – Criticism and
interpretation. I. Title.
PR6023.E833Z63 1983      823′.914      82-70556
ISBN 0-299-09230-5

For my Parents
RICHARD and ALICE DRAINE

# Contents

# ACKNOWLEDGMENTS

Those who have written before me on Lessing's works deserve foremost place in any list of acknowledgments. I particularly wish to credit John L. Carey, Annis Pratt, and Sydney Janet Kaplan, whose work has laid a foundation for all subsequent Lessing criticism. I warmly thank those who have read this manuscript and given their advice: my colleagues Walter Rideout, Eric Rothstein, Annis Pratt, and John Lyons; Claire Sprague of Brooklyn College; Anne Hedin of Indiana University; and Dee Seligman, Lessing's bibliographer.

For summer research grants, I thank the Chancellor and the Graduate Research Committee of the University of Wisconsin–Madison. For their aid in preparing materials and typing manuscripts, I thank B. J. Lins, Kathy Dauck, Dee Briley, and Cindy Townsend. For their gracious and efficient management of all aspects of this book's publication, I thank Mary Wyer, Peter Givler, and Debra Bernardi of the University of Wisconsin Press.

Finally, special thanks to Professors Alan Wilde and George McFadden of Temple University, for their guidance and encouragement over many years.

# Introduction

The career of Doris Lessing now spans thirty years and five genres. She has published fifteen novels, numerous short stories, four prose volumes, two plays, and a book of poems. Few writers are more prolific. Nonetheless, *diversity* rather than abundance is the hallmark of her career as a novelist. In fact, her variability has become a critical problem. One well might ask: Can there be artistic coherence in a body of novels that includes examples of tragedy, socialist realism, *Bildungsroman*, modernist perspectivism, parody, allegory, quest romance, parable, legend, and science-fiction saga? Where is the ideological integrity of a novelist who appears at various times a Communist, a quietist, and a mystic? Is there stability of theme in an oeuvre that at various times treats racial injustice, the corruption of liberal communism, the drift of the West towards political and ecological catastrophe, the problem of world hunger, the stultification of woman in marriage and the family, the saving potential of madness, and most recently the possibilities of intergalactic conflict and cooperation in a cosmic evolutionary experiment?

On the subject of continuity and change, Lessing has written: "This is a catastrophic universe, always; and subject to sudden reversals, upheavals, changes, cataclysms, with joy never anything but the song of substance under pressure forced into new forms and shapes."[1] With these words the extraterrestrial narrator Johor opens *Shikasta*, the first book of Lessing's space-fiction series *Canopus in Argos: Archives*. Through Johor's statement, Lessing announces not only the ontological principle of her most recent fictional space but also — perhaps unconsciously — the generative principle of her fictional career.

In the fictional galaxy of Canopus, the substance of being is one, infinite, and eternal. Yet the pressure of cosmic evolution forces that basic substance into "forms and shapes" that are multiple, finite, and ever new, ever changing, ever striving toward self-transcendence.[2] Likewise in the universe of Lessing's fiction, there is a central and abiding thematic substance, but it is constantly under the pressure of artistic evolution. A single theme persists throughout her work, but the "forms and shapes" of her novels are "subject to sudden reversals, upheavals, changes, cataclysms," under the pressure of her drive toward self-transcendence in the realm of fictional technique.

Previous critics have stressed the apparent changes in Lessing's vision and have traced the effects of these changes on her choice of form. In *The Novels of Doris Lessing*, Paul Schlueter divides Lessing's works into categories according to major themes, which he lists serially as communism among leftists in the 1930s and 1940s, racism in British colonial Africa, the dilemma of the modern "free woman," and writing itself as a therapeutic and creative reaction to the chaos of contemporary life. Viewing his book as an introductory study, Schlueter confines himself mainly to thematic analysis, and when he does deal with technique he treats it as an outgrowth of theme.

Building on Schlueter's work, Mary Ann Singleton seeks a unified view of Lessing's oeuvre in symbolic terms. Her book, *The City and the Veld: The Fiction of Doris Lessing*, traces the interaction of three motifs in Lessing's work: the veld, representing the unconsciousness of nature; the city, representing the achievements of human consciousness; and the ideal City, "a new and more unified form of consciousness, . . . the Golden Age finally at hand."[3] In Singleton's view, Lessing's style is dictated in each novel by the dominance of one of these three motifs. The veld demands a symbolic approach, the city calls forth realism, and the ideal City expresses itself in myth and archetype.

Roberta Rubenstein returns the dimension of time to a study of Lessing's career. In *The Novelistic Vision of Doris Lessing*, Rubenstein documents the shifts in Lessing's understanding of the nature of consciousness, and she argues that alterations in her ideas "led Lessing to change the form of her fiction."[4] Rubenstein marks three stages of concept and consequent form: the stage of "Breaking Down, Breaking Out" (1950–1958), the stage of "Breaking Through" (1962–1969), and the stage of "Returning to the Center" (1971–1975).

For all three of the major critics who have attempted an overview of Lessing's career, idea or image is primary; the form follows, functionally. Without offering a simple obverse to this approach, I want to call attention to the evolution of form as an imperative in itself, and as a pressure on content. While doing so, I hope to open up as well the possibility of evaluation — an element that has been conspicuously absent in Lessing criticism. When we trace the course of biological evolution, we find it possible to make distinctions between those developments which increase and diversify life in productive ways and those sports or mutations that simply do not work. In fact, the judgments we make as to what constitutes vitality, strength, or progress in the evolutionary line are enormously important to our *self*-definition, biologically, morally, politically, even metaphysically. Analogously, it is not only possible but necessary that, as literary critics, we make judgments as to what constitutes progress, health, vitality — and what constitutes their opposites — in the evolutionary line of a writer's career.

The form of Doris Lessing's fiction has certainly undergone a rapid and eventful course of evolution, but there has been no radical change in her basic themes. Lessing herself has recently denied that her work has "changed direction"; on the contrary, she declares that her themes have been constant since *The Grass Is Singing*, her first novel.[5] In an interview in 1980, she reiterates the famous statement of theme from her 1957 essay "The Small Personal Voice." She said then of her series *Children of Violence:* "I was at pains to state the theme very clearly: that this is a study of the individual conscience in its relations with the collective."[6] In 1980 she repeats, more broadly: "I always write about the individual and that which surrounds him."[7] The continuity of Lessing's vision lies in her constant attention to "the individual conscience" — the individual's limited view of and evaluation of reality, as it is related to and dependent on his or her society's conventions of perception and value. From the beginning to the end of her career, Lessing is fascinated with the dynamics of this relation and with the evolution of human consciousness through this dynamic. History is, for her, the record of the evolution of consciousness. "What interests me more than anything [in history]," she says, "is how our minds are changing."[8] Lessing's unchanging subject is itself change — in the individual and the collective consciousness.

For a writer, alterations in "ways of perceiving reality" manifest themselves openly — and often naively — in changes of form. On the other hand, a change of form itself constitutes, as much as it reflects, a change in the mode of perception — a change in the way that the "substance" of life is apprehended. Formal changes are thus both determined by the historical factors that create changes in perception, and determinant of the perceptual set of the work of art. At the balance point of these countervailing pressures is the imagination of the author, which is itself always acting under the pressure of "a need, an imperative, towards a continual striving, or self-transcendence."[9]

It is important, therefore, to trace the historical influences on Lessing's formal choices. Her commitment to Marxism forced her to grapple with the power of deterministic thinking, and that struggle manifested itself in the tragic form she adopted in *The Grass Is Singing*. Her dialectical attraction to the progressivist element in Marxism expressed itself in her use of the *Bildungsroman* structure in *Children of Violence*. Her sense of duty in upholding the tenets of socialist realism was reflected in the programmatic Marxism of *Retreat to Innocence* and the scrupulous detailings of political processes in the middle books of the *Children of Violence* series. The breakdown of her generation's Marxist faith and her struggle with relativism found a formal equivalent in the splintered and dizzying structure of *The Golden Notebook*. The influence of R. D. Laing's psycho-political theories in leftist culture of the late 1960s had its effect on Lessing's experiments with point of view and with stream-of-consciousness technique in *Briefing for a Descent into Hell*. Her study of Sufi thought and literature under Idries Shah directly influenced the structure and rhetorical strategies of *Briefing, The Memoirs of a Survivor, The Summer Before the Dark*, and *The Marriages Between Zones Three, Four, and Five*. Finally, Lessing's deep distress over world politics and world ecology in the late 1970s led her to seek a framework within which to speculate on future history, and she found such a framework in the science-fiction format of *Canopus in Argos: Archives*. In her formal choices Lessing has been highly responsive to historical and even ideological influence.

It is equally important, however, to realize that Lessing's formal choices have themselves influenced the content of her novels, and that the series of these choices has its own internal logic. While Lessing's initial move into a genre or style may be influenced strongly by ideological loyalties, her development of the potentialities inherent in each form seems to proceed by the laws of exhaustion and reaction. She pursues the possibilities and implications of each formal choice to their furthest limits; having reached the point of exhaustion, she catapults herself in nearly the opposite direction and follows the new line of formal development to its endpoint. Witness how the tragic impulse, completely fulfilled in *The Grass Is Singing*, is countered by the relatively comic thrust of *Children of Violence*. Upon finishing the third book of the series, however, Lessing recognizes that she has depleted the possibilities of the socialist realism that had permeated both *The Grass Is Singing* and *Children of Violence*. She therefore departs from the series to write a tour de force of modernist perspectivism, *The Golden Notebook* —a work that radically questions the realism and objectivity which formed the basis of the style and structure of her previous works. Returning to the *Children of Violence* series, she makes another turn-about, abandoning both socialist and modernist attitudes toward realism for a new preoccupation with the visionary and with techniques for evoking visionary experience in her novels. Moving dialectically, the evolutionary line of Lessing's technique delivers her most recently into the genre of space fiction, but this, like the other formal choices before it, is clearly only one stage in her formal development.

The use of the word "evolutionary" above ought to counsel against labeling any one of Lessing's choices of genre or technique as her definitive or perfected form. While some critics delight in arguing the inherent superiority of one of Lessing's formal modes (some prefer the "realistic" novels, others the "visionary" ones), it may be wise to follow Lessing's lead in recognizing that her moments of artistic triumph are very often moments of upheaval — moments in which the "perfected" forms are broken by the intrusion of new and unexpected imperatives. It is the history of these formal cataclysms — and of the readerly joy which they make possible — that I attempt to trace in this study of Lessing's works.

# SUBSTANCE UNDER PRESSURE

# Chapter One

# *The Grass Is Singing*
## PRESSURES OF FORM AND IDEOLOGY

There is every reason for *The Grass Is Singing* to be viewed as the most critically inviting of all Doris Lessing's novels. Since its publication in 1950, reviewers have called it "one of the best first novels of our time," "an extremely mature psychological study," a book remarkable for its atmosphere of "solitude and fear and hopelessness," "a powerful and bitter book," with "a piercing accuracy of progressive despair that is astonishing in so young a writer."[1] On the basis of emotional impact alone, the novel would seem to be remarkable.

To add to the intrigue, Lessing has published a fictional account of her struggle with guilt over the book's tone and its potential effect on its readers. In *The Golden Notebook*, Lessing's transparently autobiographical heroine Anna Wulf anguishes over the political and moral irresponsibility of her first novel, *Frontiers of War*. Anna's novel, like *The Grass Is Singing*, treats the subject of racial injustice in modern Africa by focusing on the forbidden erotic relation between a white colonial and a black servant. One might have thought that critics would seize the opportunity to re-evaluate Lessing's powerful first novel in the light of her self-recriminations concerning it. Oddly, no one has done so, and in fact there has been very little critical treatment of the novel from any angle.[2] Perhaps the critics have been as nonplussed by the contradictions and complexities of the novel as Lessing herself seems to

3

have been for the dozen years that passed between its publication and her oblique commentary on it.

When Lessing began writing *The Grass Is Singing*, she was herself a white colonial living in Rhodesia,[3] the daughter of poor British-born farmers who, like all other farmers there, employed black laborers and kept them in a menial condition. Through her own experience she knew the mind of the white settler intimately and thus could accurately and sympathetically depict the motivations and rationalizations of Mary and Dick Turner, the white couple whose failures with each other and with their black workers form the subject of *The Grass Is Singing*. At the same time, however, Lessing had reason to distance herself from her characters and their perspective on race and labor. From her early youth, she had recognized the injustice of Rhodesia's institutionalized racism,[4] and since 1942 her opinions on class, labor, and race had been highly influenced by a commitment to communism.[5]

Here we have the makings of the first level of contradiction in the text. On the one hand, Lessing intends to expose the injustices that white African farmers perpetrate against their black workers; on the other hand, she wants to present fully and vividly the mind of the white oppressor, represented here by Mary Turner. The more complete the depiction of the white woman's consciousness, the more likely the reader will sympathize with her; the more complete the sympathy for her (the oppressor), the less sharply the reader will condemn her racist cruelties. Lessing's attempt to achieve fullness of understanding at the personal and psychological level is at odds with her desire for clarity of insight at the social and political level.

The dilemma posed by Lessing's distance from her characters has its counterpart in a contradiction of broader formal imperatives. Her Marxist-humanist commitment would seem to suggest that she might adopt the conventions of socialist realism, the better to detail the material workings of an unjust social order. Indeed, a simple melodramatic structure might be best suited to present the conflict between Mary Turner and her servant Moses as representative of the larger class antagonisms between capitalist exploiter and proletarian worker, between the colonizing white race and the colonized black race. However, Lessing's own emotional involvement with her material leads her to present it in tragic terms. This is a dangerous formal choice. Lessing's political commitment requires her to identify the oppressor and the oppressed, put them in opposition, and dignify the struggle of the oppressed (in their valor and innocence) against the oppressors (in their cowardice and guilt). Tragedy, in its form and ethos, demands instead that a single hero—from *either* side—be shown as simultaneously innocent and guilty, valiant and cowardly, oppressive and oppressed. The doubleness, the ambiguity, that is essential to tragedy could easily vitiate the moral force of Lessing's desired critique of racism in Africa.

After the fact, Lessing seems to have entertained doubts as to the wisdom of casting her material in tragic form. In *The Golden Notebook*, her fictional counterpart Anna Wulf writes a mock-review of her first novel, in a convoluted expression of self-doubt:

> The simplicity of Anna Wulf's style is her strength; but it is too soon to say whether this is the conscious simplicity of artistic control, or the often deceptive sharpness of form which is sometimes arbitrarily achieved by allowing the shape of a novel to be dictated by a strong emotion.[6]

Anna later isolates and names that emotion:

> The emotion it came out of was something frightening, the unhealthy, feverish illicit excitement of wartime, a lying nostalgia, a longing for licence, for freedom, for the jungle, for formlessness. . . . It is an immoral novel because that terrible lying nostalgia lights every sentence. And I know that in order to write another, to write those fifty reports on society which I have the material to write, I would have to deliberately whip up in myself that same emotion. And it would be that emotion which would make those fifty books novels and not reportage.[7]

In the case of *The Grass Is Singing*, "that emotion" which makes the novel a novel is not nostalgia but the tragic emotion, that complex attitude which allows us both to pity the willful heroine, even in the commission of her worst crimes, and to feel a terror of her ignorant malice that can be purged only in her annihilation.[8] If she is to write a tragic novel, Lessing *must* "deliberately whip up" the guiding emotion of pity mixed with terror; a tragedy, according to Aristotle, must "excite pity and fear, this being the distinctive mark of tragic imitation."[9] Tragedy, like any other literary form, has its controlling emotion, which shapes the material into a recognizable form.

This necessity to subject her material to the distorting control of a "lying" emotion makes Anna Wulf feel inauthentic as a social critic. She tells herself that in the service of truth she should have written simply "an account of what had happened, instead of shaping a 'story'"[10] through the application of a defining emotion. Anna's attitude echoes the more simplistic theories of literature and especially of tragedy that would have been dominant in the leftist study groups that Lessing frequented in the 1940s in Rhodesia.[11] The general notion was that tragedy is a decadent, bourgeois art form—"spiritual dope traffic,"[12] in the

words of Bertolt Brecht — which reconciles the audience to the inevitability of human suffering. Brecht, whose theoretical and dramatic work
may have been known in Lessing's political circles, specifically de-
nounces the use of empathy for the tragic hero, because he believes that
identification with the hero prevents the audience from making an objective analysis of those contradictions in the social situation which ne-
cessitate both the hero's crime and its punishment.[13] Under the pressure
of such ideological opposition to tragedy, Lessing doubtless had twinges
of Anna's shame at having succumbed to the lure of tragic emotion.

It is, however, precisely this tension between documenting an injustice and giving it a tragic dimension that makes *The Grass Is Singing*
such a powerful political and artistic statement. On the political level,
the tragic form that Lessing selects helps to save the dialectical method
of analysis from being reduced, in the course of artistic representation,
to the level of a static polarity. The tragic form, with its insistence that
the hero be the conduit of antithetical forces, not the simple representative of one pole, offers an appropriate frame for the enactment of a dialectical drama. Moreover, the tragic form gives the plot a frighteningly
rapid momentum, and the gathering terror of the unavoidable culminating violence makes the novel compelling in every line. The intensity
of attention that Lessing thus commands from the reader she then channels toward questions that, inherent in the action, are also crucial to
Marxist theory.

Through the tragedy of Mary Turner's blind racism and her punishment for it, Lessing gives the reader a vision of evil. At time she seems to
illustrate the tragic (and un-Marxian) view that evil is irremediable and
inherent both in nature at large and in human nature. She seems to
demonstrate the inevitability of suffering by tracing its origin in hered-
ity, personal psychology, and the social structure. She gives very little
indication of how change — either personal or social — might be brought
about. Still, in her brutally honest depiction of the forces that sanction
racial and class injustice, she prepares the way for a recognition that
must alienate her readers from those invidious social forces and prepare
them to take a stand against them. In this novel, Lessing uses the power
of catharsis in the service of the politically responsible goal that is constant throughout her fiction, both the early Marxist-oriented novels and
the novels written long after she had repudiated Marxism: that is, to reveal to her readers that although every person's perspective has been
thoroughly determined by material forces (political, economic, social,
familial), one can nonetheless free oneself from the blinders of conventional thought in an act of re-self-possession. That act of reclaiming the
power to judge one's own experience is Mary Turner's triumph at the

end of *The Grass Is Singing*. It is a moment of awakening both to a fate and to a responsibility. Moreover, that moment is managed by Lessing so as to serve the ends of both tragedy and social analysis.

The concerns of tragedy and Marxist theory converge around the issue of how various forms of power dominate individual destiny.[14] Whether the imposing power is social, economic, political, psychological (or even, in the case of tragedy, divine), the key question is whether and how the individual can break the chain of material circumstance, which is inexorable only in the absence of a consciousness of it. In *The Grass Is Singing*, Lessing gives us a central character who is wholly unconscious of the forces that make her a racist and that will, eventually, make her responsible for the death of her black servant. Gradually, Lessing unfolds for the reader the conditions that have made Mary Turner's racism and her eventual crime "inevitable."

The sense of tragic inevitability is built into the very structure of the novel. The opening paragraph is the newspaper account of the murder of Mary Turner by her native houseboy, and we soon move to the scene of the murder. The presence of the "stiff shape under a soiled white sheet" (p. 19)[15] dominates the chapter, keeping ever before the reader's attention the fact of Mary's death. As readers we primarily share the point of view of Tony Marston, a young British man who has been only a few weeks on the farm as assistant to Dick Turner. His attitude toward the body before him and his intention toward it are ours also. Twice he calls Mary's death a tragedy, and twice he struggles with the twin emotions of tragedy. "It was mainly *pity* that agitated him," but at the same time he recognizes twinges in himself of the "*horror* and fear" that possess the other white men who have come to view Mary's body (p. 23, my italics). He suffers, in fact, under this twin burden of emotion. "Why should this happen to me," he protests — "getting involved with a damned twisted affair like this, when I have only just come; and I really can't be expected to act as judge and jury and compassionate God into the bargain!" (pp. 34–35). But that *is* his double charge — and the reader's.

In the service of both sympathy and judgment, both pity and horror, the root causes of the murder must be uncovered. As Marston stands in the presence of Mary's body, he examines his attitudes toward the tragedy.

> The important thing, the thing that really mattered, so it seemed to him, was to understand the background, the circumstances, the characters of Dick and Mary, the pattern of their lives. . . . And his chief emotion, which was an impersonal pity for Mary and Dick and the native, a pity

that was also rage against circumstances, made it difficult for him to know
where to begin. (p. 26)

Struck by the mixed emotions of tragedy — the "pity that was also rage
against circumstances" — he feels his intellect to be stunned. But appalled by the indifference of the other white men toward Mary's death,
he determines to think the situation through to full consciousness and
understanding. In his resolve, he sets a prospectus for the novel:

> He wondered how all this had begun, where the tragedy had started. For
> he clung obstinately to the belief, in spite of Slatter and the Sergeant, that
> the causes of the murder must be looked for a long way back, and that it
> was they which were important. What sort of woman had Mary Turner
> been, before she came to this farm and had been driven slowly off balance
> by heat and loneliness and poverty? And Dick Turner himself — what had
> he been? And the native — but here his thoughts were stopped by lack of
> knowledge. He could not even begin to imagine the mind of a native.
>     Passing his hand over his forehead, he tried desperately, and for the last
> time, to achieve some sort of a vision that would lift the murder above the
> confusions and complexities of the morning, and make of it, perhaps, a
> symbol, or a warning. But he failed. (p. 34)

The vision and the symbolic significance that Marston fails to achieve
in the first chapter of the novel, Lessing supplies for him in the chapters
that follow. Marston does not continue as a focus of consciousness, but
the questions and attitudes that he sets forth in chapter one organize the
rest of the novel.

Marston is convinced "that the causes of the murder must be looked
for a long way back, and that it was they which were important." Having this conviction, he shares the perspectives of both Marxism and
tragedy. The Marxist analyst looks for the causes of individual behavior
in material conditions that have far-reaching historical roots; the writer
with a tragic perspective considers each event in the light of a fate
which has been unfolding for years, or for generations. Marston likewise seeks the links of cause and effect that have created Mary Turner's
destiny. Indeed, he goes further than that — he takes a decidedly deterministic view of her character.

This term "deterministic" is a vexed one, as is well documented in
Raymond Williams's analysis of the word "determine" in his *Keywords:
A Vocabulary of Culture and Society*.[16] There Williams identifies several problems of interpretation that bear on Lessing's handling of the
issue. Williams points out that while a given condition may be seen in
retrospect to have determined a chain of events, so that the final event

seems to have been inevitable, it is quite another thing to project the sense of inevitability forward into future events. Williams warns that when such a projection occurs, "the observation of real determining factors — forces that set limits or exert pressures — can be quickly inflated into a *fatalism (determinism)* in which everything is already decided — *predetermined*, as it is often put for emphasis — and we have merely to wait for it to happen."[17]

In *The Grass Is Singing*, the reader must struggle under the weight of the predetermined, until the moment of sudden unburdening at the end of the text. At that moment of "recognition," the reader exchanges the heavy foreknowledge of events for an understanding of those events in a liberating perspective. The liberating factor is a degree of consciousness that makes both responsibility and choice possible.

In later novels, Lessing continues this pattern of subjecting the reader to an atmosphere of dark inevitability, granting deliverance only in key moments of illumination. In the five-volume *Children of Violence* series the long arm of the predetermined lies especially heavy in the first four books. There, as in *The Grass Is Singing*, a thoroughgoing determinism, influenced by both Marx and Freud, seems to deprive human beings of the freedom to make their own history, either socially or personally.

Tony Marston sees Mary Turner in such a strictly deterministic light. Setting aside the possibility of moral judgment, he says: "One can't really blame her either. She can't help being what she is" (p. 32). His statement has both a social and a psychological dimension. It is the psychological determinism that Lessing chooses to develop first. Chapter two begins a retrospective account of Mary Turner's life, told from the perspective of an omniscient narrator. Throughout the story of Mary's childhood, her parents' marriage, her childhood, and her years as a career girl in town, the analysis of her character presupposes a kind of Freudian psychic determinism. As she traces Mary's sexual aversion to a classically Freudian "primal scene" complex, the narrator concludes fatalistically: "But then there are so many people who don't want them [the joys of life]: so many for whom the best things have been poisoned from the start" (p. 49). With this passing comment, the reader is encouraged to link the "sick" elements of Mary's later character with the poisons in her early life. If in her career years she "seemed not to care for men," if she "just isn't like that, . . . something missing somewhere" (pp. 48, 51), this must derive from her identification with her mother's "contempt and derision" for her father. "She had inherited from her mother an arid feminism, which had no meaning in her own life at all" (p. 44). We are led to feel that this psychic legacy fully determines that the adult Mary will both desert her aging father and avoid intimacy with men her own age.

Moreover, the Freudian principle of repetition[18] is demonstrated in Mary's replaying the role she had seen her mother play with her father. She chooses a husband as ineffectual as her father, and begins to despair as the life that he gives her takes on the pattern of her mother's. She cannot complain to Dick, she thinks, because he "was now associated in her mind with the grayness and misery of her childhood, and it would have been like arguing with destiny itself" (p. 132). In fights with Dick, her voice "was taken direct from her mother, when she had had those scenes over money with her father" (p. 108). In scene after scene, Lessing damns Mary to her determined fate: "Mary, with the memory of her own mother recurring more and more frequently, like an older, sardonic double of herself walking beside her, followed the course her upbringing made *inevitable*" (p. 126, my italics).

Nothing is more threatening to our sense of human dignity than the idea that we are doomed to repeat the pattern of our parents and of our childhood, without the capacity to alter the shape of our own lives. When a writer premises her fiction on the idea of such inevitability and makes us follow the working out of destiny, step by step, we the readers are thrown into a state of emotional panic. The implications of such a mechanistic view of human life are simply intolerable. They are the makings of modern tragedy, in which the old-fashioned word "fate" is superseded by "how it is" and "how it must be," in our personal, our social, and our political lives.

In Lessing's own analysis, action, however tragic, is an expression not only of personal character but also of the social conditions in which character and action are rooted. One of two epigraphs to the novel reads, "It is by the failures and misfits of a civilization that one can best judge its weaknesses." The word "judge" is a strange one in the context of psychic determinism that seems to inscribe the novel. The word shows up again in Dorothy Brewster's discussion of the novel. She says, "one feels that everything—people, landscape, social order, and attitudes—has been closely observed and reflected upon, that there have been pity and indignation in the process, which make themselves felt in bitter undercurrents of judgment on the conditions that make such tragic failures possible."[19] What place do "bitter undercurrents of judgment" have in a modern tragedy? The presence of an attitude of psychic determinism might be thought to vitiate the possibility of firm moral judgment. If one uses the perspective of determinism to assess an action by an individual, one must search for the first cause, the primal action for which someone or something could be held fully responsible

—but one can never see that far back. Therefore one cannot place responsibility.

In stressing the workings of determinism on the psychological level, then, Lessing has made it difficult to construct a clear critique of white racism (or of sexism) as it manifests itself in individual actions. Since the novel focuses on the neurotic Mary Turner and her racist actions, it tends to treat acts of social injustice most forcefully as evidence of long-standing psychological disturbance, which again has its roots in a long family history. With auxiliary characters, Lessing does shift the interest to the broader social level, which would seem to give more scope for the criticism of social and political institutions. Still, even here Lessing presents the conflict of the races not so much as a social problem requiring immediate rectification, but as an instance of the intolerable "how it is": social attitudes, like psychological ones, have been inevitably determined by past conditions and attitudes.

Lessing emphasizes this social determinism by presenting the particular behaviors of individuals involved in the racial conflict as mechanical manifestations of group attitudes, of which the individual is largely unaware. Group consciousness is just as determined as personal consciousness and just as limiting. On the first page of the novel, for instance, the narrator notes the reaction of the newspaper readers to the account of Mary Turner's murder.

> People all over the country must have glanced at the paragraph with its sensational heading and felt a little spurt of anger mingled with what was almost satisfaction, as if some belief had been confirmed, as if something had happened which could only have been expected. When natives steal, murder or rape, that is the feeling white people have.
> And then they turned the page to something else. (p. 9)

The reader is being counseled, it seems, not to blame the newspaper readers for their response, but to understand that they act out of a pre-established set of group attitudes. While one may, on a personal basis, feel contempt for the mindlessness of the paper-readers, neither the tone nor the content of Lessing's passage solicits a moral judgment of them. If the group shares an attitude and a response, that is simply "the way it is"—in this social group, in this time and place.

A few paragraphs further on, Lessing returns to the subject of group response, in perfectly neutral fashion. She reports that the Turner murder was not discussed among the whites of the country, although normally "people would have been positively grateful for something to talk about" (p. 10).

> To an outsider it would seem perhaps as if the energetic Charlie Slatter had
> traveled from farm to farm over the district telling people to keep quiet;
> but that was something that would never have occurred to him. The steps
> he took (and he made not one mistake) were taken apparently instinctively
> and without conscious planning. The most interesting thing about the
> whole affair was the silent, unconscious agreement. Everyone behaved
> like a flock of birds who communicate — or so it seems — by means of a kind
> of telepathy. (p. 10)

The "bitter undercurrents of judgment" that Dorothy Brewster finds so
pervasive in the novel are certainly missing here and, I would argue, in
most of the first half of the novel. As Lessing builds the atmosphere of
tragic inevitability, there is little room for judgment, which assumes the
possibility of choice.

Lessing achieves a kind of balance in her depiction of social determinism by showing that not only the whites but also the blacks are
trapped in a set of mind dictated by their culture. For instance, the
native Moses's decision to remain at the scene of the murder is explained
in the light of his obligations as a Matabele tribesman:

> The laws were strict: everyone knew what they could or could not do. If
> someone did an unforgiveable thing, like touching one of the King's
> women, he would submit fatalistically to punishment, which was likely to
> be impalement over an ant heap on a stake, or something equally unpleas-
> ant. "I have done wrong, and I know it," he might say, "therefore let me be
> punished." Well, it was the tradition to face punishment, and really there
> was something rather fine about it. (p. 14)

Since the purpose of the novel is to reveal the limitations of the oppress-
ing white culture, however, such instances of black submission to the
native code of conduct are introduced mainly as a foil to the white code.
Here, for example, the native's code encourages him to judge his own
actions strictly and take full responsibility for them, whereas the white
code provides rationalizations for questionable actions and discourages
self-doubt. The white code is used primarily to judge others, while the
native code provides a standard for self-judgment and self-responsibility.
In one of a series of conflicts with her houseboys, for instance, Mary
Turner becomes enraged with a new native for never meeting her eyes.
"She did not know it was part of the native code of politeness not to look
a superior in the face; she thought it was merely further evidence of
their shifty and dishonest nature" (p. 95). In this scene, the native is intent upon controlling himself, whereas the white woman is wholly unaware of any need to criticize or control herself. Beyond this implied

comparison, to the dishonor of the white code, Lessing is pursuing the point that both the white woman and the black man are acting impersonally, under the firm control of cultural directives that are—at this point—beyond their comprehension.

The enslavement of the individual by the will of an impersonal cultural demand is clearly demonstrated in the first chapter. As an outsider to the colonial social system, Tony Marston "was disconcerted: the unexpectedness of these men's responses was taking him right out of his depth. He was feeling nothing that they were feeling" (p. 25). For example, Tony is shocked that the Sergeant and Slatter show no interest in learning the facts concerning the murder. In fact, they block the presentation of evidence.

> It wasn't a formal occasion, this: Tony clung to the thought. There was a court case to come yet, which would be properly conducted.
> "The case will be a matter of form, of course," said the Sergeant, as if thinking aloud. (p. 29)

Such juxtapositions demonstrate the narrator's analysis of what is behind Tony's dilemma: "The two standards—the one he had brought with him [from England] and the one he was adopting [in South Africa] —conflicted still" (p. 21). He is just one of all those English settlers who "could not stand out against the society they were joining" (p. 21). It will be only a matter of time before he learns to suppress all observations and insights that conflict with the group consciousness of the society he wishes to join. For example, after discovering blatant indications of a sexual relationship between Mary Turner and her servant Moses, Marston is momentarily appalled, but he seems to put the information out of mind almost immediately. Rather explicitly, Lessing explains why: "He would do his best to forget the knowledge, for to live with the color bar in all its nuances and implications means closing one's mind to many things, if one intends to remain an accepted member of society" (p. 31).

In this novel, then, the theme of psychic determinism in personal history is paralleled by the theme of social determinism in collective history. Lessing seems to be fusing a Freudian analysis of personal experience with a Marxist analysis of group experience. Specifically, the novel objectifies the competing themes of determinism—the Freudian, concentrating on personal history, and the Marxist, focusing on collective history—and then sets against both of these the hope for transcendence of "the determined" in Mary Turner's awakening.

There is a striking parallel to the relations Lessing establishes among these forces, in a statement on determinism by Antonio Labriola, a follower of Marx:

> First, it is evident that in the domain of historico-social determinism, the linking of causes to effects, of conditions to the things conditioned, of antecedents to consequents, is never evident at first sight in the subjective determinism of individual psychology. . . . There is no wish without its determining motive. But beneath the motives and the wish there is the genesis of both, and to reconstruct this genesis we must leave the closed field of consciousness to arrive at the analysis of the simple necessities, which, on the one side, are derived from social conditions, and on the other side are lost in the obscure background of organic dispositions, in ancestry and in atavism.[20]

In reading *The Grass Is Singing*, one focuses immediately on the psychological drama; but simultaneously, in the theme of race relations, the economic and social conditions "beneath the motives and the wish" are being uncovered. Thus Lessing illustrates the essential Marxist principle that "it is not the consciousness of men that determines their existence, but their social existence that determines their consciousness."[21]

Lessing does "leave the closed field of consciousness" to trace the family history that results in Mary's sexual aversions and then to document the social pressures that place her in such a position that her sexual oddity must be her downfall. For it is her move into marriage and life on a farm that precipitate the tragedy. Prior to the marriage, Mary has a perfectly pleasant life, well arranged to avoid the personal intimacy that is so distasteful to her. As a result, "She was a most rare phenomenon: a woman of thirty without love troubles, headaches, backaches, sleeplessness or neurosis" (p. 48). It is marriage that disturbs her happiness — pulling her out of a successful office career only to place her in the role of a farmer's wife, a position for which she is totally unsuited. Worst of all, the marriage simultaneously raises her consciousness of sexuality and hardens her aversion to intercourse — leaving her frustrated, angry, and oversensitive to the attractions of her native servant. It is her obsession with the servant that finally causes her murder.

In the words of Labriola, Lessing reconstructs the genesis of Mary's "wish" — her tragic desire — by analyzing "the simple necessities" of economics and social organization that force her into an ultimately tragic situation. A series of scenes shows how Mary's friends undermine her happiness in her single life and push her toward a marriage that is the worst thing for her. The narrator makes the point that the "friends" are acting as agents of the social order: "All women become conscious, sooner or later, of that impalpable, but steel-strong pressure to get married, and Mary, who was not at all susceptible to atmosphere, or the things people imply, was brought face to face with it suddenly, and most unpleasantly" (p. 50). Mary overhears her friends discussing her sexual inadequacy and her resistance to marriage. Her not marrying is viewed as ridiculous. According to the social system of her era, Mary is "the girl who is 'taken out.' . . . She led a full and active life. Yet it was a passive one, in some respects, for it depended on other people entirely. She was not the kind of woman who initiates parties, or who is the center of a crowd" (p. 47). Thus there is economic justice in her women friends' complaint that "she was not playing her part, for she did not get married" (p. 48). The hidden bargain is that the men will take the young women out and treat them royally if in turn the women will eventually marry and support the men in their work. "South Africa is a wonderful place: for the unmarried white woman" (p. 48), the narrator tells us. There is silence about how it is for married women there. Mary Turner's story says enough about that.

If Mary's story acts as an illustration of how socio-economic conditions impinge upon white women of South Africa, it also illustrates the Marxist principle of dialectics. Within the marriage itself, Mary shows herself to be not the simple "effect" of some static socio-economic "causes" — but to be a line of conduit along which "causes and effects are eternally changing places, so that what is effect here and now will be cause there and then, and vice versa."[22] The very factors which initially spawn her self-defeating actions are in their turn fed and strengthened by those actions. While Mary's sexual aversion to men in general causes her sexual unresponsiveness with her husband, that failure in the marriage in turn intensifies her sexual fears. Similarly, while her unquestioning participation in the racist system of labor causes her particular abuse of the farmworker Moses, her defensiveness in reaction to her injustices pushes her to become an embodiment of the cruelest aspects of that system. Moreover, the development of Mary's pattern of cruelty to her servants, and to Moses especially, proceeds always in dialectical relation to her repression of sexual desire. The more desire she develops and represses, the more cruelty she develops and acts out. And vice versa. Her commission of sadistic acts against the natives feeds her repressed desire all the more.

The strange conversion of elements in dialectical relation is also illustrated in Mary's sudden transformation from a rigid woman with "a profound distaste for sex" (p. 49) to a lascivious coquette obsessed by nothing else but sex. Likewise, there is a dialectical — and kinetic — relation between Mary's will to power and her desire to be dominated.

Thus, though with the natives "she never relaxed her will" but acted like a tyrant, with Dick "she seemed at ease, quiet, almost maternal" (p. 95). Again, dialectically, although Dick's "abasement before her was the greatest satisfaction she knew" (p. 92), she "needed a man stronger than herself" and tried to force Dick to "take the ascendency over her" (p. 177). These tendencies and countertendencies can be explained as the evidence of, on the one hand, repression of natural instinct and, on the other hand, the escape of these repressed psychic forces into the available (though restricted) channels of expression. The terminology of the dialectic, however, seems especially appropriate when we see the connection between the contradictions in Mary Turner's sexual life and the contradictions in the social structure that is the context of her life.

Just as Mary has repressed a sexual urge in order to maintain a contemptuous distance from the men she fears but depends on for support (pp. 53, 92), the white society represses the personal relation with blacks in order to control the more efficiently the powerful bodies which they fear but whose labor they require. In neither case, however, can a static relation of dominance and repression hold for long. Every assertion begets its counter-assertion, and from there the cycle of change proceeds. In fact, in this dialectical relation of repression and rebellious reassertion of the repressed lies one of the strongest affinities of tragedy and Marxist thought—the twin impulses of this novel. Kenneth Burke, in *A Grammar of Motives*, theorizes that tragedy is based on a dialectical pattern of action. The tragic hero, he says, commits an action that is an assertion of will. This assertion calls "forth a counter-assertion in the elements that compose its context. And when the agent is enabled to see in terms of this counter-assertion, he has transcended the state that characterized him at the start."[23] Burke has outlined succinctly the tragic—and at the same time the Marxist—dimension of Mary Turner's story.

Mary's "act of assertion" is her aggression against the native workers. On the one hand, her many acts of harshness against them are a mechanical manifestation of the cultural code by which whites manage their black labor force. On the other hand, her cruelties are a "counter-assertion" in reaction to her own frustrations—sexually, socially, and psychologically—as a farm wife. According to the first view, the scenes in which Mary drives the native workers, oblivious to their human needs, are typical instances of capitalist (and racist) exploitation of labor. In fact, Mary's oppressive treatment of the farm laborers could be considered a fictional gloss on Marx's famous statement on the alienation of labor. "Within capitalism," he writes, "all means for the development of production transform themselves into means of domination over, and

exploitation of, the producers; they mutilate the labourer into a frag-
ment of a man, degrade him to the level of an appendage of a machine,
destroy every remnant of charm in his work, and turn it into a hated toil,
. . . subject[ing] him during the labour-process to a despotism the more
hateful for its meanness."[24] As the agent of capitalism, Mary transforms
the natives into a farming machine and controls them with despotic
rigor. At the same time, Mary herself is one of the mechanical "means
for the development of production," and she has been transformed, by
her social indoctrination, into a "means of domination over, and exploitation of, the producers" — her black workers. Lessing stresses the point,
in fact, reminding the readers that Mary's despotism follows the South
African rule. Long before we see her abusing servants, the narrator explains that "when it came to the point, one never had contact with natives, except in the master-servant relationship. One never knew them
in their own lives, as human beings" (p. 21). Therefore Mary is completely in line in never thinking of "natives as people who had to eat or
sleep: they were either there, or they were not, and what their lives
were when they were out of her sight she had never paused to think" (p.
102). Again, when Mary delivers a scathing lecture to the natives whose
pay she is docking, Lessing tells us that the words are those of her father,
lecturing his native servants. Her attitudes, her actions, and her words
are determined by her cultural training: "they welled up from the part
of her brain that held her earliest memories" (p. 159).

Yet, at the same time, Mary's intemperance in handling her workers
represents a reaction to her personal situation. Frustrated by her husband's ineffectiveness on the farm and in the marriage, Mary fights
back by trying to assert her will over Dick's laborers. It is in carrying out
that "battle of wills" that she whips a native worker in the field because
he defied her by trying to take a drink of water. In taking this action
"she felt as if she had won a battle. It was a victory over these natives,
over herself and her repugnance of them, over Dick and his slow, foolish
shiftlessness" (p. 167). In asserting herself over all that has made her unhappy, however, she elicits the counter-assertion that will cause her
death. The whipped native controls his impulse to strike back immediately, but it is he who murders her two years later. In the broadest sense,
then, the murder of Mary Turner is the final term of a dialectic of assertion and counter-assertion on both the personal and the social level.

The last half of the book, by far the more vivid and moving portion,
represents the dovetailing of the psychological and social processes in
one unified piece of action — the gradual domination of Mary Turner by
the native Moses, her subsequent betrayal of him, and her move toward
accepting responsibility and death.

As chapter eight opens, Mary is at the end of her struggle to make her husband Dick a successful farmer. Unlike Charlie Slatter, who disregards all concerns but those that will pay off in cash, Dick has a dysfunctional love of the land, respect for his trees and his crops, and a desire to keep his own labor within reasonable limits. Dick, at one with the land he works, represents an antithetical theory of labor to Slatter's. Against Slatter's exploitative attitude, Turner posits a conservationist viewpoint, based on respect for the land and for human labor. But a synthesis between the two views is not achievable at this point. The rules of the white establishment are too strong and rigid to allow deviation by one small farmer, especially when he does not even have the support of a sympathetic wife. In Mary's eyes, Dick has first exploited her by bringing her to the harsh life of the farm and then failed her by stubbornly sticking to his idealistic and unprofitable farming practices. "Material success she would have respected, and given herself to" (p. 178); material failure brings her to personal despair and complete alienation from her husband. In this state, "she felt as if a touch would send her off balance into nothingness; she thought of a full complete darkness with longing. . . . It was at this time, when any influence would have directed her into a new path, when her whole being was poised, as it were, waiting for something to propel her one way or the other, that her servant, once again, gave notice" (pp. 194–195). Dick insists she accept Moses, the native she had whipped in the fields, as her new servant.

Now, in incident after incident, the conventional dominance of white over black is in danger of being reversed, just as the conventional dominance of male over female has been reversed in the marriage. The certainties of social relationship have been disturbed by Mary's failure to succeed as white boss in the incident in the fields, and by Dick's failure to achieve the white man's success as farmer (and as husband). The resulting uncertainties produce odd moments in Mary's relation with Moses: "She was unable to treat this boy as she had treated all the others, for always, at the back of her mind, was that moment of fear she had known just after she had hit him and thought he would attack her" (p. 196). In Kenneth Burke's terms, Mary's "assertion" threatens to beget its "counter-assertion" — and she knows it.

Moreover, Mary's unsatisfied sexual longings are played upon and awakened by the issue of dominance. What strikes her daily about the native is his muscularity, his bulk, and his stature — the masculine power that could allow him to dominate her physically. She first loses her composure with him after she observes him half naked, washing himself from a tin basin in the back yard. In this scene Lessing clearly links the themes of racial dominance and sexual repression: "She was arrested by the sight of the native under the trees a few yards off. He was rubbing his thick neck with soap, and the lather was strikingly white against the black skin" (p. 198). Later the memory of "that thick black neck with the lather frothing whitely on it, the powerful back stooping over the bucket, was like a goad to her" (p. 199). What Mary has noticed in this scene is the black-white contrast (symbol of the racial conflict), the strength that could allow the black man to dominate her, and the phallic suggestiveness of the "thick black neck with the lather frothing whitely on it." Focused as she is on these elements, Mary nonetheless represses their significance. She convinces herself that her intrusion on the native's privacy was inadvertent: "She had forgotten it was his time to wash" (p. 198). Thus rationalizing her "error," she transforms her shame for sexual interest in the native into anger at him for resenting that interest. Lessing at this point explicitly reminds the reader to take into account unconscious motivation and to remember, as well, Mary's ignorance of her own unconscious life:

> She was furious that perhaps he believed she was there on purpose; this thought, of course, was not conscious; it would be too much presumption, such unspeakable cheek for him to imagine such a thing, that she would not allow it to enter her mind; but the attitude of his still body as he watched her across the bushes between them, the expression on his face, filled her with anger. She felt the same impulse that had once made her bring down the lash across his face. (p. 198)

Mary's overt fear that she could not maintain the dominance of white over black in the arena of labor had led her to violence before; now her repressed fear that she cannot maintain dominance over the black man sexually — by asserting the right to view his naked body, without thereby admitting a sexual attraction — drives her to a frenzy of emotion.

Through imagery, the narrator tinges her irrational reactions with sexuality: "She felt as if she had put her hand on a snake" (p. 199). "She was shaking, the blood throbbed in her ears, her mouth was dry" (p. 200). "She sat tensed, wound up, her hands clenched" (p. 201). However personally Mary experiences this sexual threat, we are reminded by the narrator that this incident is not merely personal. Mary is unwittingly acting as impersonal forces dictate:

> And she was beyond reflecting that her anger, her hysteria, was over nothing, nothing that she could explain. What had happened was that the formal pattern of black-and-white, mistress-and-servant, had been broken by the personal relation; and when a white man in Africa by accident looks into the eyes of a native and sees the human being (which it is his chief

preoccupation to avoid), his sense of guilt, which he denies, fumes up in resentment and he brings down the whip. (p. 199)

From this point on, Mary is presented as the medium along which dialectical tensions move: she held "herself like a taut-drawn thread, stretched between two immovable weights: that was how she felt, as if she were poised, a battleground for two contending forces. Yet what the forces were, and how she contained them, she could not have said" (p. 208). The reader, however, understands these contending forces to be, on the one hand, the racist system of labor which demands that she remain dominant over the servant in his physical work, ignoring his humanity, and, on the other hand, the force of the sexual attraction which tempts her to recognize the human being in Moses and in fact to submit, emotionally and physically, to his greater strength of character and body.

On Mary's side, the sexual attraction is intensified by her long hidden desires to be dominated and to disprove the judgment that she is asexual, that "she is just not like that." The narrator is silent about the native's parallel personal desires, although it should be clear what imbalances of social power and privilege he might seek to redress in the sexual relation. Whatever his motives, he is very successful in gaining dominance over his white "mistress." By small increments Lessing shows how Mary relinquishes power to him — weeping before him and refusing to eat, so that he will bring her food and force her to accept it, so that he will comfort her, if only with a glass of water. In her acceptance of his ministrations, there is a confession of loss of autonomy on her part: "There was now a new relation between them. For she felt helplessly in his power. . . . She was being forced into contact, and she never ceased to be aware of him. She realized, daily, that there was something in it that was dangerous, but what it was she was unable to define" (pp. 215, 217).

The danger, however, is defined clearly enough in her dreams. "On each occasion in her dream he had stood over her, powerful and commanding, yet kind, but forcing her into a position where she had to touch him" (p. 217). Earlier she had seen him as "firm and kind, like a father commanding her" (p. 212). These two perceptions are linked with her personal Oedipal drama in a dream in which her father, ostensibly in play, forces her against his body, just as in the other dream the native forces touch on her. The father and the native eventually are joined in one dream image of simultaneous fear and attraction. When she suddenly awakens from one of these dreams and the native observes the look of fear she directs toward him, their relation is worsened. Now he can act without concealing his attitude of familiarity, insolence, and dominance. The theme of inevitability is reintroduced: "But she felt as if she were in a dark tunnel, nearing something final, something she could not visualize, but which waited for her inexorably, inescapably" (p. 232).

The tragic dimension of the story, which was emphasized in the opening scenes, here reasserts itself emphatically. Anticipating the violent denouement of the drama, Mary has already begun to understand herself as tragic heroine. First, she has recognized herself as divided between "two contending forces." Critics of tragedy universally describe the tragic hero as divided between conflicting forces — most often, the imperative of a communal standard as opposed to an impulse of the individual will rooted in personal psychology, and often in biology as well.[25] Like the tragic hero, Mary has been faced with the necessity to choose between the two forces, and she has chosen wrongly. When Mary whipped Moses in the field, thinking that she acted as a white boss must, she was actually violating the white farmer's uncodified rules about the proper management of natives. While she had made the conscious choice to obey the imperative of her community, her ignorance made her choose the improper assertion of that imperative. The assertion is an error in that instead of resolving the conflict, it provokes a counter-assertion. Mary Turner's tragic role is now threefold: to become aware of the consequences of her assertion of will, to understand the nature of her errors, and to recognize the justice of her victim's counter-assertion.

Suddenly, in the last fifteen pages of the novel, Lessing finds herself with an agenda — a tragic agenda — that she cannot strictly fulfill without sabotaging the social critique she has been developing throughout the novel. In the classically tragic situation, the hero's strength of will is insisted upon both as an ennobling virtue and as the source of his downfall. If Lessing allows readers to view Mary's act of aggression against Moses as evidence of a noble will thwarted only by an unfortunate ignorance, she will encourage in her readers an inappropriate admiration for the woman who represents the racist oppressor. In fact, in fulfilling her tragic program for the novel, Lessing has constantly stressed Mary's wilfullness in her relation with her husband, with Moses, and with the black workers. At the moment before the tragic crisis, Lessing finds this emphasis inappropriate. She reverses herself, covering the contradiction by putting the words in Mary's consciousness rather than in the narrator's:

What *had* she done? Nothing, of her own volition. Step by step, she had come to this, a woman without will, sitting on an old ruined sofa that

smelled of dirt, waiting for the night to come that would finish her. And
justly — she knew that. But why? Against what had she sinned?

The conflict between her judgment on herself, and her feeling of innocence, of having been propelled by something she did not understand,
cracked the wholeness of her vision. (p. 272)

After this statement, we cannot grant to Mary the level of critical admiration that we feel for a foolishly willful Oedipus or an impetuously
willful Hamlet. Nor can we view her personal plight with an intensely
individual interest. Mary's interpretation of her own actions turns the
reader's attention away from the personal and toward the general, the
social. We are asked to set aside our previous engagement with Mary's
personal drama and to focus nearly exclusively on the ways in which her
actions have "been propelled by something she did not understand" —
by the imperatives of a white, racist, patriarchal culture.

As Mary takes her first step toward the crisis of this tragedy-cum-
social melodrama, her growing awareness of the consequences of her
actions is represented appropriately, in dual fashion. On the level of the
personal tragedy, she realizes that she will have to die as a consequence
of her error. On the level of the social drama, the event is figured symbolically so as to generalize that consequence. What Mary suffers personally prefigures the fate of the white oppressor in Africa, as represented in the image of the Turner house: "When she was gone, she
thought, this house would be destroyed. It would be killed by the bush,
which had always hated it, had always stood around it silently, waiting
for the moment when it could advance and cover it, for ever, so that
nothing remained" (p. 272). Here and elsewhere the bush is connected
with the natives and with Moses particularly, while the house is connected with the whites and Mary especially. The fate of the house is not
so much a figure for her personal fate as for the fate of those white people who remain behind after her death. Mary dies with her back pressed
against the wall of the house — a white woman "up against the wall" of
colonial culture. Her black murderer comes out of the bush to kill her
and returns there afterward, as to his native element. Mary's last
thought identifies Moses's vengeance with the bush and what it represents: "She lifted her hands, clawlike, to ward him off. And then the
bush avenged itself: that was her last thought. The trees advanced in a
rush, like beasts, and the thunder was the noise of their coming" (p.
285). The use of the plural pronoun in the last phrase underscores the
fact that the bush is constantly identified as the natives' territory, while
the tin-and-mud house is alien territory, white territory. The successful
attack of the bush on the house of the white oppressors thus represents

and prophesies the natives' final retribution against the white race for confiscating their land. Whether the image functions simply to represent Mary's individual fear or the white man's collective fear, we are made to feel that the fear is reasonable; the final collapse is inevitable.

Confronting the inescapable in her last hours, Mary does at last have the courage to investigate the nature of her tragic error. Lessing's formulation of that error is an odd one. Mary does not consciously identify her whipping of Moses as a basic error, nor does she repent any of her specific mistreatment of him when he became her servant and the object of her sexual attention. Her realization is much more abstract and more easily generalizable to all white people in Africa. What she realizes is that she has relied on other people to set the pattern of her life, that she has given over moral as well as personal responsibility to others. (This is the tragic error of the white settlers generally. They are not evil people, but simply people who give over moral responsibility to others, to the group.) Upon this realization, Mary begins to recover the tragic dignity that her earlier professions of innocence had undone: "She rose to her feet with a queerly appropriate dignity. . . . She would walk out her road alone, she thought. That was the lesson she had to learn" (p. 279).

Given that Mary has full premonitory knowledge of her inevitable fate, her decision to walk toward death and her manner of meeting it are redeeming. Up to the last moment she is ennobled by her recognition that she must finally take responsibility for her own actions. This shouldering of responsibility seems to open her consciousness to a saving revelation and expansion of feeling. "Propelled by fear, but also by knowledge, she rose out of bed" (p. 283). Walking through the dark out onto the veranda, she sees Moses, "And, at the sight of him, her emotions unexpectedly shifted, to create in her an extraordinary feeling of guilt. . . . She felt she had only to move forward, to explain, to appeal, and the terror would be dissolved" (pp. 284–285). Like the tragic hero, she not only accepts the inevitable consequences of her acts, but also puts her actions in a moral dimension. She experiences for the first time the guilt of the woman who has betrayed a man, of the white woman who fell back on the inhuman standards of a racist society when she was suspected of having violated them. At this moment of moral awakening, her instinct is toward connection and reconciliation — "to move forward, to explain, to appeal." She has arrived at the generous and expansive awareness that characterizes the tragic hero at the moment of death.

It is as if for one half moment, the very second before her murder, Mary has effected a change, ever so slight, in the blind course of her so heavily determined existence. Whether or not Mary's death occurs within the circle of inevitability, it is clearly infused with dignity by virtue of her hard-won awakening and expansion of consciousness. Moses has "the satisfaction of his completed revenge" (p. 287); Mary dies tragically, "collapsing in a ruin of horror" (p. 285). Nevertheless, she has had her redeeming moment of comprehending fully the conditions of her death — both her own contribution to it and the native's understanding of it. Thus, at the moment of her death Mary reaches the tragic stature described by Kenneth Burke. She is enabled to see in terms of the native's counter-assertion to her violations of his humanity. She has transcended the state of ignorance that allowed her complicity in the system of racial injustice.

In the last two paragraphs, we are suddenly offered a glimpse of the parallel tragedy of the native, also carried to its completion with dignity. Whereas Mary's triumph is to discover her guilt toward Moses (and by extrapolation toward all the blacks), his is to discover his betrayal by Mary (and all whites) and to avenge himself violently. Both have triumphed over the conditions that previously had restricted their vision. Both, however, have to pay for their affront to the gods in achieving forbidden knowledge. The lightning that accompanies Moses's joy in revenge flashes like Promethean fire, a figure for the knowledge that illuminates a previously dark field of vision.

> It was black, too dark to see. He waited for the watery glimmer of lightning to illuminate, for the last time, the small house, the veranda, the huddled shape of Mary on the brick, and the dogs who were moving restlessly about her, still whining gently, but uncertainly. It came: a prolonged drench of light, like a wet dawn. And this was his final moment of triumph, a moment so perfect and complete that it took the urgency from thoughts of escape, leaving him indifferent. (pp. 286–287)

On the personal and social levels, antithetical forces have met, and after a long struggle each has been transformed. The consciousness of transformation brings tragic joy; the consciousness of the inevitability of its achievement quells that joy into a dignified acceptance. The shape of Lessing's novel has been dictated by the tragic emotions, but not at the cost of a clear political statement. The tragedy of Mary and Moses is not merely personal; it lies in their having been trapped by the collective conscience of their respective social groupings. The tragic joy experienced by Mary and Moses is available to both their races so long as individuals will struggle to break the limits to vision which are set by cultural conditioning. At the end of the novel, both Mary and Moses are helpless and solitary before their personal fates, but in the realm of consciousness they have attained freedom and dignity. The novel ends neither in the false euphoria of a utopian reconciliation nor in the devastating despair of disaster without knowledge.

Five years after publishing *The Grass Is Singing*, Lessing made a public statement about her attitude toward the two extremes that she had avoided in her first novel:

> The best and most vital works of [modern] Western literature have been despairing statements of emotional anarchy. If the typical product of communist literature during the last two decades is the cheerful little tract about economic advance, then the type of Western literature is the novel or play which one sees or reads with a shudder of horrified pity for all of humanity. . . . I believe that the pleasurable luxury of despair, the acceptance of disgust, is as much a betrayal of what a writer should be as the acceptance of the simple economic view of man; both are aspects of cowardice, both fallings-away from a central vision, the two easy escapes of our time into false innocence. They are the opposite sides of the same coin. One sees man as the isolated individual unable to communicate, helpless and solitary; the other as collective man with a collective conscience. Somewhere between these two, I believe, is a resting point, a place of decision, hard to reach and precariously balanced. It is a balance which must be continuously tested and reaffirmed.[26]

Lessing's first novel does achieve such a balance. It avoids the false optimism of a simplistic political tract; it transcends the despair of mere disaster and attains the dignity of tragedy. The balance is formal as much as it is tonal. The shape of Lessing's novel is dictated by the tragic emotions, but within that shape, political realities are contained and transformed. It belongs to Lessing's later novels to project hope for the amelioration of social ills and to open the possibility of a full liberation of human consciousness from the bonds of history.

# Chapter Two

# *Children of Violence*
## THE PRESSURE OF *BILDUNG*

In 1952 Lessing published *Martha Quest*, the founding novel of the *Children of Violence* series. Many reviewers considered the heroine to be repulsively egoistic, and thus they were less than enthusiastic about Lessing's chronicle of rebellion against provincial South African society. An anonymous reviewer for *The New Yorker*, for instance, complained about Martha's character, almost as if she were not a fictional character whom the author could "place" in moral and other terms. The reviewer seems almost scolding: "She [Martha] is quite lacking in humor and has no sense of obligation to anyone except herself. The resentment that will make her unhappy and that will bring unhappiness to all around her is already running wild in her nature, which is apparently incapable of common affection."[1] One shudders to think what such a reviewer would have to say about Julien Sorel or Stephen Dedalus. Marvin Mudrick called Martha "a mutinous, ill-tempered, unresourceful young Englishwoman from the provinces who moves through her world, with the *author's scarcely qualified approval*, in a trance of annihilating egocentrism."[2] (The appropriateness of the italicized phrase is highly debatable.) Nevertheless, Lessing stuck by her conception of a contemporary heroine and went on to complete the five-part series she had envisioned from the beginning.

*Children of Violence*, a *roman fleuve* with Martha Quest as heroine, took seventeen years to complete (1952–1969), partly because during this period Lessing published two novels outside the series and three volumes of short stories. As Frederick P. W. McDowell noted in the first major article on Lessing's work (1965), critical reception of *Children of Violence* changed radically, and for the better, as each succeeding volume revealed or heightened the irony of Martha Quest's youthful self-deceptions in former volumes. When McDowell wrote his article, four of the novels had appeared in England: *Martha Quest* (1952), *A Proper Marriage* (1954), *A Ripple from the Storm* (1958), and *Landlocked* (1965); the last, *The Four-Gated City*, would appear in 1969. In America, however, only the first two had appeared, as a single volume in 1964. "The result," he said, "has been that some American reviewers have been more lukewarm in their reception of the series than they might otherwise have been; and they have sometimes mistakenly judged Mrs. Lessing's purpose, her total view of experience, and her achievement." [3] McDowell seemed to be speaking against critics such as Elizabeth Dalton, Marvin Mudrick, and the anonymous *New Yorker* critic. Dalton gave her criticisms of Lessing's style a contemptuous edge. There is, however, some truth in these acerbic comments:

> All of this is presented as if to account for every minute of every day; the implications of all scenes are explained afterward; Martha's thoughts and feelings are set down in their fullness for page after page without any sign of the author's interest ever flagging, every nuance tracked down with an egoistic humorlessness that is the very signature of lack of style. The reader is finally brought to his knees; it takes courage to write as if Flaubert never lived. [4]

Yet Dalton seems unaware that the "egoistic humorlessness" is no more Lessing's than Frédéric Moreau's egoism is Flaubert's. The reader is continually invited to view Martha and her interminable bouts of introspection in an ironic light. Again, in the same review, Dalton shows distaste for Martha's "fierce, solipsistic vision," [5] without admitting that Martha, though very much involved in her own emotions and attitudes, is constantly trying to make sense of the events around her and to relate herself to them.

The novels themselves are anything but solipsistic — filled as they are with the textures and details of life in a particular South African town, whose inhabitants, houses, restaurants, and streets become as familiar as those of *Winesburg, Ohio*. The singular temper of particular years — 1938, 1942, 1950 — is evoked almost with a historian's care. Finally, when Martha in her self-absorption does fail to give the world its due, Lessing as narrator directs ironic judgment against her. Some of these ironies show immediately, whereas others present themselves only when

Martha herself becomes aware of them, in later volumes of the series.
McDowell was the first to credit Lessing with such complexity, arguing
that the *Children of Violence* has a "fullness of design and conception"[6]
that would allow for the "deepening irony" Walter Allen had observed
after the third volume was published.[7]

Lessing herself maintains that she planned the series as a dramatic
whole, rather than letting it develop episodically. She said in an interview after the last volume was published, "I had a fairly clear idea of
what I wanted to do. Practically all of the things I deal with in the series
were there in some degree in the first two novels."[8] The controlling images of the series (the quest, the four-gated city, the house, the tree, the
mirror, war) are introduced in the first volume, grow in resonance and
power through the succeeding volumes, and in *The Four-Gated City*
become the vehicles through which the tensions in plot and theme that
have dominated the whole series are resolved. There is an obvious integrity to *Children of Violence*, but critics have, of course, differed in their
formulations of what it is that fuses the five volumes into a whole.

Robert K. Morris holds that *Children of Violence* "works equally
well as *Bildungsroman*, autobiography, political and social history, science fiction and prophecy, and as a tentative statement of a writer committed to (and consequently alienated from) our age."[9] His is a syncretic position, incorporating the three major critical theories to date,
each of which takes its starting point from one of Lessing's statements
on her work. The first group of critics sees the series as "a study of the individual conscience in its relations with the collective."[10] Their central
text in Lessing's criticism is a passage from "The Small Personal Voice,"
where Lessing outlines her intentions for *Children of Violence:*

> I think that a writer who has for many years been emotionally involved in
> the basic ethical conflict of communism — what is due to the collective and
> what to the individual conscience — is peculiarly equipped to write of the
> dangers inherent in being "committed" . . . to something felt as some-
> thing much greater than one's self. . . . It is this conflict which I am trying
> to explore in my series of novels, "Children of Violence," two volumes of
> which have appeared. Not one critic has understood what I should have
> thought would be obvious from the first chapter, where I was at pains to
> state the theme very clearly; that this is a study of the individual conscience
> in its relations with the collective.[11]

For the second group of critics, the self-development of the individual
— the heroine — is the central theme of the series.[12] Thus the word *Bildungsroman* appears in early reviews of the first few novels and finally
receives Lessing's sanction in her "Author's Notes," printed at the end of

*The Four-Gated City.* There she states clearly, "This book is what the Germans call a *Bildungsroman.*"[13] Dilthey's definition of the *Bildungsroman* (and he coined the term) emphasizes the essentially private nature of the *Bildungsroman* hero's quest: "The *Bildungsroman* examines a regular course of development in the life of the individual, each of its stages has its own value and each is at the same time the base of a higher stage. The dissonances and conflicts of life appear as the necessary transit points of the individual on his way to maturity and harmony."[14] Thus, for the critic who follows Dilthey, the *individual* development of the hero is the critical focus, and the hero's interactions with society are means to an end — mere "transit points" on his *personal* journey.

For other critics, these interactions with society are the end itself. For them, Lessing's greatest achievement in the *Children of Violence* is that she "communicates her sense of the age in which she has lived and is living," as Granville Hicks puts it. He goes on to call her "one of the finest chroniclers of this period of history."[15] Those who stress the sociological element in *Children of Violence* might point for support to Lessing's statement in a 1963 interview with Roy Newquist:

> I'm writing volumes four and five of a series I'm calling "Children of Violence." I planned this out twelve years ago, and I've finished the first three. The idea is to write about people like myself, people my age who are born out of wars and who have lived through them, the framework of lives in conflict. I think the title explains what I essentially want to say. I want to explain what it is like to be a human being in a century when you open your eyes on war and on human beings disliking other human beings.[16]

Is it the case, then, that *Children of Violence* is all things to all critics, complete with an imprimatur from Lessing for each approach? It is true that Lessing herself calls the novel form "that hybrid, the mixture of journalism and the *Zeitgeist* and autobiography that comes out of a part of the human consciousness which is always trying to understand itself, to come into the light." But somewhat more soberly than Morris, our syncretist, she ponders upon the process by which the novelist fuses seemingly disparate elements into one piece:

> The true novel wrestles on the edge of understanding, lying on all sides desperately, for every sort of experience, pressing into use every flash of intuition or correspondence, trying to fuse together the crudest of materials, and the humblest, which the higher arts can't include. But it is precisely here, where the writer fights with the raw, the intractable, that poetry is born. . . . And when one has done with the "plot" and the characters, that is what remains: an endeavour, a kind of hunger, that passionate desire for growth and understanding, which is the deepest pulse of human beings.[17]

I want to argue here that the Marxist and sociological views of Lessing's *Children of Violence* need not conflict finally with the views of critics who see her as a psychological novelist, writing in the tradition of the *Bildungsroman* and also influenced, as she so clearly is, by Freud, Jung, and Laing. Somehow, by fighting with "the raw, the intractable," Lessing has forged a poetic expression of a paradox: the unity of personal and social *Bildung,* even as individual and society seem in dialectical opposition — the reality of individual will and freedom, even while material and spiritual evolution push men daily forward along the links of the inevitable causal chain of being. I would like to show in some detail how these disparate elements and forces are brought to aesthetic poise in each novel and in the whole series. However, I will concentrate my analysis on *Martha Quest* and *The Four-Gated City.* These two volumes are the most important of the five, introducing and bringing to resolution all the tensions that build the whole, and they are in my opinion very much superior to the middle volumes, perhaps for that very reason. There is an intensity and richness in these novels that is achieved only intermittently in the other three volumes.

The first step in giving fair consideration to the form and movement of *Children of Violence* is to knock down the straw man some critics have set up with regard to the *Bildungsroman.* In English criticism today, the *Bildungsroman* is understood to be about the cultivation and development of an individual hero. Jerome Hamilton Buckley, for example, in his *Season of Youth: The Bildungsroman from Dickens to Golding,* defines the *Bildungsroman* as a novel tracing the inner development of a particularly sensitive youth. According to Buckley, the encounter of the *Bildungsheld* with society is only one of many trials that test and train his developing soul. The *Bildungsroman,* he suggests, is "a new and unabashedly subjective literature," one of "innumerable examples in both verse and prose of what Matthew Arnold was calling 'the dialogue of the mind with itself.'" [18]

If Buckley's definition is adequate, critics who view the series as a *Bildungsroman* have been justified in neglecting the drama of the collective that Lessing has mingled with the drama of the heroine. Certainly Dilthey's definition of the genre has given critics permission to concentrate on the individual rather than the social view of the *Bildungsroman* plot, whether Lessing's, Goethe's, Dickens's, or Mann's. G. B. Tennyson neatly summarizes the five qualities that Dilthey ascribes to the *Bildungsroman.*

> (1) the idea of *Bildung,* or formation, cultivation, education, shaping of a single main character, normally a young man; (2) individualism, espe-

cially the emphasis on the uniqueness of the protagonist and the primacy of his private life and thoughts, although these are at the same time representative of an age and a culture; (3) the biographical element, usually supplied from the author's own life in what Dilthey calls the "conscious and artistic presentation of what is typically human through the depiction of a particular individual life"; (4) the connection with psychology, especially the then-new psychology of development; and (5) the ideal of humanity, of the full realization of all human potential as the goal of life.[19]

Perhaps in drawing the contrast between the classic and the romantic types of the novel, Dilthey focuses naturally on the romantic hero's escape from the bonds of social control; thus he insists upon the romantic egoism that surely is characteristic of Rousseau's, Stendahl's and Goethe's heroes. The emphasis in his definition of the *Bildungsroman* is clearly on the individual hero. However, the qualifying clause in Tennyson's second point ties the fate of the hero to the fate of his age and culture, and the final point again invites us to view the hero as representative man.

The most respected modern critics of the *Bildungsroman* amend Dilthey's definition by stressing that from *Wilhelm Meister* through the nineteenth-century English *Bildungsroman* to Mann's *The Magic Mountain*, the progress of each hero's self-development is directed toward that "moment when he ceases to be self-centered and becomes society-centered, thus beginning to shape his true self,"[20] as Roy Pascal puts it. With this revised understanding of the *Bildungsroman* form, we can begin to make sense of *Children of Violence* as a member of the genre.

Martha Quest is the *Bildungsheld* feminized and set in her own particular time and place — the 1930s on the South African veld. Like him, she is a sensitive youth, with talents and yearnings that cannot be given proper scope in the provincial setting which has been her home. Her family, like those of Wilhelm Meister, Julien Sorel, and Stephen Dedalus, is hostile to her intellectual interests and to her urge to forge herself a moral code and a vision of society that are at odds with prevailing convention. Like the *Bildungshelden* before her, Martha is superior to her family in spirit and intelligence. For example, there is a particular parallel between the first *Bildungsheld*'s view of art and Martha's. Whereas the bourgeois Meister family sells the grandfather's collection of old Italian paintings at the first opportunity, Wilhelm Meister demonstrates his appreciation of traditional aesthetic values by defending the family treasure. Similarly, whereas Martha Quest's provincial mother is revolted by modern art, Martha can "look at the work of an

Epstein with the same excited interest as at a Michelangelo" (p. 5).[21] Both authors make a critique of contemporary society at the same time that they establish the hero's distance from it. In Wilhelm's case, his family is indicted for the Philistinism and materialism that Goethe considered to be characteristic of the burgher class. Martha's mother is scored for the rigid conventionality that, as Lessing depicts it, characterizes South African society. In her handling of the incident Lessing emphasizes the mindlessness of Mrs. Quest's adoption of the attitudes of her social group:

> Her mother had said angrily that Epstein and Havelock Ellis were disgusting. "If people dug up the remains of this civilization a thousand years hence, and found Epstein's statues and that man Ellis, they would think we were just savages." This was at the time when the inhabitants of the colony, introduced unwillingly through the chances of diplomacy and finance to what they referred to as "modern art," were behaving as if they had been severally and collectively insulted. Epstein's statues were not fit, they averred, to represent them even indirectly. Mrs. Quest took that remark from a leader in the *Zambesia News;* it was probably the first time she had made any comment on art or literature for twenty years. (pp. 4f.)

Martha is, like the *Bildungsheld,* lifted above her social milieu not only in mere matters of taste, but also in her ambition to overcome convention and pursue an ideal. For Lukács, the theme of the *Bildungsroman* is the "reconciliation of the problematic individual, guided by his lived experience of the ideal, with concrete reality."[22] Martha is, like Julien Sorel and Stephen Dedalus, constantly frustrated by the disjunction between reality and her ideals, nebulous as they are. In the scenes with her friends Solly and Josh, for example, we see the way she squanders the best opportunity for intellectual companionship that her environment offers. The narrator at this point chides Martha, "whose standards of friendship were so high she was still waiting for that real, that ideal friend to present himself" (p. 6).

From the first pages, Lessing as narrator affectionately undercuts Martha's romantic ideals, quite in the fashion of Goethe with Wilhelm or Joyce with Stephen; yet the very ideals founded in naiveté do eventually carry Martha through to transcendence in the years of her maturity. The reader thus views with simultaneous dismay and respect the ideals that lead to one disappointment after another. For example, the young Martha, ignorant of the slow process by which trust is achieved among equals, is outraged that she cannot be accepted instantly by her desired political allies:

When Joss, for instance, or Mr. Van Rensberg, posed their catechisms, and received answers qualifying her for their respective brotherhoods, surely at that moment some door should have opened, so that she might walk in, a welcomed daughter into that realm of generous and freely exchanged emotion for which she had been born — and not only herself, but every human being; for what she believed had been built for her by the books she read, and those books had been written by citizens of that other country; for how can one feel exiled from something that does not exist? (pp. 78–79)

If Lessing rather confidingly lets us in on the principle behind Martha's *Bildung,* Goethe was no more subtle with his summary of what troubles Wilhelm Meister: "What is it that keeps men in continual discontent and agitation? It is that they cannot make realities correspond with their conceptions."[23]

Martha's "conceptions" have their source in literature, which is typical for the *Bildungsheld,* who is cut off from ennobling personal associations because of his isolation in the provinces. For Martha, great tomes of modern economics, sociology, and psychology take the place of Julien Sorel's romantic fare — Rousseau's *Confessions,* bulletins of Napoleon's Grand Army, and the *Mémorial de Saint-Hélène.* Nevertheless by conflating the writings of hard-nosed realists with the fancies of Shelley, Byron, Tennyson, and William Morris, Martha arrives at an ideal and an ambition as highflown and as determined as Julien's.

The emblem of her ideal is the four-gated city. As the aspiring Jude Farley conjures up a New Jerusalem in his vision of Christminster beyond the fields of Marygreen, so Martha sees a vision of a gleaming white city "somewhere between the house on the kopje and the Dumfries Hills" (p. 120). Lukács says the soul of the hero, destined as it is to reconcile the real and ideal, "carries within itself, as a sign of its tenuous, but not yet severed link with the transcendental order, a longing for an earthly home which may correspond to its ideal — an ideal which eludes positive definition but is clear enough in negative terms."[24] Thus, the first thing Martha knows about her dream city is who does not belong there: "Outside one of the gates stood her parents, the Van Rensbergs, in fact most of the people of the district, forever excluded from the golden city because of their pettiness of vision and small understanding. . . . In Martha's version of the golden age there must always be at least one person standing at the gate to exclude the unworthy" (p. 11). In the volume *Martha Quest,* Martha hardly gets beyond the stage of negation. Her experience, however, does contribute to the building of the city, which in symbolic terms occurs in the fifth volume, since through exposure to life she clarifies her sense of what human limitations the citizens of her city must overcome. Her exposure to leftist politics, for example, makes her long for that city "where people who were not at all false and cynical and disparaging, like the men she had met that afternoon, or fussy and aggressive, like the women—where people altogether generous and warm exchanged generous emotions" (p. 120). Out of negation she begins to conceive a vague notion of the virtues that would characterize "the white-piled, broad-thoroughfared, tree-lined, four-gated, dignified city where white and black and brown lived as equals, and there was no hatred or violence" (p. 120).

For Martha, the vision of the heavenly city situated somewhere on the other side of apocalypse is somehow tied to her moments of illumination in childhood. It is as if these ecstatic experiences put her in touch with values and visions that are part of the order of experience to which the four-gated city belongs. Lukács speaks of the soul's "not yet severed link with the transcendental order," as if the experience of transcendence were to be not so much achieved as rediscovered. Similarly, for Martha there is a sense in which the spiritual site of illumination and the four-gated city are territories from which she has been temporarily exiled. When she achieves ecstasy she feels herself rediscovering lost knowledge. Martha's intimations of immortality occur in youthful moments of re-absorption into nature, moments when she painfully re-learns the smallness of her given place in the cycles of the universe. The epiphanies of Richard Feverel and Stephen Dedalus seem easy, even self-deluding, by comparison with Martha's. In rendering this experience, Lessing exhibits her characteristic attitude of sober groping after unsentimentalized reality. She begins by describing the physical stillness and quiet in the setting, which both condition and express Martha's preparation for ecstasy.

> The mealies swayed and whispered, and the light moved over them; a hawk lay motionless on a current of blue air; and the confused and painful delirium stirred in her again, and this time so powerfully she did not fear its passing. The bush lay quiet about her, a bare slope of sunset-tinted grass moving gently with a tiny rustling sound; an invisible violet tree shed gusts of perfume, like a benediction; and she stood quite still, waiting for the moment, which was now inevitable. . . . There was a slow integration, during which she, and the little animals, and the moving grasses, and the sun-warmed trees, and the slopes of shivering silvery mealies, and the great dome of blue light overhead, and the stones of earth under her feet, became one, shuddering together in a dissolution of dancing atoms. She felt the rivers under the ground forcing themselves painfully along her veins, swelling them out in an unbearable pressure; her flesh was the earth, and suffered growth like a ferment. . . . She knew futility; that is,

what was futile was her own idea of herself and her place in the chaos of matter. What was demanded of her was that she should accept something quite different; it was as if something new was demanding conception, with her flesh as host; as if there were a necessity, which she must bring herself to accept, that she should allow herself to dissolve and be formed by that necessity. (pp. 51–53)

Martha apprehends this experience in religious terms as a "benediction," an incarnation ("demanding conception, with her flesh as host") and a kind of advent (she stands still, waiting for the moment when the event will arrive, as it does in an ecstatic "shuddering" that St. Theresa would recognize). Like any mystic experience, Martha's moment demands acceptance and submission. At the same time, she feels the experience primarily as a natural process that flows through her body in the same way it flows through the air, grass, trees, stone, and sky that are so clearly presented in concrete terms.

In Martha's version of a blessed but natural union of herself and nature lies the wisdom that she will fully command only at the end of her quest. The vision is one of an organic unity, in which Martha participates, fully subject, like animals and inanimate nature, to inexorable natural pressures. By the end of *The Four-Gated City*, Martha will see herself as a cooperative subject in the same evolutionary process that drives forward the development of animal species and river beds. She will "suffer growth like a ferment," in hopes that her developing capacities will contribute to a better future for her race. Since Lessing's final view of the universe is organic and evolutionary, it is fitting that she should present the child Martha as possessing the seeds of her final wisdom. In fact, the very terms of her experience will be repeated in later epiphanies: light, stillness, integration, rivers flowing through veins, ferment. Here Lessing echoes Goethe's romantic organicism when he suggests that the task of the young Meister is not to acquire wisdom from the world but rather to develop his innate virtues and talents through experience. Significantly, Meister says, in the midst of his apprenticeship, "The cultivation of my individual self, *entirely as I am*, has from my youth upwards been constantly though dimly my wish and purpose."[25] Likewise, Martha's task through the long *Bildungsroman* of *Children of Violence* is to develop herself entirely as she is, as epitomized in the moment of her ecstatic epiphany of nature in *Martha Quest*.

Yet the difficult knowledge that Martha obtains in her youthful vision is nearly impossible to retain in consciousness. Though the flower of wisdom is growing within her, she can recognize it only in heightened moments. As Annis Pratt notes in her essay on the nature epiphany, "Women and Nature in Modern Fiction," the sensations of the epiphany again "crop up in Martha's dreams, in moments of intensity and despair as her quest from marriages and childbirth through divorces and solitude unfolds."[26] But the full impact of total being-in-the-moment is not felt until the last pages of *The Four-Gated City*, when at last Martha has learned the route to this experience so that she will be able to find it again.

What then are the impediments to full vision? These, too, are indicated in the central passage on the nature epiphany. There is "a necessity, which she must bring herself to accept." Yet she fights that acceptance with her futile "idea of herself and her place in the chaos of matter." Martha thinks she has discovered the necessity that governs her development, and therein, she thinks, is the key to her identity. From her reading in social science, "Martha had gained a clear picture of herself, from the outside. She was adolescent, and therefore bound to be unhappy; British, and therefore uneasy and defensive; in the fourth decade of the twentieth century, and therefore inescapably beset with problems of race and class; female, and obliged to repudiate the shackled women of the past" (p. 8). Gindin and other critics quote this passage as if it were Lessing's analysis of the relation between Martha's character and her environment.[27] However, as I want to demonstrate, there is a wide discrepancy between Martha's view of herself and the one Lessing conveys to the reader. As narrator, Lessing often reports Martha's views of her situation, without committing herself to definite agreement or disagreement with those views. It is in her highly ironic juxtapositions of these views (Martha's naive theories) and the subsequent plot (the hard realities) that Lessing makes her unspoken comment on the inadequacies of Martha's self-analysis. Lessing seems to hold in balance compassion for Martha's state of ignorance, and amused dismay at her folly.

The naive child of the veld certainly is unequipped intellectually and emotionally to counter the materialism of her readings in sociology and psychology — and especially to put into perspective the determinism they suggest. "Well, if all this has been said," Martha moans desperately, "why do I have to go through with it? If we *know* it, why do we have to go through the painful business of living it?" (p. 8). The whole drift of modern thought seems to be toward despair, and it carries Martha along:

> For the feeling of fate, of doom, was the one message they all had in common. Martha, in violent opposition to her parents, was continually be-

ing informed that their influence on her was unalterable, and that it was
much too late to change herself. She had reached the point where she could
not read one of these books without feeling as exhausted as if she had just
concluded one of her arguments with her mother. . . . There were, at this
very moment, half a dozen books lying neglected in her bedroom, for she
knew quite well that if she read them she would only be in possession of yet
more information about herself, and with even less idea of how to use it.
(p. 9)

Martha is therefore in terror of life before it begins — disgusted at the
thought of being fated into marriage, motherhood, varicose veins, and
suburban mediocrity. Naturally, then, she feels constantly cornered,
sensitive as she is to the pressures that society is exerting on her, she
thinks, in the service of some inexorable fate.

Everybody seems to want to mold Martha. Eager for experience, she
keeps falling under influences, discovering too late her loss of autonomy. Her mother wants to make her into a sweet English girl, the Cohen boys want to educate her as a socialist, her beau Donovan thinks he
can transform her into a fashionplate, and the crowd at the Sports Club
expects her to adopt the group style. Having given up the notion of directing her own life (after all, the books said it was all determined
ahead of time), she leaves herself prey to collective pressures. Martha
unwisely abdicates responsibility, as Lessing stresses in her authorial
comments. For example, as Martha, having allowed Donovan to rear-
range her dress for a dance, passively awaits his decision as to how the
rest of the evening will proceed, Lessing adds this authorial judgment:
"For this way of hers, submitting herself to a person or a place, with a
demure, childish compliance, as if she were under a spell, meant that
she did not consciously expect or demand: she might dream about
things being different, but that, after all, commits one to nothing" (p.
149). She had fallen into a "rich and pleasurable melancholy" (p. 167)
that absolved her from the necessity to exert her will against the will of
others.

The Sports Club, where Martha learns to conform, is Lessing's emblem of collective pressures on the individual. There one lives a role — a
chorus-line role at that, not a star part. One is, according to sex, either
one of the wolves or one of the girls, making oneself sexually available
according to group conventions. "But it did not matter with whom one
danced; it was all impersonal: one moved trancelike from one man to
the next . . . and kissed; and always in the same way." For Martha, the
only one who seems at all conscious of how this enforced sexual
behavior demeans the spirit, "each kiss was a small ceremony of hatred"

(p. 157). Through half-unwilling compliance to the group, "her own idea of herself was destroyed" (p. 157). "She was feeling lost, self-abandoned" (p. 182). More pernicious still than the required patois, dress, and sexual play is the regulation of social attitudes. Although she thinks their motives base, Martha does not effectively oppose her friends when they attempt to ostracize the Jew Adolph King. Moreover, in spite of the fact that she considers the war fever of the young men to be childish, she finds herself dreaming about her own heroism in the trenches. These surrenders to collective pressures are inevitably followed by disgust at herself.

If in her early days of reading social science Martha had merely dreaded falling into conventional patterns, she now returns to her reading to gain an excuse for her actual failure to resist them. Lessing clearly counsels the reader to withhold approval:

> In the meantime, she continued with the process of taking a fragment here and a sentence there, and built them into her mind, which was now the most extraordinary structure of disconnected bits of poetry, prose, fact and fancy; so that when she claimed casually that she read Schopenhauer, or Nietzsche, what she meant was that she had deepened her conviction of creative fatality. She had in fact not read either of them, or any other author, if reading them means to take from an author what he intends to convey. (p. 200)

This illicit use of the concept of fate is not new to the *Bildungsroman*. Wilhelm Meister himself falls into it and is counseled by a mysterious stranger, clearly Goethe's spokesman. Wilhelm is advised that the idea of fate is a ready excuse for every kind of folly or self-indulgence; however, respect is due only to the man "who labors to control his self-will." There is no denying that "every thing that happens to us leaves some trace behind it; every thing contributes imperceptibly to form us. Yet often it is dangerous to take a strict account of that. For either we grow proud and negligent, or downcast and dispirited; and both are equally injurious in their consequences. The safe plan is, always simply to do the task that lies nearest us."[28] The stranger's knowledge is finally attained by Martha Quest only at the last line of *The Four-Gated City*, when she realizes "Here, where else, you fool, you poor fool, where else has it been, ever. . . ."

In the meantime the young Martha lives not in the present but in some ideal realm compounded of what she would like to believe about the present and what she hopes for the future. Lessing has strongly emphasized the traditional quality of the *Bildungsheld*, self-delusion. Martha makes all the mistakes of Pip, Wilhelm, and Stephen Dedalus.

She overestimates her capacities, makes impossible resolves and then neglects them, suppressing her intuitions when they suggest she ought to deny herself a present pleasure, and formulates romanticized images of her experience. "She arranged the facts of what was occurring to fit an imaginative demand already framed in her mind" (p. 184). The narrative is full of such phrases as "she dismissed the thought at once," "she shrugged away the thought," and "or so she thought." When some shameful fact cannot be denied, Martha typically falls into a spell of lethargy, as if she thinks she can anesthetize herself and thus avoid the pain of reality.

> Martha did not want to think of these things, she was turned in on herself, in a heavy trancelike state. Afterwards she was to think of this time as the worst in her life. What was so frightening was this feeling of being dragged, being weighted. She did not understand why she was acting against her will, her intellect, everything she believed. It was as if her body and brain were numbed. (p. 23)

Martha's participation in the Sports Club merely accentuates this tendency toward moral lethargy. Lessing's depiction of the group and of Martha in the group almost seems like a deliberate illustration of some remarks by Jung, the great philosopher of the relation between individual and collective — Lessing's stated subject in the *Children of Violence* series.[29] In the essay on rebirth he points out that identification with a group is one of the easiest routes to spiritual transformation, though its effects are likely to be short-lived. Martha, unconsciously seeking to recover the sense of oneness that her mystic experience had given her, is attracted to groups, which offer an instant sense of belonging and a collective ideal, no matter how paltry. First she joins the Left Book Club, then the Sports Club. In *Landlocked* and later volumes, the Communist Party is her refuge. Robert Morris amusingly accuses Lessing of setting up a kind of bowling match in which one group after another is the target pin. As he puts it, "One group, . . . one structure, one ideology, then another, offers a way of life potentially attractive, sound, certain; but all are ultimately disillusioning, unable to satisfy those inherently mystical, partially absurd and chaotic longings and stirrings within Martha; that sense of being alive and knowing it, and wanting something, someone to prove it."[30] Jung explains why the group experience will inevitably disappoint the sensitive individual:

> A group experience takes place on a lower level of consciousness than the experience of an individual. This is due to the fact that, when many people gather together to share one common emotion, the total psyche

emerging from the group is below the level of the individual psyche. If it is a very large group, the collective psyche will be more like the psyche of an animal, which is the reason why the ethical attitude of large organizations is always doubtful. . . . In the crowd one feels no responsibility, but also no fear.[31]

Jung's last words are echoed in Lessing's description of the release Martha feels as a girl at a local dance: "For the few minutes the music lasted, every person on the verandah lost self-consciousness and became part of the larger whole, the group; their faces were relaxed, mindless, their eyes met those of the men and the women they must meet and greet in the dance with an easy exchange. It was no longer their responsibility; the responsibility of being one person, alone, was taken off them" (pp. 73–74).

Later, in a less rustic setting, the dances of the Sports Club become an outlet for baser emotions than those allowed expression in the Van Rensburgs's country dance. Under cover of the group, Perry, one of the young men, may humiliate a black waiter by insisting that he perform a native war dance to the tune of the song "Hold him *down*, the Zulu warrior"(p. 206). When the incident gets ugly, Perry simply claims an innocent desire to give everyone a good time. Martha is astonished that the group joins him in a sentimental grievance against the uncooperative black. The pack mindlessly upholds its class interest in maintaining hostility against the blacks at a constant level. Furthermore, when their class interest makes a new demand, entrance into the war, they even manage to tie this new demand to the need to keep the blacks powerless.

> They were saying, devoutly, that things looked like trouble; they did not define this, for it meant what it would have meant to Mr. Quest—they would shortly be expected to defend the honour of Britain in some way or another. It would have been difficult for them to define it in any case; they never read anything but the newspapers. . . . Soon, however, one of them said that if there was going to be a war, then there would be trouble with the niggers. His voice had that intense, obsessive note which means that the speaker desires a thing although he may be claiming the opposite. (p. 203)

Martha is as infuriated by the men's apish eagerness to go to war as she is by their viciousness toward the blacks. And her disgust finally propels her toward the rebellion from the collective toward which she has been tending since her rebellion from her parents and from farm district society. She can finally say she is finished with the Sports Club and everything it stands for (p. 208).

Martha has arrived at a crucial stage in her journey toward self-realization. She has reached the point at which the *Bildungsheld* must disavow association with the false values of a decadent milieu. Wilhelm Meister must learn to be dissatisfied with the frivolity and artifice of the theater group, Pip must recognize the shallowness of the money-centered life in the city, Stephen Dedalus must disentangle himself from the smothering embrace of the church, and Martha must repudiate the Sports Club, with its racial prejudice, war-mongering, and rigid sex roles. Again Jung lends support to the *Bildungsroman* pattern, claiming that the first fruit of self-development "is the conscious and unavoidable segregation of the single individual from the undifferentiated herd." To become a personality, he says, one must individualize. And only a personality can contribute anything valuable to the collective.[32]

Jolande Jacobi aptly describes an aspect of Jung's theory that corresponds precisely with Lessing's theme, when she says that Jung's theory tries "to bridge the opposition between individual and collectivity through the full personality rooted in them both."[33] Martha is Lessing's representation of such a personality. Moreover, Jung is convinced, as Lessing seems to be, that "the change in the collective does not begin with propaganda and mass meetings, or with violence. It begins with a change in individuals."[34] Martha's refusal to participate in war fever or in oppression of the blacks can be seen, then, as a first step in a possible reformation of her group. Clearly, we are watching Lessing orchestrate a double *Bildung* — the intertwined development of individual and society. As Martha develops individually, she pushes forth the development of her culture.

Realistically, however, Lessing does not give indications of easy or rapid change in this group's attitudes toward race and war. Social inertia parallels Martha's personal resistance to change. In fact, in the five-volume series, progress on both social and individual fronts is very slow, with hope prevailing fully only at the end of *The Four-Gated City*. Here, toward the end of *Martha Quest*, Martha is left feeling "rage at herself for her ineffectiveness" in the social sphere (p. 210). What is even more maddening is her inability to resist the impulse to behave, "inevitably, inexorably, exactly like everyone else" (p. 211), as when she participates in the group's purge of Adolph King. There is bitter irony in the fact that she not only returns to the Sports Club after her determined repudiation of it but also tacitly endorses its most low-minded impulse, its racism.

Roy Pascal describes Mann's similar handling of the relation between individual and collective in *The Magic Mountain*. There, Pascal says, "the alternatives facing his characters represent the dilemma of a whole nation."[35] His hero, moreover, is "not an abstract, ideal summation of the dominant characteristics of a group . . . but an average man of the middle class, who experiences the dilemma of his times in a peculiar, individual way, and whose achievement is limited, imprecise, provisional."[36] Martha has her struggle with race prejudice, as when she is threatened by the fact that a black man in her office makes a salary not much less than her own; and she has her fight with war fever, dreaming of being a Florence Nightingale to the troops. But for the most part, Lessing sets Martha above her social group in terms of her comprehension of social issues and the development of her moral conscience. Martha therefore often offends the reader with her constant irritability, "spasms of resentment" (p. 2), and priggish repudiation of one friend after another, because of their supposed deviation from an ideal standard. Lessing might have done well to follow Mann's lead and allow Martha to participate more directly in the prejudices and delusions that were typical of her social group. Perhaps, though, Lessing felt that to bring about in Martha a complete transformation of racial, political, and sexual attitudes would be an overwhelming narrative task, and unrealistic as well. Consequently, Lessing arranges her narrative so that Martha meets city society already equipped with an advanced social conscience, tutored by the Cohen boys and their extensive library of modern social science.

Martha Quest thus has her vision of the ideal city well in mind as she meets the trials and obstacles that impede her quest to find it. The two major obstacles that I have discussed so far — the social pressures of a corrupt society and her own sense of being without free will — are standard impediments to the quest of the *Bildungsheld*. To these is added the stumbling block of sex, and here Martha is thoroughly thwarted. Wilhelm Meister, Richard Feverel, and Pip have to learn to control lust and to value highly the spiritual traits that will make the fair lady a better helpmate than the dark beauty could be. But the conflict between body and spirit is resolvable for them through a wise marriage. For Martha the conflict seems unresolvable. Neither the free indulgence of sexual urges outside marriage nor the controlled fulfillment of body and spirit in marriage is a possibility for her.

The sexual dilemma first presents itself in the opening scenes of the novel, where Martha is pictured sitting on the steps of her verandah, just opposite to her mother and a woman friend. "She was reading Havelock Ellis on sex, and had taken good care they should know it" (p. 2). Martha thinks she knows what she opposes in these women. She despises their "loathsome, bargaining, and calculating" attitude toward sex; she is disgusted by their conventional admonitions that she must "make men respect her" if she intends to "do well for herself."

The opposition between the conventional pressure to participate in the marriage market and her unconventional urge toward sexual freedom seems clear enough. In striking out for the city, she expects to be able to live out her choice. Martha, "a girl whose first article of faith was that one was entitled to lose one's virginity as romantically and as soon as possible," finds, however, that an affair embarked upon for its shock value fails to touch her real sexual nature. Retreating in grief from her first sexual attempts, she finds herself repossessed by fears about sex that somehow don't fit into her simple schema of convention versus freedom. As she had in adolescence, she anxiously fears the loss of her perfect body. Looking in a mirror or lying in her bath, "she thought of the ugly scar across her mother's stomach, and swore protectively to her own that it would never, never be so marred" (p. 146). Her own attractive body "made her remember the swollen bodies of the pregnant women she had seen, with shuddering anger, as at the sight of a cage designed for herself. Never, never, never, she swore to herself, but with a creeping premonition" (p. 57). Whether she plays the marriage game or claims her rights to "free love," she is trapped by nature's curse on her sex — or so she thinks.

Martha is left will-less, passively stricken before equally repugnant options. This dilemma seems unresolvable. Moreover, her dissatisfaction as a woman is not limited purely to her physical fate; she rejects as well her social options. She will not contentedly submit to a husband in the fashion of the women of the district. On the other hand, she scorns the attempts of modern women to participate with men in work at the same time as they raise their families. She is repelled by the harried, fussy women of the Left Book Club:

And Martha heard that fierce and passionate voice repeating more and more loudly inside her, I will *not* be like this; for comparing these intelligent ladies, who nevertheless expressed resentment against something (but what?) in every tone of their voices, every movement of their bodies, with the undemanding women of the district, who left their men to talk by themselves while they made a world of their own with cooking and domesticity — comparing them, there could be no doubt which were the more likable. And if, like Martha, one had decided to be neither one nor the other, what could one be but fierce and unhappy and determined? (p. 117)

Lessing builds a heavy irony into Martha's final capitulation to the conventional female role. A letter from her mother, stuffed with racist clichés, makes Martha feel "caged and imprisoned." That dangerous conviction of fatality, along with Martha's too passionate (and unexamined) revulsion against her mother, leads Martha to conspire in her own entrapment by the marriage she had not been able to contemplate without loathing. Putting down the letter, she calls the Sports Club and accepts an invitation to a dance, where she meets her future husband. At the dance she falls prey to impulses that she has long sought to locate outside herself, denying that they had been appropriated as her own. While in the past she has expressed disgust at the idea of selling herself on the marriage market, she now sells her companionship to visiting athletes for the price of a dinner and an assuagement of loneliness. Whereas in the past she insisted that her longings to be carried off like booty by a strong man were simply echoes of a social demand (p. 77), she now begins to own up to her desire for a man to whom she could defer (p. 223). Although even still she resents the man's objectification of her body, she suppresses these feelings in the interest of getting engaged. In all these ways she is disloyal to her former conception of herself.

Martha's former confidence in herself as rebel receives its final ironic blow in the joyless marriage scene. Her euphoria, so often singing its triumphal march at the ends of chapters and sections of the novel, is finally dispelled, as it has so often been ironized, and depression falls like a weight on the scene. We recall the close of part one, when Martha strikes out for the city: "And a door had closed finally; and behind it was the farm, and the girl who had been created by it. It no longer concerned her. Finished. She could forget it. She was a new person, and an extraordinary, magnificent, an altogether *new* life was beginning" (p. 80). The daughter of the farm, however, selects a husband in the same manner as her mother, and for the same reasons. As later books will emphasize, this marriage is the product of war, like the Quests'. Martha is simply one person caught up in the emotional frenzy caused by the coming conflict. In her whirlwind courtship she hardly has time to notice that one couple after another in the Sports Club is falling into marriage, unconsciously grasping for a last-minute idyll before the war. It is not the individual will of an autonomous heroine that controls this movement in the plot, but rather the will of the collective and of that inevitability which works through the personal history of each individual. A feeling of fatality — always Martha's bane — saps her of the strength to resist the course of events: "She said to herself that now she could free herself, she need not marry him: at the same time, she knew quite well she would marry him; she could not help it; she was being dragged towards it, whether she liked it or not" (p. 243).

The novel ends on a bitter note, with the joyless thoughts of Mr. Maynard, the marrying official:

Poor kids, let them enjoy themselves while they can — He shook himself furiously; this was a first infection from that brutal sentimentality which poisons us all in time of war. He recognized it, and dismissed it, and walked on, more slowly. Four more weddings to get through. Well, he thought cynically, that would be four divorces for him to deal with, in due time. Five, counting the one he had just finished. (p. 247)

And his prediction is accurate. Martha has ended in being duped by her era, by sex, and by her own personal history. But her *Bildungsroman* is not over. As Goethe says of his often-erring hero, "He in whom there is much to be developed will be later in acquiring true perceptions of himself and of the world."[37] In Martha's story there are four more novels, in which will be revealed the primitiveness of this stage of her own consciousness and the distance that exists between this state of society and the four-gated city.

Chapter Three

# *The Four-Gated City*
## THE PRESSURE OF EVOLUTION

While the critics are aware that Lessing has called her series a *Bildungs-roman*, a number have quarreled with the label. Dagmar Barnouw, for instance, explains that it is necessary for a *Bildungsheld* to move toward a meaningful choice, and in the world of *Children of Violence* such a choice does not seem to be available. "The first four volumes of the *Children of Violence* are not *Bildungsromane* in the strict sense of the concept," Barnouw writes. "Matty is neither moving toward a choice, a determining decision she will make at one time or the other, nor is the fact that she is incapable of such a choice integrated into the substance and structure of her development."[1]

On the contrary, both the plot and the system of tropes which structures the five-novel series show Martha moving through a series of stages, each climaxed by either a willed decision or an acquiescence to destiny. Indeed, the question of whether active choice or passive acceptance is the appropriate response to life is the chief issue on which the whole series is based. In the early books, especially, Martha is continually choosing the wrong things — marriage to Douglas, abandonment of her child, marriage to Anton — while fate delivers to her door every good she is later to cherish — the birth of her child, the affair with Thomas Stern, her friendships with Maisie and Athen, and the association with the Coldridge household, her ultimate means of salvation. Through images of entrapment, of change without change, and finally of growth, conversion, and evolution, Lessing develops a metaphoric

46

apologia for her concept of self-development. Although Goethe emphasized the necessity for organic rather than willed self-development, most writers in the *Bildungsroman* tradition have sanctioned the active striving and romantic rebellion of their heroes. Lessing retreats from this late-romantic idea of *Bildung,* returning to Goethe's original insight that the hero must develop naturally out of what he is and that, to that end, receptivity is fully as important a trait as assertiveness. Martha thus finally learns that growth cannot be willed but can be nurtured, enhanced, and protected from impediments.

Lessing's depiction of Martha's organic self-development comes as a shock to readers schooled to admire and relish the dramatic revolts of Stephen Dedalus and Julien Sorel. Patricia Spacks, for example, finds Martha lacking in heroic stature precisely because she holds back from full rebellion: "If Martha Quest, then, figures as a heroine, she must be a heroine of a very peculiar sort. She stands for nothing, defies nothing successfully, cannot endure her condition without self-defeating gestures of escape. She is passive when she should be active, obtuse when she should be perceptive. Her heroism consists merely in her suffering and her rage, not in any hope or promise of effect."[2] In contrast to Spacks's view, I contend that by holding back from decisive action, personal or political, the young Martha keeps herself open to the wisdom that Thomas Stern and others bring to her, while at the same time she gives herself time to feel the stirrings of the desires and intuitions that require development if she is to come to true maturity.

D. J. Enright, for his part, does not quarrel with Martha Quest's seeming passivity, but he complains that "there is no true—no artistically true—connection between the Martha Quest whom we first met as a fifteen-year-old in the novel named after her and the old woman whose death on a contaminated island somewhere off Scotland is casually mentioned in the 'Appendix' to *The Four-Gated City.*"[3] That the *Bildungsheld* could change, even markedly, should not be surprising to Enright. It is common that the *Bildungsheld* undergoes a conversion experience and sheds the callow skin of youth. As Count Jarno explains to Wilhelm Meister, there is bound to be a marked appearance of difference between a man's youthful character and his mature self.

> "It is right that a man, when he first enters upon life, should think highly of himself, should determine to attain many eminent distinctions, should endeavor to make all things possible; but when his education has proceeded to a certain pitch, it is advantageous for him, that he learn to live for the sake of others, and to forget himself in an activity prescribed by duty. It is then that he first becomes acquainted with himself, for it is conduct alone that compares us with others."[4]

According to this model, Martha Quest gives up youthful rebellion, self-assertion, and idealism — all of which *seemed* the defining traits of her selfhood — only to find herself more truly in "an activity prescribed by duty." Upon joining the Coldridge household, Martha gives up her self-absorption, extending herself outward to tend the needs of the writer Mark Coldridge, his disturbed wife Lynda, and the two emotionally battered children, Francis and Paul. It is in the course of living for the sake of these others that she comes to know and develop her defining talents, her clairvoyance and her capacity to save others from coming disaster. These talents are an outgrowth of the capacities shown by the very young Martha Quest. Mark revives in Martha her youthful vision of the four-gated city and helps her to see that this city can be, indeed must be, a reality in the time of world catastrophe. Lynda restores to Martha her youthful capacity to see things outside the frame of "normal" vision; the perceptions that Martha becomes attuned to give Martha the knowledge necessary to her role as savior of the special children. Similarly, the young people, Francis and Paul, force Martha to recall both her youthful fury against the blindness and stubbornness of authority and her willingness, in youth, to take terrible personal risks in order to live outside the net of that authority; such recollections prepare Martha to defy governmental authorities and risk her life in an attempt, at the time of the Catastrophe, to establish a counter-society on Faris Island.

There is, it seems, a great deal more continuity in the presentation of Martha Quest than Enright gives Lessing credit for. This continuity, moreover, is established largely through metaphor — a device that one hopes Enright would admit as "artistically true." Through the imagery of growth and evolution that pervades *Children of Violence*, Lessing prepares the reader to follow Martha and her society through stages of growth that lead finally to a virtual metamorphosis. Failing to see the continuity in Martha's development, Enright misses too the continuity in the parallel development of Martha's society. He complains, for example, that the apocalyptic events chronicled in the Appendix to *The Four-Gated City* are "not in accordance with the rest of 'Children of Violence.'"[5] Enright can be refuted by an examination of the imagery that threads through the series, prefiguring and expressing the gradual evolution of both individual and collective.

The best image to start with is the image of the growing tree,[6] an image that Lessing seems to have borrowed, from Goethe, as the central running motif of her series. Expounding to his fellow actors in *Hamlet*, Wilhelm declares: "To me it is clear that Shakespeare meant, in the present case, to represent the effects of a great action laid upon a soul unfit for the performance of it. In this view the whole play seems to me to be composed. There is an oak-tree planted in a costly jar, which should have borne only pleasant flowers in its bosom: the roots expand, the jar is shivered."[7] For Wilhelm, the image of the tree expanding beyond the capacity of its container is a warning against his tendency to embark on projects for which he has no natural, but only a romantic, inclination. At each step of his self-development, he must ask if he is fitted for the task before him, if it suits his soul and gives room for the development of his genius. He makes mistakes — trying to fit himself into the role of actor, which is beyond his talent, and trying to create happiness for Mignon and the Harper, a task that is beyond human skill. His self-development comes to fruition when he has fitted the roots of his soul to a suitable vessel — a society of friends who will give spiritual support, a wife who will temper his romantic impulses, and, most importantly, an ambition that is matched to his talents and his opportunities.

Doris Lessing has also used the symbol of the growing tree as a standard by which to measure the development of her *Bildungsheldin*, Martha Quest. In every novel of the series there is a tree or a group of them that is emblematic of a particular stage in the opening of her consciousness. The young Martha has a tree that she calls her own and that she later visits as if it were a shrine. This tree, "hard under her back, like a second spine," has roots sunk deep into the African soil, and it is the solid post against which she leans as she reads *The Decay of the British Empire*, Engels's *Origin of the Family*, and other books aimed against the social milieu in which she finds herself placed. The firm-rootedness of the tree, in tension with the uprooting impulse of the revolutionary literature she reads, reassures the rebellious but frightened girl. The tree is a locus for her unconscious knowledge that the African landscape, along with her experience of natural rhythms there, is the root and support for everything good that will grow within her in later years. When she confronts threats to her identity, it is important to have that past to lean back on, as the young Martha leaned back on the tree.

As Martha pursues an independent life in the city, she is caught by impulses that flow not from her inner nature but from the social rhythms of a corrupt society — the impulse to marry as a solace in the time of war-making, the desire for material luxury as a substitute for spiritual health, even the falsely romantic urge to create a political utopia (especially false in Martha's case, since it involves the rejection of her daughter and of her own nurturing capacity). While Martha is far from her inner self, pursuing these inappropriate goals, the image of the tree is held at a distance. Her world is far from nature now; she is shut up in stuffy offices or enclosed in the boxes of a middle-class suburb.

Nonetheless, at moments of pain, when Martha fleetingly feels the distance between her innermost urgings and her daily reality, she often glimpses a tree outside a window or beyond a gate.[8] Or, as she stands under the shelter of a tree, she momentarily opens herself to a fresh vision of things. For example, in a scene from *A Ripple from the Storm*, Lessing uses the image of dust to indicate the aridity of Martha's life as wife and comrade to Anton, the Communist group leader, along with the image of the tree to express the continuing presence of her inner urge toward growth, threatened as it has been by lack of tending:

> The smell of dry dust filled her nostrils; an odour of dry sun-harshened leaves descended from the darkening gum trees above. She thought — and it was a moment of illumination, a flash of light: I don't know anything about anything yet. I must try to keep myself free and open, and try to think more, try not to drift into things. (*RS*, pp. 171–172)

At last, through her relationship with Thomas Stern, Martha learns to live from the roots of her being. Thomas is, literally, a tree-nursery man, and the hut where he makes a shelter for his lovemaking with Martha is the city base for his nursery: "From this centre she now lived — a loft of aromatic wood from whose crooked window could be seen only sky and the boughs of trees, above a brick floor hissing sweetly from the slow drippings and wellings from a hundred growing plants" (*L*, p. 98). As Martha relearns the rhythms of her own body and of nature, she luxuriates in natural sensations. The descriptions of setting thus proliferate, as Lessing reflects Martha's consciousness of life around her, and references to trees abound — jacarandas, trees festooned with golden shower creeper, on the veld or in town, luxuriant or dusty.

Finally, the maturing Martha, having abandoned Africa and her political connections, sits in a small bedroom in Bloomsbury and watches "the structure of the sycamore tree disappear in spring green" (*FGC*, p. 199). Day and night she charts its quiet, hidden growth. In the Coldridge household Martha has been transformed from a self-centered girl to a generous woman nurturing a family of sad children and emotionally disturbed adults. Her bedroom is her only privacy in this house where she owns nothing and no one. So the tree outside her window becomes her mandala, the symbol of her potential growth:

> There she was, in her room, empty, at peace. She watched other people developing their lives. And she? In every life there is a curve of growth, or a falling away from it; there is a central pressure, like sap forcing up a trunk,

along a branch, into last year's wood, and there, from a dead-looking eye, or knot, it bursts again in a new branch, in a shape that is inevitable but known only to itself until it becomes visible. (*FGC*, p. 201)

This is a freer image than Wilhelm's oak in a jar. He had to find the proper form to contain his growth; there is a conservative, curbing impulse in his metaphor. (One may imagine Wilhelm having to be pruned now and again to fit his chosen container, the Society of the Tower.) Martha's metaphor, in contrast, is organic and progressive. She must follow the impulse of her own growth, when it comes. In the meantime, she must watch and wait, not force or prune. Whereas for Wilhelm the shattering of the jar would be the moment of defeat, for Martha such a moment is a triumph.

*Children of Violence* is a series of episodes in which Martha Quest comes to recognize that she is enclosed by a containing structure (metaphorically, a cage, a net, a shell, or a room) in which she will be stifled and out of which she must break. The net is different in each volume, but the struggle and the metaphors for it remain the same. Martha escapes the family web, only to fall under the net of the Sports Club and its expectations. In *A Proper Marriage*, two forces threaten to trap her — the claims of the utopian vision she had fostered as a girl, now exerting pressure on her in the form of the Contemporary Politics Discussion Circle, and the opposing claims of her marriage and maternity. In her first exposure to the socialist group, which will absorb nearly all her energy for the next decade, Martha feels "the old fear as if nets were closing around her" (*PM*, p. 194). As she will later learn, every social group has its net — a set of beliefs, expectations, and vocabulary in terms of which life must be experienced — and in committing oneself to the group, however tacitly, one agrees to live under the net. What Martha seems to intuit is that no group with a dogma can foster the free and organic development of personal or social potential. Thus, although in *The Four-Gated City* Martha finally works with others to foster the developing psychic abilities of the race, she performs her service outside the nets of any dogmatic group. When confronted with the demands of the Contemporary Politics Discussion Circle, then, the young Martha acts instinctively for her survival when she tries to shake "herself free of this mesh of bonds before she had entered them; she thought that at the end of ten years these people would still be here, self-satisfied in their unconformity, talking endlessly" (*PM*, p. 194). The irony is that for a long time she will be with them.

While Martha is on one front resisting her political destiny, her biological destiny (as she sees it) simultaneously threatens to overwhelm her. Suddenly, Lessing's prose is full of images of entrapment, as Martha's pregnancy calls up her old fear of inevitability. When Martha thinks of her child growing in the womb, she does not link this process with the free growth of trees or plants. Rather, she mourns for the "doomed" child "bubbling continuously in its cage of ribs" (*PM*, p. 131) and continually refers to her womb as a prison. Birth, however, is no release. If "the web was tight around her" (*PM*, p. 99) while she was pregnant, afterwards "there was this band of tension, felt deeply as a web of tight anxiety, between her and the child" (*PM*, p. 201). But even the fact that "she would be bound for months and months of servitude, without any escape from it," is nothing to the "bored thought that this was a baby like any other, of no interest to anybody, not even herself" (*PM*, p. 152).

The underlying anxiety, for which pregnancy becomes almost a symbol, is the still unresolved dilemma of determinism. What could be more determined, more repetitious, than the cycle of generations?

> And now Martha was returned . . . into her private nightmare. She could not meet a young man or woman without looking around anxiously for the father and mother: that was how they would end, there was no escape for them. She could not meet an elderly person without wondering what the unalterable influences had been that had created them just so. She could take no step, perform no action, no matter how apparently new and unforeseen, without the secret fear that in fact this new and arbitrary thing would turn out to be part of the inevitable process she was doomed to. She was, in short, in the grip of the great bourgeois monster, the nightmare *repetition*. (*PM*, p. 77)

The ferris wheel outside her window is, then, negatively an emblem of fate's cyclic repetitions; but, when feeling trapped by marriage, she "looked at the wheel steadily, finding in its turnings the beginnings of peace. Slowly she quietened, and it seemed possible that she might recover a sense of herself as a person she might, if only potentially, respect" (*PM*, p. 24). Critics have focused on the ferris wheel as a negative symbol, representing the mindlessness of a bad marriage and the endless circles of procreation and family life—"like a damned wedding ring," as Martha herself thinks crossly (*PM*, p. 29).[9] However, even in *A Proper Marriage*, Lessing foreshadows through this image a positive theme that she will develop fully in *The Four-Gated City*. Lessing believes that one cannot find freedom by jumping off the wheel of fate; rather, one must "hold on" (a frequent phrase in Martha's mouth) and live each moment through. Therefore a pregnant Martha is affirming an instinct for life, rather than denying it, as several critics suggest, when she revolves "on the great wheel as if her whole future depended on her power to stick it out" (*PM*, p. 92).

When Martha rebels against the idea of repetition, the uses of which she will discover in *The Four-Gated City*, she commits the one irrevocably wrong act of her youth, the repudiation first of her pregnancy, then of the child she has borne. Through this repudiation Martha intensifies her self-division.

> She was essentially divided. One part of herself was sunk in the development of the creature, appallingly slow, frighteningly inevitable, a process which she could not alter or hasten, and which dragged her back into the impersonal blind urges of creation; with the other part she watched it; her mind was like a lighthouse, anxious and watchful that she, the free spirit, should not be implicated; and engaged in daydreams of the exciting activities that could begin when she was liberated. (*PM*, p. 127)

This split between the rational watcher and the irrational, impersonal experiencer widens as the years go by, until in *The Four-Gated City* Martha seeks out a psychiatrist to help her come to terms with the division.

In the meantime, the youthful Martha is almost proud of her ability to maintain a distance from her feeling self. Her compartmentalizing of experience is expressed in images of shells, rooms, walls, and houses.[10] In her political work, for example, Martha becomes aware of how her double self operates:

> She was engaged in examining and repairing those intellectual's *bastions* of defence behind which she sheltered, that *building* whose shape had first been sketched so far back in her childhood she could no longer remember how it then looked. With every year it had become more complicated, more ramified; it was as if she, Martha, were a variety of soft, *shell*-less creature whose survival lay in the strength of those *walls*. (*PM*, p. 94, my italics.)

While Martha remains aware of the need to keep a lighthouse keeper's vigilance over her separate selves (*L*, p. 14) she is warmed by the presence of her friend Maisie, who "always understood by instinct what was going on underneath everybody's false shells" (*L*, p. 14). Nevertheless, she admonishes herself that "she must keep things separate" (*L*, p. 14). This need is figured in her dreams and fantasies of being a housekeeper who attends a large house filled with people who must not leave their own rooms or be suffered to "meet each other or understand each other, and Martha must not expect them to. She must not try to explain, or build bridges" (*L*, p. 15). Lessing suggests that this separating off, though ultimately life-denying, is nevertheless a temporary necessity for Martha. In fact, as is the case often in *Landlocked,* Lessing is rather too obvious in her use of dream symbolism and in her directions to the reader as to how to evaluate the dream.

> Martha's dreams, always a faithful watchdog, or record, of what was going on, obligingly provided her with an image of her position. Her dream at this time, the one which recurred, like a thermometer, or gauge, from which she could check herself, was of a large house, a bungalow, with half a dozen different rooms in it, and she, Martha (the person who held herself together, who watched, who must preserve wholeness through a time of dryness and disintegration) moved from one room to the next, on guard. These rooms, each furnished differently, had to be kept separate — *had* to be, it was Martha's task for this time. For if she did not — well, her dreams told her what she might expect. The house crumbled drily under her eyes into a pile of dust. (*L*, p. 14)

Before her exodus from Africa, Martha could not integrate the separate rooms of her experience except through the unifying power that belonged to Thomas Stern. Precisely as a result of his tutelage, however, Martha learns to feel dissatisfied with a divided existence, so that in London she no longer feels content to live the sterile and divided life that seems typical of her generation. At the beginning of *The Four-Gated City,* Martha arrives in London and goes to the house of an old pal, Jack. She feels simultaneously attracted and repelled by his neat little box of a room: "People like her, for some reason, in this time, made rooms that were clean and bare and white: in them they felt at home, were safe and unchallenged. *But she did not want to feel like this*" (*FGC*, p. 49). Later, she realizes that, for her, rooms become containers for discrete emotions and that her life is unbalanced because she is unable to hold together various emotions and insights. At one time her room in the Coldridge house is filled with an atmosphere of death tempting her to suicide. Weeks later it is "all sexual fantasy, anger, hatred" (*FGC*, p. 201). The basement flat, where the supposedly mad woman, Lynda, lives, is at one time a refuge and days later a threat: "The basement flat, its occupants, were isolating themselves in her mind, as if it was a territory full of alien people from whom she had to protect herself, with whom she could have no connection" (*FGC*, p. 221).

Martha finally comes to realize that the walls of these rooms must be broken down. While tending Lynda through a period of madness, Martha has a moment of revelation.

Now she understood very well what it was Lynda was doing. When she pressed, assessed, gauged those walls, it was the walls of her own mind that she was exploring. She was asking: Why can't I get out? What is this thing that holds me in? Why is it so strong *when I can imagine, and indeed half remember, what is outside?* Why is it that inside this room I am half asleep, doped, poisoned, and like a person in a nightmare screaming for help but no sounds come out of a straining throat? (*FGC*, p. 494)

If the walls that block out a clear perception of unified experience could be broken down, there would be no need for Lynda's bizarre pantomime.

The message that cries out from Martha's stream of thought for her own recognition is Forster's dictum, "Only connect!" As Selma Burkom shows with special reference to *The Golden Notebook*, this need for integration is always one of Lessing's central themes.[11] One begins to see the relevance of the dervish teaching story used as the dedication to *The Four-Gated City:*

Once upon a time there was a fool who was sent to buy flour and salt. He took a dish to carry his purchases.

"Make sure," said the man who sent him, "not to mix the two things — I want them separate."

When the shopkeeper had filled the dish with flour and was measuring out the salt, the fool said: "Do not mix it with the flour; here, I will show you where to put it."

And he inverted the dish, to provide, from its upturned bottom, a surface upon which the salt could be laid.

The flour, of course, fell to the floor.

But the salt was safe.

When the fool got back to the man who had sent him, he said: "Here is the salt."

"Very well," said the other man, "but where is the flour?"

"It should be here," said the fool, turning the dish over.

As soon as he did that, the salt fell to the ground, and the flour, of course, was seen to be gone.

The story expresses the paradoxical difficulties that Martha faces in the Coldridge household. Practicality would seem to dictate that opposites — for example, the insane Lynda and her sane family — be kept apart. However, when one fixates on the task of separating one aspect of the world from another, both aspects — the salt and the flour — may be lost to you, as both Lynda and her son are almost lost to each other, to life, and to the larger Coldridge household. In coming to this insight, Martha is beginning to recover the mystic experience of her youth — the "slow integration, during which she" and all her environment "became one, shuddering together in a dissolution of dancing atoms" (*MQ*, p. 52). She is beginning to accept the challenge to see life whole — the challenge which she has not been able to accept up to this time.

With Thomas Stern she finds herself living from one center for a brief time, but she loses the ability when he goes away. Again, when she first reaches London, in a delirium of hunger and fatigue, she remembers the Arnoldian wisdom that "it is a question of trying to see things steadily all the time" (*FGC*, p. 35). In this heightened state she enters an intense sexual experience with Jack and discovers that the "normality" that others accept is a condition of disparateness, both within the parts of the self and between the self and others. For Martha and Jack, the condition of normality is one to be outgrown by those who are capable of reaching a higher state. Sex is the vehicle that Jack recommends. Through his tutelage Martha discovers that "when the real high place of sex is reached, everything moves together" and disparateness is overcome (*FGC*, p. 64). Finally, after exploring madness with Lynda, Martha realizes:

> There is something in the human mind which makes it possible for one compartment to hold Fact A which matches with Fact B in another compartment; but the two facts can exist side by side for years, decades, centuries, without coming together. It is at least possible that the most fruitful way of describing the human brain is this: "It is a machine which works in division; it is composed of parts which function in compartments locked off from each other." Or: "Your right hand does not know what your left hand is doing." (*FGC*, p. 523)

The machine has its revenge, however, when it begins to switch from Fact A to Fact B without warning. Marion Vlastos points out that here, as throughout her work since *The Golden Notebook*, Lessing echoes or perhaps borrows the concepts of R. D. Laing, the radical British psychiatrist who believes that schizophrenia is an extreme protest by sensitive individuals against the society's demand that they constantly divide off approved perceptions from disapproved ones.[12] Vlastos quotes Laing in a statement that could act as a gloss for *The Four-Gated City:*

> It has always been recognized that if you split Being down the middle, if you insist on grabbing *this* without *that*, if you cling to the good without the bad, denying the one for the other, what happens is that the dissociated evil impulse, now evil in a double sense, returns to permeate and possess the good and turn it into itself.[13]

In *The Four-Gated City*, images of conversion between negative and positive electrical states express the wonder and the danger of this phenomenon. Part Three begins with a selection of "Various Remarks about the Weather from School Textbooks." These are statements about the composition of air, which according to Lessing is shocked by the action of lightning into losing its nitrogen to the soil: "A lightning flash is only a spark which bridges cloud and earth or cloud and cloud. But in order for this spark to happen, one place must be negatively charged and the other positively charged" (*FGC*, p. 290). Out of the conflict of negative and positive impulses, lightning fire is born. This image is a figure for psychological processes that operate by means of conversion or dialectic. In the Coldridge household a number of people undergo "conversions" from one "pole, or opposition point" to another — in political or personal terms. Mark "switches" (note the vocabulary of electricity) from an aristocratic liberalism to Communism and finally through both to a cynical idealism. Martha feels herself flipping from love to hate, from left to right, and wonders what the "pressure" or the "switch" is that causes the change. Moreover, she begins to think that this phenomenon is not purely personal. Just as she had noted that the impulse to separate things off into neat little rooms was characteristic of her generation, she now notices that the time when she is susceptible to conversion is a time when a great many people are breaking out of past patterns. "It was a year of protest and activity and lively disagreement — . . . change, breaking up, clearing away, movement" (*FGC*, p. 292). But Martha realizes that this change may not be progressive. It represents a conversion of energy but not necessarily a push in the right direction.

Jack is the first person through whom Martha becomes aware of an impersonal energy that operates like electricity. Her love-making with him is described at first in terms of currents and pulses of the sea (the metaphor for her affair with Thomas Stern) but these terms are simultaneously the terms of electrical energy. Martha begins to see Jack as an "instrument" that focuses a "high alert tension" and acts as a dynamo to wash the lovers "through and through by currents of energy" (*FGC*, pp. 61, 62, 64). However, while Jack positively acts as the instrument that makes both lovers "conductors or conduits for the force which moved them and lifted them" (*FGC*, p. 495), he at the same time hints to the uncomprehending Martha about the negative potential of this energy. He mentions that it is necessary to maintain firm control of these processes, for there "is a sort of wavelength you can tune into" and it is as apt to be the wavelength of hate as the place of love:

> "If you can get beyond *I hate* — then you find, *there is hatred, always there*. You can say, I am going into hatred now, it's just a force. That's all,

it's not anything, not good or bad, you go into it. But man! — you have to
come out again fast, it's too strong, it's too dangerous. But it's like a thousand volts of electricity."(*FGC*, p. 60)

When Martha consciously tries to recover the state of receptivity that
she had accidentally entered as a girl on the veld and with Jack in London, she finds herself victimized by the "pairs of opposites," which continually switch on and off in her mind. She finds herself gripped by
sadistic impulses, then suddenly by masochistic fantasies. She finds herself using the language of anti-Semitism and as suddenly repudiating
her own statements. Gradually she comes to see that these are "what all
those books call 'the pairs of opposites.' . . . Every attitude, emotion,
thought, has its opposite held in balance out of sight but there all the
time. Push any one of them to an extreme, and boomps-a-daisy, over
you go into its opposite. . . . A body is a machine for the conversion of
one kind of energy into another" (*FGC*, pp. 539, 550).

Especially through the second and third sections of the novel, when
she is trying to share the energy of madness with Lynda, images of vi-
bration, wires, dynamos, volts, currents, tension, and fields or grounds
fill Martha's narrated monologue. When she becomes aware that it is
possible for individuals to share the same "wavelength" or to tap into
each other's stream of thought, these electrical images mix with images
of electronic communication.[14] The brain is likened to a radio and the
various pools of universal emotion are called stations, bands, or wavelengths. Thoughts or emotions may be "in the air" for sensitive individuals to "pick up" or "tune in to." At best, these metaphors point to a sort
of Jungian pan-psychism. Martha understands at one point, for instance, that Jack brings to her a timeless range of sexual responses, and
that she can connect these with a pool of universal sexual energies that
she shares with others:

> There was woman coming to man for sex, and her reactions, which were
> expected, known, understood. There was woman experiencing this new
> thing, sadism, masochism — succumbing to it then holding it off, refusing
> it, looking at it. And different from either, an impersonal current which
> she brought from Mark, who had it from Lynda, who had it from . . .
> the impersonal sea. (*FGC*, p. 496)

Negatively, these metaphors can be used to account for madness.
Lessing, influenced by R. D. Laing, reflects here his notion that the so-
called mentally ill are those who are particularly receptive to reality
and able to hear the thoughts of other people by simply tuning in to

their wavelengths. Operating at the threshold of human capabilities, these special individuals are sometimes unable to control their experiences:

> There were people whose machinery had gone wrong, and they were like radio sets which, instead of being tuned in to one programme, were tuned in to a dozen simultaneously. *And they didn't know how to switch them off.* Even to imagine the hell of it was enough to make one want to run, to cover one's ears. (*FGC*, p. 518)

Even if the sensitive "receivers" are not overloaded by being attuned to too many wavelengths at once, they may still be destroyed if they become stuck on a channel that transmits only negative messages. This is Martha's metaphor for Lynda's state. As a girl Lynda had been too aware of the hatred that adults directed against her, and she learned to hear too exclusively the self-hater, the inner voice that echoes and amplifies the criticisms that come from outside the self. Moreover, everyone conspired to deny her the knowledge her specially developed senses gave her. Since no one wanted to hear that Lynda's stepmother hated her, everyone denied that she did—and particularly denied that Lynda could possibly sense such a fact, even if it were true.

It is suggested that the alarming number of people who have nervous breakdowns in the novel do so because like Lynda they are being worn down by the tension between society's pressure to repress a body of knowledge that lies within them and the opposite pressure of the knowledge, which wants to force itself out into the open. In earlier volumes of *Children of Violence*, Lessing repeatedly expressed this tension, in the image of a well that is filled with an emotion ready to overflow at any moment, threatening to pour through the "cracked surface" of a social facade.[15] In *The Four-Gated City*, Lessing abandons that image in order to express the conviction that there was once access to the insight or emotion in question and that it has been deliberately suppressed. Martha therefore speaks of putting experiences into cold storage and of burying evidence, and later of conducting a salvage operation to recover lost perceptions, of opening locked doors and rediscovering once-known territories.

These metaphors become so vivid that the reader almost comes to believe in the existence of a literal "tempting, dangerous, glamorous territory lying just behind or interfused with this world of . . . landscapes, shores, countries forbidden and countries marked Open, each with its distinctive airs and climates and inhabitants living and dead, with its gardens and its forests and seas and lakes" (*FGC*, p. 462). Martha lives this fantasy — and the one about an empty, lit space to be found at the center of her consciousness — so intensely that the fantasy becomes as real for the reader as the Coldridge house itself, which in turn becomes a bit fantastic, a symbol of Martha's divided self. In depicting the reality of her character Martha, Lessing adheres to her statement of belief in "The Small Personal Voice": "I define realism as art which springs so vigorously and naturally from a strongly-held, though not necessarily intellectually-defined, view of life that it absorbs symbolism."[16]

It is important to keep this perspective on Martha's metaphors, if we are not to reject as simply insane her conviction of having developed a special ability to hear the thoughts of others. For example, Martha describes a time when she begins to hear Paul's thoughts. She says that she seems to have switched on to a radio channel that carries Paul's fantasies. She begins wondering whether she is picking up Paul's words in their original form or whether some mechanism might be translating his feelings into words. She speaks, too, of the law by which "one did not hear something, pick up something that one didn't know, or was prepared to accept, already" (*FGC*, p. 371). While Martha is thinking in terms of the radio metaphor, her speculations may seem bizarre. But she finally states the case in pedestrian prose: "Perhaps it was more a question of remembering — that was a more accurate word, or idea" (*FGC*, p. 371). All the metaphors of cold storage, salvage operations, hidden territories, and radios express one psychological fact — that society and our own instincts for self-protection cause us to repress the great bulk of what we perceive, but that through great effort we may remember these perceptions and achieve extraordinary insights into reality. If we were to be conscious of all we already know, reality would be so much more than we now know that it would be as if whole new countries had suddenly appeared next to the one we have consciously lived in.

Now perhaps we can understand the relevance of the epigraph to part one, a passage from Rachel Carson's *The Edge of the Sea*:

> In its being and its meaning, this coast represents not merely an uneasy equilibrium of land and water masses; it is eloquent of a continuing change now actually in progress, a change being brought about by the life processes of living things. Perhaps the sense of this comes most clearly to one standing on a bridge between the Keys, looking out over miles of water, dotted with mangrove-covered islands to the horizon. This may seem a dreamy land, steeped in its past. But under the bridge a green mangrove seedling floats, long and slender, one end already beginning to show the development of roots, beginning to reach down through the water, ready to grasp and to root firmly in any muddy shoal that may lie across its path. Over the years the mangroves bridge the water gaps between the

islands; they extend the mainland; they create new islands. And the currents that stream under the bridge, carrying the mangrove seedling, are one with the currents that carry plankton to the coral animals building the offshore reef, creating a wall of rocklike solidity, a wall that one day may be added to the mainland. So this coast is built. (*FGC*, p. 2)

As the mangrove root connects shoal to shoal, extending the mainland, so Martha's salvage operations recover territory and add it to her personal "landscapes, shores, countries" (*FGC*, p. 462). And as with the mangroves, this change is "being brought about by the life processes of living things."

A whole series of metaphors links Martha's development with the natural evolution of living things growing beyond the previous limits of their nature. These images begin in the first volume, *Martha Quest*, when in her moment of difficult knowledge, Martha "felt the rivers under the ground forcing themselves painfully along her veins, swelling them out in an unbearable pressure; her flesh was the earth, and suffered growth like a ferment. . . . It was as if something new was demanding conception, with her flesh as host" (*MQ*, pp. 52–53).

The tension in this experience, the image of fluid straining against a swelling vessel, and the suggestion of rebirth are repeated toward the end of the volume, when Martha remembers a scene from the farm. In a passage that fittingly retains the pastoral simplicity of an idyll, while it moves toward a distasteful over-ripeness, Martha encounters an image that exhilarates her, though at this point she cannot understand what it signifies.

> She saw, as if the deep-green substance of the leafage had taken on another form, two enormous green caterpillars, about seven inches long, the thickness of a wrist; pale green they were, a sickly intense green, smooth as skin, and their silky-paper surfaces were stretched to bursting, as if the violence of this pulsating month was growing in them so fast (Martha could see the almost liquid substance swimming inside the frail tight skin) that they might burst asunder with the pressure of their growth before they could turn themselves, as was right and proper, into dry cases, like bits of stick, and so into butterflies or moths. They were loathsome, disgusting; Martha felt sick as she looked at these fat and seething creatures rolling clumsily on their light frond of leaves, blind, silent, their heads indicated only by two small horns, mere bumpish projections of the greenish skin, like pimples — they were repulsive, but she was exhilarated. She went home singing. (*MQ*, p. 199)

These creatures are participating in their proper cycle of development; yet, repulsively, they push their development beyond its former bounds,

stretching their skins to the limit. This image becomes a model not only
for Martha's unorthodox process of self-development but also for the
evolution of the human race. In *Landlocked*, Martha's teacher Thomas
Stern suggests that the pains of her life are simply her straining against a
"frail tight skin" like the caterpillar. Perhaps, he proposes, there may
come one day a mutation that will allow a transformation in the human
race such as the caterpillar's metamorphosis from crawling insect to
butterfly. "Perhaps that's why we are all so sick. Something new is trying to get born through our thick skins" (*L*, p. 116). The loathsomeness
of the "fat and seething creatures" is analogous to the seeming madness
of the many persons who compose the vanguard in a process of psychic
evolution. "I tell you, Martha," he says, "if I see a sane person, then I
know he's mad. You know, the householders. It's we who are nearest to
being—what's needed" (*L*, p. 116).

These caterpillars with overexpanded skins are about to become
butterflies. Lynda, Martha, and Thomas Stern are "in the main line of
evolution," yet society rejects them because of their highly developed
psychic capacities.

> In spite of . . . society's never having been more shrilly self-conscious than
> it is now, it is an organism which above all is unable to think, whose essen-
> tial characteristic is the inability to diagnose its own condition. It is like
> one of those sea creatures who have tentacles or arms equipped with
> numbing poisons: anything new, whether hostile or helpful, must be
> stunned into immobility or at least wrapped around with poison or a cloud
> of distorting colour. (*FGC*, p. 451)

Thus poisons, drugs, and hypnosis become images of all those processes by which society prevents the natural course of human evolution.
Martha observes this poisoning process at work in her first meeting with
a member of the British upper class. The first thing she notices about
Henry Matheson is his complacency. To his discomfort, she reproaches
him: "You're drugged, you're hypnotised, you don't seem to be able to
see facts when they're in front of you. You're the victim of a lot of slo-
gans" (*FGC*, p. 30). This encounter leads her to the conviction that she
must "live in such a way that I don't just—turn into a hypnotised animal" (*FGC*, p. 98).

Like everyone else, Martha does allow herself to be hypnotised, but
through Lynda's tutelage she learns to waken herself. Awakening
means remembering all that society has required she forget; even
harder, it means seeing at every moment all of an experience, not just
the part that society requires one to focus on. There is a long passage of

intense, almost surreal description, in which Martha goes out for a walk, having awakened her sensibilities. The prose alternates between the raptures of full perception and the tortures of seeing other people who are blinded and poisoned, uncomprehending. At the sight of the sky and the foliage she exclaims:

> Let me keep this, let me not lose it, oh, how could I have borne it all these years, all this life, being dead and asleep and not seeing, seeing nothing; for now everything was so much there, present, existing in an effulgence of delight, offering themselves to her, till she felt they were extensions of her and she of them, or at least, their joy and hers sang together, so that she felt they might almost cry out, Martha! Martha! for happiness, because she was seeing them, feeling them again after so long an absence from them. (*FGC*, pp. 505–506)

On the other hand, she is repelled by the humans, because they are such a perversion of what they naturally should be. A long Swiftian passage depicts the sluggish creatures in all their vileness. Finally Martha identifies the worst horror about these "defectively evolved animals":

> The eyes had a look which contradicted their function, which was to see, to observe, for as she passed pair after pair of eyes, they all looked half drugged, or half asleep, dull, as if the creatures had been hypnotised or poisoned, for these people walked in their fouled and disgusting streets full of ordure and bits of refuse and paper as if they were not conscious of their existence here, were somewhere else: and they were somewhere else, for only one in a hundred of these semi-animals could have said, "I am here, now, and conscious that I am here, now, noticing what is around me." (*FGC*, p. 506)

A bit more prosaically, Martha had seen the same vision when she ate dinner with Henry Matheson, her would-be benefactor: "It was like talking to – well, the blind, people blinkered from birth" (*FGC*, p. 33). Nonetheless, blindness and stupor are not confined to the upper class; they are human afflictions wherever society has had its effect on the individual.

Martha herself battles continually to waken herself from lethargy and impercipience. At the very brink of her final moment of vision, Martha feels "herself as a heavy impervious insensitive lump that, like a planet doomed always to be dark on one side, had vision in front only, a myopic searchlight blind except for the tiny three-dimensional path open immediately before her eyes in which the outline of a tree, a rose, emerged, then submerged in dark" (*FGC*, p. 591). How far she is, at this point, from the children of the coming apocalypse, who will not only luxuriate in the sun, sea, and flowers that presently surround them but also sense the sounds and sights of distant places. Indeed, these survivors of the apocalypse will awaken to heights of perception heretofore unknown. From her station on Faris Island, after the disaster, Martha will report:

> It is a place with a rare fine air, a "high" air, if I can use that word. Sometimes it seems that inside ordinary light shimmers another kind of brilliance, but very subtle and delicate. And the texture of our lives, eating, sleeping, being together, has a note in it that can't be quite caught, as if we were all of us a half-tone or a bridging chord in some symphony being played out of earshot with icebergs and forests and mountains for instruments. There is a transparency, a crystalline gleam.
>
> It is the children who have it, who are sensitive to it — being with them means we have to be quick and sensitive ourselves, as far as we can be. (*FGC*, pp. 645–646)

These children are Martha's butterflies, born out of the straining of their thick caterpillar skins (*MQ*, 199; *L*, p. 116). They are the mutants by way of radiation who were predicted by the students on the Aldermaston March (*FGC*, p. 414). They are the response to a necessity that man acquire new organs of perception, as the Sufi prophet Idries Shah says in the passage used as epigraph to part four of *The Four-Gated City*. Shah states in flat prose the belief that Lessing has been expressing metaphorically:

> Humanity is evolving towards a certain destiny. We are all taking part in that evolution. Organs come into being as a result of a need for specific organs. The human being's organism is producing a new complex of organs in response to such a need. In this age of the transcending of time and space, the complex of organs is concerned with the transcending of time and space. What ordinary people regard as sporadic and occasional bursts of telepathic and prophetic power are seen by the Sufi as nothing less than the first stirrings of these same organs. The difference between all evolution up to date and the present need for evolution is that for the past ten thousand years or so we have been given the possibility of a conscious evolution. So essential is this more rarified evolution that our future depends on it. (*FGC*, p. 448)

Martha, with her intermittent access to heights of perception, is, as one of the new children reports, "a sort of experimental model" of which nature has had enough now that the clairvoyant children have been born. She has done her duty as part of the evolutionary line. Like the sycamore tree, Martha waited for her "curve of growth" to develop, until "from a dead-looking eye, or knot, it bursts again in a new branch, in a shape that is inevitable but known only to itself"(*FGC*, p. 201). She was admirably persistent in nurturing the growth of her extrasensory skills — surrounded as she was by a society hostile to such growth. After all, "how long did roots live under a crust of air-excluding tarmac?" (*FGC*, p. 8). The condition of her growth has been a willingness to move in response to the rhythms of life, a fluid sort of patience. "She had learned that one thing, that most important thing, which was that one simply had to go on, take one step after another: this process in itself held the keys" (*FGC*, p. 588). The steps may seem to take one in repetitious circles, but when all the working-through is done "you start growing on your own account" (*FGC*, p. 454). In the meantime, repetition, the turning of the ferris wheel, affords the finest wisdom that one may achieve. Martha's final wisdom comes through a voice that has repeated in her brain since the first vision of her girlhood. It says that beauty, transcendence — whatever she is seeking — is "here, where else, you fool, you poor fool, where else has it been, ever . . ." (*FGC*, p. 591).

If the novel proper ends with a vision of beauty in the present moment, the Appendix takes the reader over to an apocalyptic future time in which prophecy is fulfilled. The metaphors of poisoning that have appeared in the whole series intensify throughout *The Four-Gated City*, culminating in Lynda's vision of a contaminated England, looking like "a poisoned mouse lying dead in a corner" (*FGC*, p. 566). She also sees a "kind of frozen dew" that covers everything with "a faintly phosphorescent or begemmed stillness" (*FGC*, p. 566). In the Appendix these images are fulfilled in accounts of England's contamination by radiation after a nuclear accident. In fact, the exiled Martha speculates that before the catastrophe everyone had an unconscious foreknowledge of coming disaster. The accuracy of these prophecies, along with the appearance of the predicted special race of children, seems to point toward the existence of the "certain destiny" of which Idries Shah spoke. Thus Martha was right when she suspected that life was inexorably determined by forces beyond her control, but she was wrong to fear these forces and to believe that inevitability was inimical to the human race. Martha had thought that inevitability implied the worthlessness of human will and consciousness. But now she learns that it is possible for her to live with dignity in harmony with the will of evolution.

There is a difference between fatalistic resignation and a fruitful receptivity. One may, Martha discovers, accept the demand that the future be conceived in one's own flesh (*MQ*, p. 52). One may be one's own midwife and assist the future in its birth. One may, like the mangrove, throw off seeds that will ultimately join the mainland (the dominant society) to the islands (groups of innovators, such as the children on Martha's island). Or one may refuse, like Mark Coldridge.

Thus, inevitability is Janus-faced. While it destroyed the will of some, others "it quietened and sobered; made them grow fast, developed them" (*FGC*, p. 601). The attitude of fatalism that plagued the young Martha Quest, causing her to lie down and let fate march over her, also victimizes Mark Coldridge, author of the utopian novel, *A City in the Desert*. Affected by the "fatalism, the determinism, which is so oddly rooted in [Communism] that revolutionary party" (*FGC*, p. 148), he falls from idealism into nihilism and loses his will. He, like Martha and Thomas Stern before him, imitates Nasrudin of the Sufi fable: When a chill runs through him, he becomes convinced that he is dead and just lies on the grass while wolves eat his donkey (*L*, p. 213). It may seem illogical to retain one's sense of free will in the face of determinism, but that is what the wisdom of the tale and of *Children of Violence* counsels. If one gives up believing that one's decisions and acts matter, one ends a cynic like Mark, moaning, "What point has there ever been?" (*FGC*, p. 653). On the other hand, if one follows continually the drift of events, using intelligence and imagination to chart a survival course, one may, at last, like Martha arrive at an island where even "the face of the world's horror could be turned around to show the smile of an angel" (*FGC*, p. 643).

While the jaded Mark only dreams mawkishly of the ideal city about which he had once written a prophetic novel, Martha actually labors to bring it about. As a girl she had envisioned "a noble city, set foursquare and colonnaded along its falling, flower-bordered terraces," a fabulous and ancient city where children of all races play together among white pillars and tall trees (*MQ*, p. 11). As an adult she is haunted by the image of the ideal city, the purity of which contrasts so painfully with the actual, rotten capitals of Zambesia and England. This double vision is incorporated in Mark's novel *A City in the Desert*, vaguely reminiscent of Borges's "Tlön, Uqbar, Orbius Tertius." As a "shadow city of poverty and beastliness" threatens to overwhelm the ideal city, it is protected by its gardeners, the hidden keepers of an ideal order:

> A great number of the inhabitants spent their lives in the gardens, and the fountains and parks. Even the trees and plants were known for their properties and qualities and grown exactly in a relation to other plants, and to people and buildings; and it was among the gardeners, so the stories went,

that could be found, if only one could recognize them, most of the hidden people who protected and fed the city. (*FGC*, p. 140)

Through the metaphor of the gardeners, the dilemma of Martha's private *Bildung* — and that of the collective as well — is resolved. She learns to come to terms with the inner order of experience and thus is able to save a number of people from destruction. It is on account of her intuition of the coming apocalypse that a small number of people are sequestered on an island, where the gifted children of a new age are born. These children she refers to as "our guardians." The prophecy of Mark's novel seems due for fulfillment when Martha sends the most gifted of these children, Joseph, to become a gardener in Nairobi, the city in the desert where Francis heads a colony of refugees from the holocaust. And with these gardens we return to the guiding metaphor of organic growth. The order of the garden is natural, but human gardeners must learn the principles behind that order and tend it continually.

In accepting the natural order of life, Martha Quest has not simply given up choice, as Barnouw suggests; rather, she has given up egocentric willfulness in order to exercise choice wisely in the service of a collective *Bildung*. She is not passive to the point of despair, as Spacks asserts, but rather she waits until the time for action is ripe — she knows the value of latency. Moreover, far from there being "little positive meaning" in Martha's attempts to free herself from the horrors of her past, the movement of her life is positively redemptive. Finally, through the metaphors that thread through the five-novel sequence, Lessing supplies what critic Enright did not see: an "artistically true . . . connection between the Martha Quest whom we first met as a fifteen-year-old in the novel named after her and the old woman" who nurtures the children of violence.

In an interview given just after the publication of *The Four-Gated City*, Lessing expressed a strong faith in the future of mankind, even though that future may be born out of violence. "Maybe out of destruction there will be born some new creature. I don't mean physically. What interests me more than anything is how our minds are changing, how our ways of perceiving reality are changing. The substance of life receives shocks all the time, every place, from bombs, from the all-pervasive violence. Inevitably, the mind changes."[17] Images of growth, evolution, and energy conversion present her hope, while images of enclosure, constriction, blindness, poisoning, and stupor present the obstacles to that hope, which is finally embodied in the image of the four-gated city and its hidden gardeners. In the struggle between the human desire for good and all within us that holds us back from attaining it,

the good will prevail. That vision is nowhere more vivid than in Martha
Quest's report of a year on her island:

> During that year we hit the depths of our fear, a lowering depression
> which made it hard for us not to simply walk into that deadly sea and let
> ourselves drown there. But it was also during that year when we became
> aware of a sweet high loveliness somewhere, like a flute played only just
> within hearing. We all felt it. We talked about it, thinking it was a sign that
> we must be dying. It was as if all the air was washed with a bright prom-
> ise. Of what? Love? Joy? It was as if the face of the world's horror could be
> turned around to show the smile of an angel. It was during this year that
> many of us walking alone or in groups along the cliffs or beside the inland
> streams met and talked to people who were not of our company, nor like
> any people we had known—though some of us had dreamed of them. It
> was as if the veil between this world and another had worn so thin that
> people from the sun could walk together and be companions. When this
> time which was so terrible and so marvellous had gone by some of us began
> to wonder if we had suffered from a mass hallucination. But we knew we
> had not. It was from that time, because of what we were told, that we took
> heart and held on to our belief in a future for our race. (*FGC*, p. 643)

# Chapter Four

# *The Golden Notebook*

## THE CONSTRUCTION OF
## A POSTMODERN ORDER

Smoothly, organically, the metaphors of *Children of Violence* trace the metamorphosis of a progressivist faith. Like Thomas Stern's caterpillar, Martha Quest's political commitment to leftist politics stumbles awkwardly along for a while, becomes overburdened and ugly, retreats into the chrysalis of the Coldridge household, and emerges transformed into the vision of psychic evolution that dominates the coda of *The Four-Gated City*. At the midpoint of that cycle of change which now seems so fluid in its progress, Lessing stepped aside from the *Children of Violence* series to write a book about the terrors of destruction and stress of reconstruction undergone by the creature in the midst of such a metamorphosis. In 1962, four years after writing *A Ripple From the Storm*, the third book of the Martha Quest quintet, Lessing published *The Golden Notebook.*[1]

*The Golden Notebook* tells the story of Anna Wulf's transformation of personal and political consciousness, and it marks as well a transformation in Lessing's artistic identity. With this novel, the writer who once held "the view that the realist novel, the realist story, is the highest form of prose writing; higher than and out of the reach of any compari-

This chapter first appeared as "Nostalgia and Irony: The Postmodern Order of *The Golden Notebook,*" *Modern Fiction Studies* 26 (Spring 1980): 31–48. *Modern Fiction Studies,* © 1980 by Purdue Research Foundation, West Lafayette, Indiana 47907.

son with expressionism, impressionism, symbolism, naturalism, or any other ism," the writer who had proudly identified her writing with the novels of Tolstoy, Stendhal, Dostoevsky, Balzac, Turgenev, and Chekhov,[2] suddenly and emphatically rejects both "the conventional novel" and the modernist novel[3] as models for her own. Seemingly overnight, the caterpillar becomes butterfly — the traditional novelist becomes not merely a modern novelist, but a postmodern novelist. In this new and powerful identity, Lessing reshapes the form of the novel, giving it a postmodern order.

In postmodern fiction,[4] form is forced to acknowledge and accommodate the force of chaos, the source and destroyer of all form. Thus it is a kind of fiction ideally suited to express the simultaneous destruction and reconstruction that occurs within the psyche in times of personal and social metamorphosis. The postmodern writer realizes that in all realms of life chaos and order are constantly impinging on one another in a process of continual transformation. It becomes the novelist's task to provide a fictional form that can give ample scope to this dynamic interplay of order and chaos.

In *The Golden Notebook*, Lessing succeeds in creating such a form. In her new identity as a postmodern writer, she refuses to put a lid on chaos; neither does she let chaos freely reign. Instead she shapes the novel so that its structure and story express the powerful tension between chaos and order — a tension that characterizes the postmodern consciousness.[5]

The reader's first impression is one of dissonance. The complicated, highly ordered superstructure of the novel is clearly at odds with the apparent disorder of the content within that structure. This form-content split in the novel in turn mirrors the heroine's awareness of the split between the forms (social, artistic, emotional, intellectual) of her own consciousness and the experiential chaos that these forms attempt to control. It is important to realize, however, that this pair of parallel contrasts, so immediately apparent to the reader, is actually an oversimplification. There is more to the content of Anna's notebooks than mere chaos, if what we mean by chaos is utter formlessness. Rather, the various notebooks contain material that has been liberated from outworn forms and that holds its state of formlessness only as potentiality, beginning quickly to move toward new and provisional form, toward the constitution of a new cosmos. Thus there is no final *opposition* in the novel between chaos and form. Rather, chaos itself is seen to be continually destroying forms while moving itself to create new ones. Chaos and form are inextricably bound to one another in a dialectical process.[6] Toward the end of the novel, Anna herself imagines two people in the process of falling out of form into chaos: "Both cracking up because of a deliberate attempt to transcend their own limits. And out of the chaos, a new kind of strength" (p. 400). Outmoded form is broken by the force of chaos, primordial being, but the matter of chaos regroups itself into a new form, based on new values or strengths.

In Anna's first line of dialogue, she declares, "As far as I can see, everything's cracking up" (p. 9). The structure of the novel is designed to emphasize this fragmentation. The four colored notebooks reflect the four aspects of life that Anna can no longer reconcile with one another; her success as a published novelist (Black), her failure in political work (Red), her efforts of imagination (Yellow), her struggle to revise her own self-concept (Blue). In addition to these notebooks, written in the first person by Anna, there is a framing novel, called "Free Women," about the Anna who writes the notebooks. The four notebooks and the novel are additionally split each into sections and arranged in a neat pattern: "Free Women" 1, Black 1, Red 1, Yellow 1, Blue 1; "Free Women" 2, Black 2, Red 2, Yellow 2, Blue 2, etc.[7] Lessing accomplishes several purposes by this dizzying arrangement of the novel's parts. First, she reflects the fact that, for Anna, existence has fragmented and threatens to return to an undifferentiated state of chaos. However, the mathematically neat arrangement of the splintered parts of Anna's experience suggests that in the face of threatened chaos, she is overreacting by imposing an order in her novel that does not properly belong to the material. Finally, Lessing suggests to the reader that while the many parts of the book treat separate subjects, they are actually unified by an underlying pattern, which their odd juxtaposition is designed to highlight.

The first striking element of that pattern is that each notebook (as well as "Free Women") starts just as "the stage sets collapse"[8] in one theater of Anna's life, leaving her without a context within which to play her part. That is, each notebook begins as one form of her life begins to yield to chaos. The drama of each notebook is her battle not to be seduced by "a lying nostalgia" (p. 61) — a yearning for the recovery of the sense of form, the stage illusion of moral certainty, innocence, unity, and peace. In effect, this yearning is a desire for unreality and nonexistence. Since the yearning can never be fulfilled, it always leads to painful frustration and often to nihilism and despair.

Although Anna's nostalgia for moral sleep is acute, it is countered by an aspiration toward full, waking consciousness. In the battleground of each notebook, moreover, consciousness conquers, and Anna takes a victory, in existentialist terms. For her, as for Camus, "everything begins with consciousness and nothing is worth anything except through it."[9] In Anna's case, full consciousness means facing up to the power of chaos and accepting its effect on her life. Yet Lessing does not let the case rest there. More acutely than her precursors Camus and Sartre, Lessing senses that every bit of ground gained for consciousness is saturated with irony — and that an excess of irony easily leads to bitterness, cynicism, and despair.

If the plot of each notebook concerns Anna's struggle to subdue her nostalgia for form and attain consciousness of chaos, the hidden and opposing plot of the novel as a whole concerns her struggle against the poisoning cynicism that accompanies her new knowledge. In the first three notebooks — Black, Red, and Yellow — Anna as a lone character moves from naiveté, through awareness, to cynicism, withdrawal, and loss of faith. Moreover, in the process of writing each of these three notebooks she loses confidence, becomes disoriented, doubts her own veracity, and finally despairs of communicating at all. In the Blue Notebook, on the other hand, there is a slow movement away from detachment, ennui, and self-consciousness toward commitment, passion, and unself-consciousness. This positive movement flows into the Golden Notebook, where Anna, by opening herself to chaos and emotion, achieves a mature vision that is simultaneously ironic and committed, detached and involved. In the overall dynamic of the novel, the detachment and irony that accompany awareness of chaos finally come to balance with the attachment and warmth that accompany commitment to the forms we impose on chaos.

Within each notebook, then, there is a pattern of opposition between nostalgia and awareness, as between their concomitants, pain and irony. In an analogous but larger pattern, the first three notebooks, where awareness is bought at the cost of irony, are opposed by the Blue Notebook, where moral and emotional passions reawaken. The Golden Notebook is the vehicle through which these antitheses are channeled into dialectic. Failure to take account of this dialectical structure is bound to result in a distorted reading of the major themes of the novel. "Living inside the subjective highly-coloured mist" (p. 122) of any one notebook, the reader is apt to be so intensely struck by a theme or attitude that he will fail to appreciate the countertheme or countertone developed elsewhere in this long and sometimes perplexing novel.

I propose an unorthodox method of examining the workings of this dynamic in the novel — that is, to unshuffle Lessing's deck and take a look separately at each colored notebook and the novel "Free Women." This is to play Anna's game — to "name" the pattern of each notebook, rescuing it from chaos, as she would say (p. 402). So long as we take care to return the pieces to their splintered condition, we should do justice to both impulses in the novel — the one toward form and the one toward chaos.

## THE BLACK NOTEBOOK

In the first of the notebooks, Anna's yearnings for an ideal order are twice frustrated. In the past that she chronicles, her younger self aspires to save the exploited blacks of Africa from racial oppression; she imagines the establishment of an ideal society in which peoples of all colors would participate equally. In the present, an older Anna has an equally idealistic aim — to discover the complete truth about her past and to render it with absolute objectivity in writing. Both these impulses toward perfect order encounter resistance from chaotic matter: in the past, human jealousies and passions had defeated Anna's first efforts at social reorganization, and in the present her desire for truth is frustrated by the unreliability of memory and language. Anna realizes that her elaborate and very rational plans for existence are not to be supported by reality. The whole of *The Golden Notebook* is an exploration of what happens emotionally after that moment of revelation and frustration.

In the Black Notebook, Anna becomes aware of two stages of her reaction — the first, a nostalgia in which she prolongs the sense of loss and yearning; the second, a bitter cynicism, in which she allows disappointment to immobilize her both morally and emotionally. To the existentialists Camus and Sartre (who often seem to echo through these pages),[10] both reactions seem natural, though destructive. For Camus, nostalgia is simply an "appetite for the absolute"[11] so strong that one will stoop to any self-deceptions in order to satisfy it. In his writing, as in Anna's, this feeling is oddly linked with the romantic lure of chaos and anarchy. "A lying nostalgia" leads Anna to "a longing for licence, for freedom, for the jungle, for formlessness" (p. 61). Denied her ideal of perfect moral order, Anna can imagine no alternative other than "the death that we all wanted, for each other and for ourselves" (p. 135). If she and her friends "have been half in love with easeful Death," it is for reasons similar to those of the romantic poets. A childlike inability to accept limits to the satisfaction of their extreme yearning for an absolute order sometimes leads the romantics and Anna to a form of "nihilism, an angry readiness to throw everything overboard, a willingness, a longing to become part of dissolution" (p. 62).

Like the thwarted romantic, too, Anna excuses her imaginative poverty by positing a literary golden age — some past and better time when poetic inspiration was freely available, as it is no longer. In this self-serving piece of myth-making, Anna follows the lead of another frustrated romantic, the melancholy Matthew Arnold, envying those writers "born in days when wits were fresh and clear / And life ran gaily as the sparkling Thames; / Before this strange disease of modern life, / With its sick hurry, its divided aims / Its heads o'ertax'd, its palsied hearts, was rife."[12] She complains, echoing Arnold: "The novel has become a function of the fragmented society, the fragmented consciousness. Human beings are so divided, are becoming more and more divided, *and more subdivided in themselves,* reflecting the world, that" it has become impossible to write a great novel on the old model—"the only kind of novel which interests me: a book powered with an intellectual or moral passion strong enough to create order, to create a new way of looking at life" (p. 59). Against the dissolution of individuals and society into chaos, Anna wishes to posit an alternative force, a movement toward a new order that will grant new meanings. In fact, she feels it her duty as an artist to create such order.

Ironically, Anna despairs of fulfilling her artistic role just as she has begun to create the conditions for performing it. In her memoir of the Mashopi summer (Black Notebook 1, pp. 55–135), Anna is conducting a devastating critique of her former artistic stance, which had been undermined by romanticism, nostalgia, and cynicism. These false attitudes had poisoned the novel that she had made out of her Mashopi memories, *Frontiers of War.* Now, however, Anna is trying to diagnose the sickness in her own literary sensibility, in the hope of a cure. As narrator of the Mashopi memoir, she devotes herself carefully to depicting and criticizing the emotional atmosphere of that time and place—as gauged by the tones of people's voices. The predominant tone, the same one that permeated *Frontiers of War,* now threatens to infect the Black Notebook: "I am again falling into the wrong tone," she admits. "And yet I hate that tone, and yet we all lived inside it for months and years, and it did us all, I am sure, a great deal of damage. It was self-punishing, a locking of feeling, an inability or a refusal to fit conflicting things together to make a whole; so that one can live inside it, no matter how terrible" (p. 63).

Perhaps it is fear of that tone that makes her avoid the Mashopi memories in Black Notebook 2 (pp. 243–254). If anything, however, the cynicism deepens in Anna's parody of her agent's letters, in her self-mockery when discussing *Frontiers of War,* and in her sarcastic sniping at an American television agent who suggests that the novel be turned into a musical. In the last line of Black Notebook 2, though, Anna comes to an important realization. Thinking back over her appointment with the woman from American television, she recognizes that there was only one honest moment — when she broke through all the ironic parrying and aggressively announced to the conservative American that she was a Communist. "Yet I feel ashamed and dissatisfied and depressed" (p. 254). The choice is between earnest commitment and ironic detachment, and Anna is uncomfortable with either. Her commitment and earnestness reveal that she is naive enough to believe in order and meaning; yet her detachment and irony suggest that she is reacting defensively to the breakdown of order and meaning. Neither stance is fully acceptable to her, at this point. However, social sanctions clearly favor the ironic attitude. Irony, mockery, parody — these are all considered more civil than the earnest response. Thus Anna is ashamed at her own forthright statement of her political belief.

While the second section of the Black Notebook ends with Anna's dismay at her own earnestness, the third section (pp. 353–382) opens with an illustration of how society scorns such earnestness and sanctions cynicism. Anna tells about an incident in which an old woman's righteous fury over the killing of a pigeon was mocked mercilessly by bystanders in the park. The social group made an outcast not of the "pigeon-murderer" but of the person who remained sufficiently committed to standards of decency to feel outrage. This incident leads Anna to recall the pigeon-shooting episode at Mashopi, in which Paul Blackenhurst is the "pigeon-murderer" and Anna and Maryrose represent the outraged woman. Taking the gang out to shoot pigeons for pie, Paul callously shoots the birds and then leaves them to stink in the sun, all the while speculating aloud on the naturalness of injustice and pain. As he mockingly draws an analogy between the violence of the hunt and the violence between the races in Africa, Anna's friend Maryrose turns against him:

> "I don't find it humorous," said Maryrose.
> "You never find anything humorous," said Paul. "Do you know that you never laugh, Maryrose? Never? Whereas I, whose view of life can only be described as morbid, and increasingly morbid with every passing minute, laugh continuously? How would you account for that?" . . .
> "You weren't laughing. I listen to you a lot . . . and I've noticed that you laugh most when you're saying something terrible. Well I don't call that laughing." (pp. 367–368)

Paul is a lapsed idealist, suffering from his consciousness that the benevolent order he has wished for is not present either in nature or in society. Faced with blood, destruction, injustice, he cannot remain impassive.

He must choose between outrage and laughter. Because he, of all the Mashopi group, is the most "civilized" and self-conscious, he chooses the response that earns him the greatest social respect — a bitter but humorous irony. For example, at the end of the shooting, when it is obvious that everyone is sickened both by his conduct of the hunt and by his cynicism, Paul characteristically strikes a parodic pose, mocking both his own callousness and the earnest disapproval of his friends: "And now let's make tracks fast for the pub. We shall just have time to wash the blood off before it opens" (p. 370).

After chronicling this memory, Anna tries on Paul's pose, attempting to write a series of parodies of her own *Frontiers of War,* but just as she ultimately rejected her earnestness with the television agent, she here becomes disgusted with her own irony. Completely stymied, Anna gives up on the whole attempt to create or control her own attitudes toward her experience. She rejects all the efforts so far in the Black Notebook on the grounds that they have been distorted by either wrongheaded earnestness or sterile irony. She almost penitently fills Black Notebook 4 (pp. 449–450) with "objective" newspaper cuttings referring to violence and death in Africa.

The majority of the Black Notebook is an attempt to eradicate the "wrong tone" that she believes to have distorted her memory and her writing. At the end of the notebook, however, Anna faces what Robert Scholes calls "fallibilism," the realization that all human perceptions and all records of these perceptions are fallible, imperfect, inexact, relative rather than absolute. Therefore, there is no such thing as the "wrong tone" — or alternatively, all tones are equally wrong. With this realization, Anna feels herself at a dead end.

Aside from the newspaper reports, the fourth Black Notebook consists only of a two-page entry in Anna's writing — an account of a dream that expresses Anna's artistic despair. She dreams that her Mashopi memories are being made into a film but that each scene seems distorted by the director, even though the dialogue is accurate. Earlier, Anna had appealed to the medium of film as the most objective (and thus truthful) of the arts, and she had set filmic accuracy as the standard for her writing. The dream at the end of the Black Notebook suggests that even the film has lost its authority as an accurate reflection of reality. Even film is filtered through a human consciousness (the director's) and that means the film cannot convey experience directly, "objectively." There is an obvious analogy between the director's relation to the film and Anna's relation to her writing. Therefore, it is quite significant that Anna does not argue with the director's statement that "it doesn't matter what we film, provided we film something" (p. 450). She seems to have accepted the assumption that all perceptions are relative and the conclusion that it is futile to try to find the "right" view of reality or to record it in film or writing. This is a positive achievement for Anna, but only a partial one, because it leads her to feel "total sterility" as a writer. Anna has recognized the absence of an abiding order in life, in art, and in the relation between the two, but she has not yet learned to allow the energy within disordered matter to regenerate her art, to become the driving force of a new kind of creativity.


## THE RED NOTEBOOK

In the Black Notebook, Anna has lost her faith in both memory and art, learning that neither can adequately order her world. In the Red Notebook, she loses faith in another source of order, the Communist Party. Even as the Red Notebook begins, Anna is aware that her naive enthusiasms as "the Party fanatic" are being undercut by the observations of "the dry, wise, ironical political woman" within herself (p. 141). The notebook is the record of Anna's gradual acknowledgment that, in the words of Maryrose, "We believed everything was going to be beautiful and now we know it won't" (p. 140). In daily life as a Party member, Anna finds that her nostalgia for old and worthy dreams is being undermined by the pressure of cynical awareness. As Comrade John puts it, "The reason why we don't leave the Party is that we can't bear to say good-bye to our ideals for a better world" (pp. 141–142).

Anna and her friends are tending the flame before a temple that the gods have deserted. They try to believe in the power of the Communist Party to provide wholeness, "an end to the split, divided, unsatisfactory way we all live" (p. 142); yet they already know that it has lost its redemptive power. Moreover, lingering at the defunct temple is dangerous to one's health. Anna's first symptom is a vague nausea whenever she hears Party officials — the priests of the political order — lacing their doctrinal pronouncements with overtones of irony, sarcasm, and malice. While other comrades seem unperturbed at the double-think jargon and ironic tones, Anna, with the prophet's sensitivity, realizes that the political temple has been transformed into Babel: "Words lose their meaning suddenly. I find myself listening to a sentence, a phrase, a group of words, as if they are in a foreign language — the gap between what they are supposed to mean, and what in fact they say seems unbridgeable" (p. 258). Within the Party, irony has become a prevailing quality of mind, so that it is no longer possible to hear or to read a sentence without wondering whether it is meant "as parody, irony, or seriously" (p. 259). Anna calls this "the thinning of language against the density of our experience" (p. 259). If the ratio of language to experience has changed, however, it is not language that has thinned; rather, subjective experience has thickened. On account of the breakdown of a single, absolute order of meaning (whether religious, political, or metaphysical), the modern mind has developed nets of suspicion, perversity, and duplicity, which divide each moment of experience into multiple versions and interpretations of the original. Language — linear and discrete — begins to seem inadequate to express the myriad layers of possible meaning held in a single consciousness.

The symbol for the crisis of meaning is a story introduced in Red Notebook 2. It is an account of how Comrade Ted, dedicated Communist and British schoolteacher, travels on vacation to Moscow and is summoned by Stalin to advise him on the current Soviet policy toward Great Britain. In 1952 when Anna first reads it, she is confused by her own multiple reactions: "When I first read it, I thought it was an exercise in irony. Then a very skillful parody of a certain attitude. Then I realized it was serious" (p. 259). Anna further recognizes that the story represents a suppressed fantasy of her own, so that her confused reaction to the story mirrors her inner confusion about her own Communist idealism. Just as Black Notebook 4 shatters the faith in art and order that has been in question throughout the notebook, so Red Notebook 4 destroys Anna's faith in the order provided by the Communist ideal. This last section of the Red Notebook is devoted to a "true" version of the story Anna had read five years earlier. This time, because the Communist faith is dead not only for Anna but for most of her comrades, there is no question of ambiguity. Comrade Ted, now called Harry Mathews, is revealed clearly to be a naive fool, and the story ends with his disillusionment. Anna closes the notebook rather than confront the feelings of loss that the story arouses in her. In this notebook as in the Black one, Anna gives up when she perceives that the forms she has relied on have finally disintegrated. In her relation to her past and to politics, Anna is not strong enough to endure the time of disintegration and recognize the energizing force of chaos.

## THE YELLOW NOTEBOOK

In the notebook devoted to fiction, Anna moves further toward acceptance of chaos by acknowledging, if only tentatively, the evidence of her own art work, the novel "The Shadow of the Third." While her literary and political ideals were broken in the Black and Red Notebooks respectively, here in the Yellow Notebook it is the ideal of love that is shattered. Anna's novel traces the love affair of Ella (an acknowledged self-projection) and Paul Tanner (a fictional version of Anna's lover, Michael). In the novel, Anna mercilessly exposes the self-deceptions and illusions that make Ella's love possible. However, at the moment when it becomes clear that Ella is self-deluded and self-destructive, Anna as narrator recoils from her creation. Astounded by what she has discovered about herself, she breaks off the narrative. Then, abruptly, she resumes it in the form of a *prospectus* for a novel. This act of distancing allows Anna to continue to explore the tension within herself between her yearning for an ideal love and her realization that there is no basis for such a love.

In Ella she represents her romantic, idealizing self — the part of her that wishes to "put her intelligence to sleep" and float in a dream world of love and trust (p. 183). In Paul she represents her more conscious self — the disappointed idealist. He, like Anna in Mashopi or Ella after her abandonment, feels disgust and bitterness in the face of the suffering in the world. This is the legitimate emotion that accompanies consciousness of the distance between the real and the ideal. Whereas Anna condemns herself and short-circuits her emotions whenever she feels despair or nausea before the facts of existence, she is able to allow her fictional surrogate Paul to push the emotion far enough to reveal its positive potential. If all seems ugly to Paul just before he takes action toward realizing an ideal, the ugliness is, as Nietzsche puts it, "the form things assume when we view them with the will to implant a meaning, a new meaning, into what has become meaningless: the accumulated force which compels the creator to consider all that has been created hitherto as unacceptable, ill-constituted, worthy of being denied, ugly!"[13]

After this nausea at existence, there are three alternatives: nostalgia, cynicism, and action. The first two have been explored and repudiated in the Black and Red Notebooks. Paul now recommends action: "You and I are the boulder-pushers. All our lives, you and I, we'll put all our energies, all our talents, into pushing a great boulder up a mountain. The boulder is the truth that the great men know by instinct, and the mountain is the stupidity of mankind" (p. 182). The echoes of Camus's Sisyphus can hardly be accidental. For Camus, Sisyphus is the absurd hero, lucid, conscious of the futility of his labor, yet defiantly "stronger than his rock."[14] Likewise, Paul, often convinced that "ultimately the boulder-pushers don't help anything," nevertheless "works like a madman, out of a furious angry compassion" for humanity. Although dedicated completely to a humanist ideal, Paul, like Sisyphus, has no comfort from illusions that his labors cause progress. In this way, Anna's character Paul gives fictional form to the existential attitude counseled by Camus: the "struggle implies a total absence of hope (which has nothing to do with despair), a continual rejection (which must not be confused with renunciation), and a conscious dissatisfaction (which must not be compared to immature unrest)."[15] These are the attitudes that Paul embodies in the Yellow Notebook.

Unable to accept the starkness of the call to action which she herself has given her character Paul, Anna rejects it in favor of the very reactions Camus counsels against. Given an ideal that seems unreachable, Anna responds not by struggling in dignity like Sisyphus or Paul but by succumbing to despair, renunciation, and immature unrest. In the Yellow Notebook, these inadequate responses are given form in stories — Anna's novel about Ella and her attempt at death after the failure of her idealized love affair with Paul, Ella's novel about a man who commits suicide when he despairs of fulfilling "the impossible fantasies of a distant future" (p. 151), and Anna's notes for stories and novels in which all loves founder because "women's emotions are all still fitted for a kind of society that no longer exists" (p. 269). At this stage of her development, Anna and her characters renounce life because they cannot tolerate the distance between their ideals and reality. Once more, too, this frustrated idealism extends to Anna's attitude towards art — here, as in the Black Notebook, her own. In the last line of the notebook ("If I've gone back to pastiche, then it's time to stop"), Anna renounces her fiction-making because it does not live up to her ideal of art.

## THE BLUE NOTEBOOK

Where the Yellow Notebook ends, the Blue Notebook begins: "I came upstairs from the scene between Tommy and Molly and instantly began to turn it into a short story. It struck me that my doing this — turning everything into fiction — must be an evasion. . . . Why do I never write down, simply, what happens? . . . Obviously, my changing everything into fiction is simply a means of concealing something from myself" (p. 197). At the onset of the Blue Notebook, as at the beginning of each of the others, one of the values that determines Anna's identity is being called into question. At the beginning of the Black Notebook, Anna was on the edge of emotional collapse on account of the shame she felt over the novel that had made her career; as the Red Notebook began, she realized the insanity of her desire to throw herself into the arms of the Communist Party just as she had fully realized its corruption; when the Yellow Notebook opened, Ella was brooding over her status as a divorced woman, considering whether to perform the expected role of husband-hunting divorcée, or not. In each of these three notebooks, Anna-Ella conducts a long battle with nostalgia for the lost condition of naive commitment to an order of meaning, achieves consciousness of the outwornness of old values and the demand for new ones, but finally succumbs to despair. The task of creating a wholly new vision of her world seems just too formidable for her.

In contrast, here in the Blue Notebook the realization that a new viewpoint is necessary comes at the onset, with Anna's resolution, "I shall keep a diary." Since fiction-making has seemed to her an evasion of truth, she will take reportorial accuracy rather than imaginative force as her new artistic goal. In doing so, she opposes not only her own romantic notions about art but also those of her analyst, called Mother Sugar because of her tendency to sugar-coat reality. Mother Sugar values instincts and emotion, intuition and imagination, dreams and fiction, insofar as they provide hints and visions of an ideal, transcendent order. Moreover, according to her, "the artist has a sacred trust" (p. 202), the revelation of this higher order of reality to a less sensitive public. In opposing this theory, Anna is equally romantic — but in the direction of chaos rather than order. Insisting on the value of the "raw unfinished quality in [her] life" (p. 203), Anna allies herself with those romantics who revel in disorder and uncertainty, struggle and innovation, because these are proofs of their responsiveness to a turbulent reality within which conflict and contradiction are ever in process of resolution. As she listens to Mother Sugar talk about a "true artist" and a "real woman," Anna realizes that such absolute ideals are inconsistent with her developing view of life and art. Anna chooses the diary notebook form precisely to exorcise the ghost of her old idealizing self. She hopes to purge her mind of distorting dreams and illusions, by recording only the *facts* of experience.

Within the diary day, Anna faces some facts she has been skirting for a long time. First she discovers that the Communist ideal is being pursued in Russia and even in London by means of lies, repression, torture, and murder. She herself has pursued the noble goal by questionable means — delivering lying lectures and helping to publish books that perpetuate the myths of the Party. She realizes, furthermore, that in the service of her ideal of perfect love she has repressed herself with her lover, Michael, just as she has repressed herself in relation to the Party: She has denied anger and disappointment, ignored evidence of mutual disaffection, and manufactured a myth to protect a dream. Now, questioning Mother Sugar's Jungian model of archetype and individuation, Anna protests that she is "afraid of being better at the cost of living inside myth and dreams" (p. 402). She refuses any longer to fit her private experience to patterns that serve an ideal but deny her reality. As Anna comes to recognize her disillusionment with Communism, romantic love, and Jungian psychology, she begins to approach the saving attitude of the Golden Notebook—dedication to the values once attached to these ideals, but without hope of realizing them in an ideal order of things. Thus, without abandoning an ethical perspective, she shifts gradually away from the romantic's "desire of the moth for the star"[16] toward the existentialist's alert awareness of existence just as it is. The notebook form is obviously appropriate; Camus recommends to the absurd man the task of simply describing (not analyzing) "the ever virgin landscape of phenomena,"[17] and Sartre's Roquentin chooses the notebook form as the medium best suited to help him "bring certain circumstances to light" without the intervention of fantasy or phrase-making.[18] Similarly, Anna resolves simply to "write down, as truthfully as I can, every stage of a day" (p. 283).

Through this method, Anna transforms herself from a passive sufferer under illusion to the destroyer of illusions. In every sphere, she violates her former creeds, in spite of priestly warnings that her soul is in danger. At first tormented by dreams in which her impulse to destroy is imaged as a malicious, spiteful dwarf, she finally learns to see that figure—and herself—as the principle of joy-in-destruction (p. 408). Through Anna's dreams, Lessing seems to give her approval to Nietzsche's Dionysian wisdom, which counsels "joy in the destruction of the most noble and at the sight of its progressive ruin; in reality joy in what is coming and lies in the future, which triumphs over existing things, however good."[19]

This anticipation of some new creation beyond the moment's devastation is echoed in Anna's image of the new man, already disfigured but potentially transfigured by the forces of destruction: "there's a crack in that man's personality like a gap in a dam, and through that gap the future might pour in a different shape—terrible perhaps, or marvellous, but something new" (p. 405). In this image Anna affirms the protean powers that she will find embodied in Saul Green and Tom Mathlong; implicitly, at the same time, she rejects the sterility of Paul Blackenhurst and all others who try to block the future by locking emotion. Once Saul has awakened her fully to passion—whether longing, jealousy, hatred, or joy—she can fight back against Paul's cynicism with a conviction she has never felt before. After Saul, Anna appropriately imagines Paul no longer as an alluring, suave young lover but as a dead spirit who threatens to possess her and freeze her emotions. In Nietzschean spirit, she now feels horror of people who seek to avert the pain and tumult of emotion by weakening it at the source. She sees the fallacy in the thinking of those "people everywhere [who] are trying not to feel" (p. 466), those who choose to limit emotion because they cannot endure its chaotic energy long enough to let the emotion learn its natural form.

The education of the emotions is, of course, a slow and dangerous process, which must be pursued with care. Rather than plunging naively into expression of any given emotion (as Saul often does), one may have to feel emotions deeply but slowly, tentatively. Anna summarizes: "It is possible that in order to keep love, feeling, tenderness alive, it will be necessary to feel these emotions ambiguously, even for what is false and debased, or for what is still an idea, a shadow in the willed imagination only . . . or if what we feel is pain, then we must feel it, acknowledging that the alternative is death. Better anything than the shrewd, the calculated, the non-committal, the refusal of giving for fear of the consequences" (p. 467).

Saul Green and Tom Mathlong represent for Anna two styles of putting her self-admonition into effect. The two stand respectively for romantic fervor and postromantic detachment, for idealism and realism, for belief and unbelief, for egoism and altruism, for self-indulgence and self-control. Saul, the romantic egoist, initiates Anna into the chaos of a personality beset by contradictory drives and contradictory perceptions; Mathlong teaches her how to channel and employ these tempestuous energies.

While the majority of critics take Saul Green to be Anna's sole savior and source of wisdom for the future, I see him as the first and indispensable factor in a series of conditions that lead her to a wisdom rather different from his. Saul lectures Anna on the importance of allowing ourselves to be naive and foolish; he insists that we "believe in our beautiful impossible blueprints;" he forces Anna to create again. In these ways he is constructive, yet lacking the control and subtlety that characterize Mathlong and, eventually, Anna herself. In his easy devotion to the feeling of the moment, he allows himself to shift wildly from one emotion to another, refusing to bear with any feeling long enough to allow it to take on form and purpose. Although here, as elsewhere in Lessing's work, temporary madness is regarded as a necessary condition in the passage from illusion to enlightenment, Saul wants to prolong the intermediate stage indefinitely. "Suppose I prefer being crazy," he challenges Anna. "What then?" (p. 491). The answer to Saul's question lies in his behavior to Anna and in the novel he writes after leaving her. As Anna's lover he is irresponsible, unjust, and often positively cruel. Saul's libertinism is only the most obvious of many ways in which he demonstrates his lack of self-control. Anna does learn from Saul to feel deeply, even

when feelings conflict with one another; at the same time, however, her
position as Saul's potential victim teaches her to control her emotions in
the interest of survival. Ultimately, her efforts to hold out against disintegration of personality (which has claimed Saul) strengthen her and
give her the staying power to parlay Saul's gift of a first line into a novel
— *The Golden Notebook* — that recognizes the dual claims of individual
and society, experience and language, commitment and detachment,
order and chaos. In contrast, Saul debases the first line Anna gives him.
His novel, demonstrating the futility of both free thought and ideological orthodoxy, rivals Anna's repudiated *Frontiers of War* in its nihilism
and morbidity. The violence of Saul's novel is directed toward oblivion;
the violence in Anna's new novel destroys forms in order to liberate material for a new creation.

Clearly, as the Golden Notebook ends, Anna is more mature, more
life-affirming and more creative than her mentor Saul. His schizo-
phrenic leaping from role to role has been just the sort of madness calculated to cure Anna's excessive sanity. She has always kept herself within
the confines of a few narrow roles; she has divided her perceptions into
separate notebooks; she has made a false dichotomy between fiction
and reportage. Saul forces her into a chaotic state of dreams and visions, where she embraces the fullness of her experiences including, at
last, all the roles she has denied herself. Through these roles she finds
herself venting the passions that she has consistently denied herself in
the past. However, Saul seems powerless or unwilling to control his passage from role to role, while Anna defends herself from being possessed
by destructive spirits (such as that of Paul Blackenhurst) and aspires toward possession by a benevolent one. Out of memory and imagination,
she tries to conjure and claim for herself the spirit of Tom Mathlong —
"the man who performed actions, played roles, that he believed to be
necessary for the good of others, even while he preserved an ironic
doubt about the results of his actions" (p. 510). Mathlong balances
Saul's gifts to Anna of passion and flexibility with his own gifts of detachment and commitment.

The key characters in Anna's struggle bear a dialectical relation to
one another, each figure contributing a factor essential for her development, but carrying it eventually to such an extreme that it becomes a
danger from which another character must rescue her. Young Anna, in
her excess of naive idealism, seeks and finds her opposite, the highly
conscious and cynical Paul Blackenhurst. In her fiction, Anna similarly
pits the credulous Ella against the wary and world-weary Paul Tanner.
Since both Pauls become thoroughly disillusioned and bitter, their influence on Anna must be counteracted by Saul Green's earnest passion.

Saul's impulsive, impotent flailings are balanced, in turn, by Tom Mathlong's deliberate, effective actions. The opposites finally resolve within Anna herself, the first and last term of the dialectical process. At the end of the Blue Notebook, Anna has at last synthesized a balanced self; she declares her resolve to put "all of myself in one book" (p. 519).

## THE GOLDEN NOTEBOOK

Anna's task in that one book, the Golden Notebook, is to confront the relativity of the values with which she has been presented and to transcend the knowledge of relativity by becoming responsible for her own set of revaluations. As Anna puts it, "I was faced with the burden of re-creating order out of the chaos that my life had become" (p. 530). Immediately following this insight, Anna is struck with a terrifying vision that tempts her to give up her task of ordering and embrace nihilism, or fixation on chaos. A film projectionist (a "projection" of her own self-doubt) runs films of her life before her eyes, attempting to convince her that all versions — all possible perceptions — of individual scenes of memory are equally fictional and thus equally false. But Anna resists, battling her way to a responsible assessment of the relation between experience directly perceived through the filter of her consciousness ("what I had known") and experience distorted by a will to fit the perception into a preset order of meaning ("what I had invented"). Anna affirms the ordering function of her mind at the same time as she realizes the possibility that it will sometimes lead her into distortions of experience.

In a controversial article attacking Lessing for her romanticism, Michael L. Magie faults Anna and Lessing for irresponsibly "turning this defeat [the realization that knowledge cannot be perfectly objective and sure] into a triumph by asserting that she can invent truth and create herself."[20] This is a significant distortion of Anna's position. It is true that Anna wishes her imagination could create a valid and absolute order of reality, but she recognizes her own wish as a self-indulgent fantasy: "I was thinking that quite possibly these marvellous, generous things we walk side by side with in our imaginations could come in existence, simply because we need them, because we imagine them. Then I began to laugh because of the distance between what I was imagining and what in fact I was" (p. 545). Always she tests her imagination and valuations against observed reality, even as she recognizes the fact that observation itself is personal, relative, dependent on the constitution and experience of the mind that perceives. Anna and Lessing are not at all romantic in the sense that Magie claims they are: Neither claims that imagination creates reality out of whole cloth. But both are romantic in the ambiguous manner of Nietzsche. Like him, Lessing recognizes the pain of losing a coherent world view, once thought to be absolute. She depicts Saul surrendering to self-pity over it ("My God, what we've lost, what we've lost, what we've lost, how can we ever get back to it, how can we get back to it again"), but Anna overcomes the loss, with the "small painful sort of courage which is at the root of every life" (pp. 538, 543). Confronting the place in herself "where words, patterns, order, dissolve," she resolves to "preserve the forms, create the patterns" within which brute experience can take on meaning—simply because that is the condition of existing at all as a human being (p. 542). To settle finally for chaos and non-meaning is to become subhuman. To insist on the universal truth of one order of meaning is to pose as superhuman. The human task is to shape the chaos of empirical reality into a personally valid order of meaning. By adopting this latter attitude, Anna finds what Nietzsche calls the "means of *enduring it*: the revaluation of all values. No longer joy in certainty but in uncertainty: no longer 'cause and effect' but the continually creative; . . . no longer the humble expression, 'everything is *merely* subjective,' but 'it is also *our* work! — Let us be proud of it.'"[21] Here, then, the novel finds its moral center—in Anna's commitment to the personal task of creating order and meaning in the one, immediate life that is her own.

## "FREE WOMEN"

No longer bound to find *the* truth—because she knows truth to be relative—Anna is free to present *her* truth, with renewed conviction. She has recovered that creative faith in her own vision that naiveté once supplied, but she has reconciled that faith with awareness of the limiting conditions of her vision. Anna's novel "Free Women" reflects this reconciliation. Its very existence attests to Anna's recovered faith in her perceptions and her imagination; yet, the placement of the novel against the notebooks that were its source reflects Anna's awareness of the relativity of every act of vision. She is willing to reveal, in the novel, her perception of a pattern in her past life, provided that she can simultaneously put on record, through the notebooks, the sense of chaos that she was experiencing when she was actually living that life.

In writing "Free Women," Anna seems to heed Saul Green's advice: "I was thinking that if you could simplify it in your mind, boil it all down to something, then you could take a good long look at it and beat it" (p. 546). What she takes a good long look at — and represents in fiction — is that pattern in her life which the Black, Red, and Yellow Notebooks had more faintly revealed: her need to create order, her obsession with chaos, her tendency to "crack up" under these conflicting pressures, and finally her temptation to give up the struggle to obtain a balanced vision. The objectification of this pattern does indeed allow Anna to "beat it." Although the character Anna in "Free Women" succumbs to fatigue and refuses to write any longer, her creator — Anna of *The Golden Notebook* — has learned to avoid that possible scenario for herself. Refusing to dead-end in cynicism, she has learned to balance chaos and order, irony and commitment, awareness and faith. She is, at last, the woman who can compose "a book powered with an intellectual or moral passion strong enough to create order, to create a new way of looking at life" (p. 59). *The Golden Notebook* is that novel.[22] The ultimate expression of her balanced perspective is the novel as a whole, which refuses to settle for an easy view of any of the issues it raises, but rather creates for the reader that tension among versions of the truth which Anna must learn to recognize, tolerate, and transcend. Formally, this complex relation of truths to one another is embodied in the arrangement of the five notebooks against one another and "Free Women."

What Camus says of any creator's oeuvre applies in microcosm to Anna's six-part work:

> Too often the work of a creator is looked upon as a series of isolated testimonies. Thus, artist and man of letters are confused. A profound thought is in a constant state of becoming; it adopts the experience of a life and assumes its shape. Likewise, a man's sole creation is strengthened in its successive and multiple aspects: his works. One after another, they complement one another, correct or overtake one another, contradict one another too. . . . But viewed all together, they resume their natural grouping. . . . If those [works, which may, in isolation, seem failures] all have the same resonance, the creator has managed to repeat the image of his own condition.[23]

"Viewed all together," the parts of *The Golden Notebook* create an image not only of Anna's *personal* condition but also of a *public* condition, called the postmodern consciousness. This state of mind is a jumble of contradictory moods — a wrenching nostalgia for the comfort of past forms, a paralyzing fear of the formlessness of the present, a despairing sense of emptiness and futility, a positive will to confront chaos — all often counterpointed by a public pose of defensive "cool." The postmodern sensibility is that of Anna Wulf, who "could feel herself, under this shape of order, as a chaos of discomfort and anxiety" (p. 331). Lessing's novel continually acknowledges chaos, nonetheless noting our human urge to impose willed forms on chaos, and demonstrates the need for the individual to establish an ambiguous relation to the two poles of chaos and order. The dynamic of the novel pushes the reader and the central character Anna Wulf toward a state of saving schizophrenia — a state that permits her commitment to practical goals, visionary ideals, art, work, altruism, social organization, logic, and order, while at the same time allowing her to acknowledge and even honor all that accompanies chaos — creation, destruction, randomness, power, potential, vitality, and emotion.

The form of Lessing's novel embodies this saving schizophrenia in that it is many times split, yet in such a way as to reveal the underlying — saving — shape of one woman's experience. That shape is not a fixed form but a continual movement away from outworn forms into chaos and toward new form. Acceptance of this creative flux is one of the prerequisites of postmodern art. The creation of a text patterned and textured so as to express it is Lessing's triumph in *The Golden Notebook*.

Chapter Five

# Briefing for a Descent into Hell

## COMPOSITION BY CORRESPONDENCE

When she published *Briefing for a Descent into Hell* in 1971,[1] Doris Lessing had a right to be resting on laurels. Her most recent novel, *The Four-Gated City* (1969), had brought to wild and satisfying climax the five-part series, *Children of Violence*; this successful completion of the series won her critical acclaim as the most imaginatively gifted of living English novelists in the central tradition of realism. *The Golden Notebook* (1962), the one novel she had written outside the *Children of Violence* series during the years of its composition, had earned high critical marks on different grounds—as an experiment in narrative technique and prose style. The reading public expected that the newest novel would live up to the standards set by earlier ones—full and intriguing characterization, a clear narrative stance, meaningful action, subtle and timely themes, and an effective (if not particularly graceful) prose style. *Briefing* gave readers pause on all counts. Its characters were sparsely drawn, the pattern of narration was inconsistent, the action multilayered and jumbled, the theme so simple and timeless as to be perhaps too obvious, and the prose style highly erratic.[2] Lessing seemed not so much to have reversed her previous practice as to have disintegrated it.

Nowhere is this falling away from a previous wholeness and unity more evident than in the handling of plot. Depending on how one

counts, there are from two to five plot levels in *Briefing*, and their relation to one another is problematic. The initial scene defines two of these
levels and suggests a connection between them. On the opening page, a
hospital admissions sheet dated August 15, 1969, describes an amnesia
patient, later to be identified as Charles Watkins, classics professor at
Cambridge. Immediately following brief reports on Watkins's condition, from a nurse and doctor, we shift to a timeless ocean scene in
which a sailor, "poor Charlie," gives an account of his wanderings after
the pirating of his ship by a cosmic force embodied in a kind of spiritual
space ship, the Disc or Crystal. By virtue of the names and of the simple
juxtaposition of stories, Charles Watkins and poor Charlie would seem
to be identified with each other. Very early on, the doctors do record
that the patient is hallucinating the voyage. The reader assumes that
poor Charlie's story is merely a metaphorical account of some more primary reality belonging to Charles Watkins, victim of a nervous breakdown. During most of the first forty pages, in which there are five
switches between hospital and sea, the sailor's narration is a jumble of
indistinct images and literary allusions — difficult to correlate with one
another, repetitious, and often incoherent. The firmly objective stance
of the doctors' reports and the dreamlike quality of the sea story help to
maintain the reader's assumption that the "real world" of this novel is
the hospital housing Watkins and that the secondary or imaginary
world is the ocean of his dreaming self, poor Charlie.

At the end of Charlie's fifth section, however, his story shifts from
present tense to past tense, and Charlie's vague, timeless memories of
being at sea are replaced by a detailed, moment-by-moment account of
his adventures in locating the fortress City that holds a potential landing station for the Crystal. Suddenly the novel is charged with excitement and authenticity, as the sailor vividly describes his explorations of
the City, his battles with its inhabitants (rat-dogs and apes), his struggle
to resist the temptation of their bloodlust, and his efforts to keep clean a
landing place for the redemptive Crystal. Although the content is fantastical, the style is realistic, anchoring each suspenseful moment in a
clear temporal sequence and situating each concrete detail in a coherent spatial framework. All these changes prompt the reader to reverse
his previous account of the relation of the two narrative levels. At the
opening of the novel we are led to believe that Charles Watkins needs to
"come to himself" and recognize the world of sailor Charlie as a mere
nightmare from which it would be desirable to awaken. However, by
the end of the gripping description of Charlie's experience on land in
the City, it is the flat world of the hospital that seems inauthentic by
comparison to the more vivid and more attractive world of the City of
the Crystal. The length of the section alone — sixty pages (pp. 40–101)

with only a one-page return to the hospital context — induces the reader to develop attachments to the realm of the City, subverting the realistic framework of the hospital.

Having negotiated this reversal in the primacy of narrative levels, Lessing now perversely proceeds to undermine the newly established narrative base of Charlie's action adventure. First she disorients the reader by introducing an incident that jars against the tone and narrative suppositions of the previous material. Charlie's adventure has drawn on the motifs of two compatible genres: space fiction (the fantasy of higher powers coming in a ship from outer space to interfere with human destiny) and time travel (the deserted stone city, so similar to the great mystery cities of archaeology — Teotihuacan, Chichen-Itza, Knossos; the barbarous, caveman-like humans who eat the flesh of their own babies; and the canny rat-dogs and apes, animals who seem to be early items in the chain of evolution toward human consciousness). Suddenly we flip into a fairy-tale fantasy in which "a great white bird" gives Charlie a piggyback flight over the city, before standing guard over his efforts to clear the square for the landing of the Crystal. The giant guardian bird, so powerful and benevolent, seems a figure out of children's fantasy. Entering incongruously into the space fiction/time travel narrative, the fairy-tale figure calls into question the solidity of Charlie's world. We are forced to return again to the initial narrative framework — the assumption that Charles Watkins, while in hospital, is hallucinating a nonsensical dream world without claim to our serious belief. We are thus quickly distanced from a narrative line that had come gradually to command our primary loyalty.

At this highly vulnerable moment, we are called upon to make *another* radical shift in gears. Charlie is whisked into the Crystal and begins a long (fifty-six-page) section of mystical meditation and vision. This section, with its vague, exclamatory style, has only one claim on the reader's attention — the labored earnestness of its approach to spiritual experience. Even that small foothold in the meditative world slips when Charlie's sober reflections give way to a preposterous fantasy about the place of the Greek gods in saving modern man from his spiritual ignorance. The offensively silly story of the jokester gods, played in the tone of farce, once more undermines the reader's confidence in the status of the narration. Are we listening in on the thought stream of a demented Charles Watkins, whose metaphorical productions — Charlie, the City, the Crystal, and the clowning gods — are merely a symptom of maladjustment to a commonplace reality? Or is Watkins a vehicle through which a transcendent reality manifests itself in these various guises?

It becomes clear that Lessing has been switching narrative frames precisely in order to generate that question. She explores the issue fur-

ther through numerous upheavals of narrative ground. We undergo
birth and infancy with a first-person narrator (one of the gods' messengers? Charlie? Watkins?), return to Watkins's experience in the hospital,
then confront a long series of letters to the doctors describing Watkins's
life before his amnesia attack. Only sixty pages from the end of the
book, a totally new tale is introduced, Charles Watkins's story of his
World War II mission for the Allies in Yugoslavia. The novel ends with a
final variation in narrative stance, a move to the third person for an objective rendering of Watkins's decision to undergo shock therapy, an
event that puts an end to the multiple layers of narration. After the
shock therapy, there is only one "hero" — Charles Watkins, a very ordinary man who repudiates his recent extraordinary imaginations and
memories by apologizing to friends for being "such a bore" while not in
"full possession of his faculties." The stories of Charlie as sailor, explorer, mystic, and potential messenger of the gods fade into the background and appear to be nothing but the useless fantasies of Watkins's
unwell mind.

This reductive movement in the narrative is countered, however, by
the gradual gathering of a meaning that transcends the "main" plot.
That meaning inheres neither in the fate of Charles Watkins at the end
of the linear action nor in his evaluation of his situation, but rather in
the interconnections of situations, characters, and action among the
several versions of his story. Moreover, Lessing's manipulation of the
parts of the narrative has much to do with the reader's perception of this
interconnection. At some time during the course of the novel, each level
of narration has been undermined in some way — by conflict with other
levels or by stylistic oddities that tend to alienate the reader. If no single
level of action can be relied on, then one begins to seek meaning not by
determining the definitive meaning of any one of those parts, but by
submitting to stages of narration, each of which opens up several lines
of inquiry which may lead eventually to spiritual insight.

Lessing has made of her novel a kind of mystical teaching-story, and
it is clear from the first epigraph to the novel (from the Sage Mahmoud
Shabistari, a fourteenth-century Sufi) as well as from thematic evidence
that she takes as her models the teaching stories of the Sufi masters. At
least since 1964, Lessing has been an admirer of Sufi master Idries
Shah,[3] and in *Briefing* she begins to imitate the Sufi strategy of using
teaching-stories to change the spiritual disciple's mode of perception — a
strategy she learned from Shah. In *The Way of the Sufi*, Shah explains
that the traditional teaching-stories of the Sufi dervishes are designed so
as to have many planes of significance. He notes that the Sufi habit of
arranging the story so that there are many layers of meaning often offends beginning students, "who tend to prefer being told that a story has

one message or one use only."[4] If the willing Sufi novice balks at the ambiguities of a story designed to be "capable of revealing, according to the stage of development of the student, more and more planes of significance,"[5] so much the more does Lessing's reader balk when presented with a fiction that has multilayered plots as well as multiple interpretations of each plot.

Lessing's story, like those of the Sufi teachers, is designed to lead its audience to the perception of a hidden harmony among elements of life that initially appear to be incongruous. Sufism is a name for Islamic mysticism, a way of seeking to lift the veil of appearance that masks true Being. It is a method of pursuing *gnosis*, the wordless knowledge not only of God but also of the essential unity of God and all that man calls God's creation. One of the most important assumptions of Sufism is that humanity is in a state of lamentable ignorance of that unity—an ignorance which it is the goal of Sufi life to dispell. The first words of Idries Shah's *The Sufis* (the book through which Lessing was introduced to Sufism[6]) are an epigraph from a twelfth-century Sufi master: "Humanity is asleep, concerned only with what is useless, living in a wrong world."[7] This too is the assumption of *Briefing for a Descent into Hell*, in which Charles Watkins is humanity asleep to the truth and at the same time seeking to awake to knowledge of it. Throughout the novel, the Sufi emblem of sleep is employed in its dual aspects. On the one hand, sleep symbolizes the state of spiritual unconsciousness. As Charles Watkins sleeps the days away in hospital, he comes to resent the people who have conspired to keep him asleep all his life, from babyhood on. He realizes, "I must wake, I *know* there is something more awake than this, I *know* I have to be awake and be, but . . . I never learned to live awake. I was trained for sleep" (pp. 149, 153). Paradoxically, however, it is through sleep that he will awaken to spiritual reality. His daily life keeps him so insulated from ultimate concerns that he will not be able to become awakened without a mental breakdown and the freedom of consciousness provided only in sleep. For him, "Awake is asleep" (p. 165)—daily life is spiritual unconsciousness; whereas his "sleep is awake"—in the sleep of his mental breakdown he can dream his way toward knowledge and spiritual wakefulness. There again the text echoes Sufi symbolism, which holds that "the road to annihilation [the Sufi word for the desirable absorption of the individual into the One] may be travelled sleeping."[8]

Lessing takes her hero Charles Watkins—and her reader—on a spiritual journey toward the knowledge of the Sufis. In constructing her novel on the Sufi model, she uses the symbolism of Sufi scripture and imitates the teaching strategy of her Sufi master Idries Shah. He is, in Lessing's opinion, "a master of the difficult arts of deliberate provoca-

tion, slight dislocation of an expected sense, use of the apparently banal
— to make one read a thing again, and more carefully."[9] That is, passages in Shah's writings that on first reading seem annoyingly dislo-
cated, trite, repetitive, or unoriginal can be seen in the light of his
whole work to be signposts pointing to a hidden meaning, demanding a
special quality of attention. In using this technique, Shah follows in the
long tradition of Sufi writings, in which the secret sense of the text is en-
coded in allegory, puns, and even cipher.[10]

Lessing is as much a practitioner of deliberate provocation as Shah,
and for similar reasons. As Sufis, both cherish a conviction that the
deepest truth is unsayable but that contact with that truth entails awakening to the essential harmony of all things. Acting the role of Sufi
teacher, Lessing is responsible not to tell the truth directly (for this is
held to be impossible) but to prod her students into a state of alertness
and receptivity to that truth.

Through the disjunctions of her text she *provokes* her readers to a
heightened state of attention, in hopes of calling to their notice hidden
patterns of correspondence among the characters, scenes, levels of plot,
metaphors, and allusions in her novel. These patterns of correspondence amount to a thematic statement, an affirmation by Lessing of
that idea of correspondences which underlies the teachings of Platonism, Swedenborgianism, theosophy, symbolism, Sufism, and many
other forms of mysticism.

According to the theory of correspondences, all elements of the universe, spiritual and material, derive from the same primal life impulse;
therefore, they all ultimately form a harmonious whole that parallels in
macrocosm the unity of that first moment, or point, of Being. Within
the harmony of the completed universe, moreover, there are myriad
correspondences among the things that exist; a particular odor, a tone, a
color, a sound, may all be aspects of one note in the total harmony of being. In *Briefing for a Descent into Hell*, it is Lessing's overt thesis that
man has lost sight of his place in this essential harmony. The novel's
hero, Charles Watkins, is charged with the role of teaching this lesson to
humanity. In visions, the very gods inform him "that there is a Harmony and that if they [human beings] wish to prosper they must keep in
step and obey its Laws" (p. 133). He learns also that all people, as final
products of that first moment of being, are ultimately still part of it;
they "are a whole, they form a unity, they have a single mind, a single
being" (p. 120). Individuality must be understood to be subsumed under the larger units of the cosmic harmony; "there was no such thing as
judges, but only Judge, not soldiers, but Soldier, not artists, but Artist.
. . . For since any category anywhere always beat on its own wavelength of sound/light, there could not be individuals in this nourishing

web. Together they formed one beat in the great dance, one note in the song. Everywhere and on every level the little individuals made up wholes, struck little notes, made tones of colour" (pp. 110 f.). These statements are alive with echoes from the writings of mystics devoted to the doctrine of correspondence.

It is easy enough to see that the many essay-like statements of belief in cosmic harmony convey Lessing's own convictions and form the dominant theme of the novel. It is less obvious, however, that the novel itself is constructed as a kind of object lesson for the reader. Discordant on the surface, the text nonetheless discloses a whole series of corresponding elements that together form a microcosm of the universal harmony. Many of the most glaring oddities of Lessing's novel are actually her prods to the reader. The apparent incongruities provoke the reader to look for and find the overriding unity of all elements in the whole.

In the mystic vision of things, no one fact or interpretation is reliable or significant unless it is viewed as part of the total Truth — as one note in the Harmony. So with Lessing's novel, no one level of narration is true or meaningful until it is correlated with the others.

This correlation begins most easily with the sets of characters. At one point in his enlightenment, Charles recognizes that his separate identity is partly illusory: "My mind was the facet of a mind, like cells in a honeycomb. Letting my mind lie dark there, quiescent, a mirror for light, I could feel or sense or recognize a pulse of individuality that I had known once as poor Charlie or Felicity or James or Thomas. Pulses of mind lay beating and absorbing beside my own little pulse, and together we were a whole" (p. 112). The Charles who is experiencing the ecstasy of union with the Crystal feels as identified with his wife of a former life in Cambridge as he does with his own past identity on another level, as the sailor "poor Charlie." If we separate the plot into four main levels, we can chart connections among characters within the "honeycomb" of the novel:

| PLACE | CHARACTERS | | | |
|---|---|---|---|---|
| Hospital, 1969 | Charles Watkins | Felicity Watkins | Constance | Nancy Thorne |
| Ocean, timeless | I, poor Charlie, Jonah, Jason, Odysseus, Sinbad Ulysses | | Conchita | poor Charlie's Nancy |
| City, timeless | I (explorer) | Bloody Woman 1 Felicity | Bloody Woman 2 | Bloody Woman 3 |
| Yugoslavia, WW II | I (British soldier) | | Konstantina | Vera |

The reader is made to recognize the hero as one man in many guises. He is first of all Charles Watkins, a mental patient suffering from both amnesia and hallucination; we learn about him through medical reports, through his conversations with hospital staff, through letters from friends to the doctors, and through the record of his thoughts and visions while ill. This record is itself a narrative anomaly: sometimes it seems to be the transcription of Watkins's thought stream by an omniscient but effaced narrator; at other times Watkins speaks of having to "be careful to set down my mind's movement accurately" (p. 53), as if he were keeping a diary; quite late in the book, Watkins's doctor asks him to try to write down his thoughts, as if the patient had done no previous writing, and the Yugoslavian "memory" is given as the result of this effort. While Watkins seems to be in some way the voice behind all the first-person narratives, he calls himself variously Jonah, Jason, Odysseus, Sinbad, Ulysses, and most often "poor Charlie" (using his own first name). As the sailor who climbs to the City of the Crystal, he refers back to his sailing self as "poor Charlie" but no longer calls himself that, as if to indicate a partial transformation of identity. Finally, Charles Watkins offers the London doctors the Yugoslavian episode as a memory of his wartime experience, although information provided to the doctors by Charles's war-companion Miles Bovey would suggest that none of the Yugoslavian experience is Charles's "own" — but rather, experience he has appropriated imaginatively from Miles Bovey.

Just as Charles Watkins changes form as a character but retains a core identity in all the imaginative episodes, so do the women who surround him. His wife Felicity, for example, provides Charles with domestic tranquility (and the name underscores her emblematic status) but in that very capacity she seems to block Charles's spiritual progress. She acts uninterested in her husband's life outside his home, the intellectual life that has been leading him to insights concerning universal harmony, and in the hospital she does not care to learn about Charles's mental journeys — only about his possible return to normalcy. It seems that, if Charles has been trying for years to respond to an urgent sense that there is something else he should be doing (p. 302), Felicity has been no help, returning him always to the norm of contented home life. In his imaginative role as the explorer of the City of the Crystal, Charles meets another Felicity, who tempts him to eat bloody meat, thus disqualifying him for union with the Crystal. Although the second Felicity is a much darker image than the first, they are presented as similar in that they both hold their men back from a spiritual purpose (in Watkins's case, awakening to universal Harmony and the need to teach its lessons to others; in the explorer's case, preparing a landing site for the Crystal, the symbol of Harmony). Felicity, as Cambridge wife and as the bloody woman of the explorer's adventure, is archetypally Circe, the woman who uses sensuality to lure men away from his higher duties to intellect and spirit. The view of Felicity as evil temptress, occurring in Watkins's fantasy projection, is countered in the more objective reportage of the doctor's conversations with the wife Felicity. There she reveals Watkins's frequent absences from home (during which, as Constance Mayne's letters reveal, he was carrying on an exploitive affair with her, his ex-student). Felicity's coolness and reticence concerning Charles, combined with Constance's portrait of him, suggest that he has been imperceptive enough to fail to see his wife fully — fixing her instead in stereotypes that express his immature resentment of her.

Just as Felicity's two incarnations are to Charles archetypally one, so Constance Mayne and her counterparts are one. Constance is the other woman, met during the course of work, sharing interests with Charles that he cannot share with his wife, engaging Charles in an affair that makes him not only an adulterer but the father of an illegitimate child. She is a woman toward whom and because of whom Charles feels guilt. Nonetheless, although she may be, in Charles's eyes, a temptress, she has shown "constancy" in her love, whereas he has been only superficially and transiently involved. Moreover, she has demonstrated constance, or consistency, in putting into action the theoretical insights of her professor Charles Watkins. When he claimed in a lecture that Greek was the only language worth studying, Constance immediately dedicated herself to a degree in Greek. Later, when he suggested that if she were concerned about the fate of women and slaves she should do something about it, she dropped her studies and "became a shop steward and a communist" (p. 235). Constance becomes bitter when she realizes that Watkins himself is inconstant in his devotion to his own principles. (His negligence of both wife and mistress during the conduct of the affair is just one manifestation of his inability to remain faithful to his own ideals and choices.)

Charlie the sailor is also inconsistent in his attentions to his mistress Conchita. Like Watkins, Charlie already has a wife when he takes Conchita (Constance) as mistress. Charlie's yearning for Conchita is a cause of guilt; like Constance Mayne, Conchita is faithful to her lover Charlie. He has twinges of guilt whenever he recalls that she has relegated herself to a nunlike chastity because of his wanderings from her (p. 25).

By name and function, Conchita and Constance correlate in turn with Konstantina, the Yugoslavian Partisan with whom Charles Watkins "recalls" sharing love, comradeship, and political commitment. Like Constance and Conchita, Konstantina is the symbol of an ideal of

constancy which Watkins seems to want to love, but which he nonetheless betrays. Konstantina is, like Constance, a worker toward an ideal—
in this case, the liberation of her country. Towards her he feels the same
attraction, devotion, suspicion, and guilt that characterize his relation
to Constance and Conchita. He loves her and admires her—in fact, he
idolizes her—yet he is convinced that conditions will shortly defeat
their love. He tries to bear in mind that the primacy of the war effort
will shortly separate them. Yet it is not the war effort which defeats the
love. Rather, Konstantina is killed as she tries to defend Charles from
the slicing horns of a female deer defending her territory because she is
about to give birth. Figuratively, the mistress defends the husband from
the severity of the claims of family, and she is destroyed in the process.
Given that Charles's Yugoslavian story is exposed as a fabrication, it
seems reasonable to interpret the story of Konstantina's sacrifice as a
glamorized version of the story of Constance's sacrifice; Constance destroyed her own life by protecting Charles from the consequences of his
extramarital affair, in that until shortly before his breakdown she kept
from him the fact that she had borne their son illegitimately. Constance, like Konstantina, upholds the ideal of constancy and in so doing
exposes Charles's inconstancy. (Charles feels guilt every time he thinks
of the fact that Konstantina died to save him from the deer but he made
no move to save her.)

Yet Charles prefers to see his mistresses, like his wife, as an impediment to his spiritual growth. The linkage of the two types of woman in
Charles's mind is revealed late in the novel, when Felicity shows Doctor
Y a letter that Charles had written her in their courting days. In the letter, Charles identifies the blond Felicity with the dark-haired Konstantina. He pictures Felicity in Konstantina's setting: "I keep thinking of
you in a big forest somewhere with the sunlight coming down through
branches and you and your bright shining head and you smiling at me"
(p. 219). Then, he further lessens his grip on the familiar archetypal division between fair-haired, virtuous wife and dark-haired, seductive
mistress. He becomes confused over who was fair and who was dark,
seeing only one common denominator among the several women he refers to as "she": He fears them all as potential Circes to his Odysseus. He
tries to believe that Felicity will not "keep me a pig in [her] pen," as his
former loves had done (or so he thinks). He hopes that she will not be,
like Konstantina, a temptress: "Not like that dark one, black hair and
white teeth and red lips—those are the colours for pig-keepers. And in
war time too. . . . *She* died, and so could never lock me in her stye"
(p. 220).

The Circe reference reinforces the by now over-determined image of the wandering hero in search of a noble goal who is in danger of giving up his quest because of family, love, lust, or romance. Each temptation is represented in the person of a woman. There are the "three women, all intimately connected with [him], alike, sisters perhaps," who tempt him to defile himself in the forest, near the Crystal (p. 70). Later he names them and looks for them to reappear: "In this paradisical forest Felicity and Constance and Vera were not represented at all, yet as my thoughts hung over the memory of what had been there, a compulsion or pressure or need grew into them: a demand from the excluded, a claim" (p. 105). In this passage, the allegorical significance of the many women in Charles's stories becomes apparent. When he looks for the three bloody women who have tempted him to give up his quest for the Crystal, he thinks of three women who belong here instead: Felicity (simple happiness), Constance (consistency of ideal and action), and Vera (truth). These are "the excluded, a claim." Felicity, Constance, and Truth are the qualities that Charles Watkins needs if he is to fulfill the "claim" laid on him by Rosemary Baines—the claim that he must remember the message that he has to deliver to humanity. The problem is that in his undeveloped spiritual state, Charles does not know how to balance the claims of Felicity, Constance, Truth, and finally Remembrance (Rosemary). The claims of the one seem to "exclude" the claims of the other. (In serving Constance, he betrays Felicity; if he throws himself into living out his ideals consistently, he fears that he will have no energy for simple happiness.)

Charles's fear of each of the women is a symbol of his fear of the spiritual qualities that have laid a legitimate claim on his life. Charles never understands fully how his view of the women in his real and imaginative life is distorted by the inadequacy of his spiritual insight. In his enlightened state (in the hospital) he believes in the primacy of categories over individuals: "There was no such thing as judges, but only Judge, not soldiers, but Soldier, not artists, but Artist" (p. 110). But he does not fully draw the inference that in his own life there is no such person as Felicity (his wife), but only Felicity as a quality which both supports him and puts demands on him; no such individuals as Constance, Conchita, or Konstantina, but only Constance as an ideal and a claim on his actions. And as for Vera, or Nancy Thorne, or poor Charlie's Nancy—they manifest that elusive quality of Truth: They exist "on the side" of where Charles must daily exist, just out of reach of recognition. The fantasy character Vera is Konstantina's friend, never a focus in the story but ever present. Nancy Thorne, Felicity's friend, has never been a lover of Charles but at a moment of insight he realizes that "he might have married her." Similarly, in explaining his hallucination to Dr. Y,

Charles proclaims that Poor Charlie's Nancy could be as much his wife as Felicity.

If Charles had been able to understand how the claims of Felicity, Constance, Vera, (and finally Remembrance-Rosemary) could be reconciled, he might have fulfilled the task of his own spiritual integration, and as a result he might have done better justice to each of the actual women whose (unwitting) role it has been to call him back to his task. The many women in Charles's life have all held their places in the great effort to return Charles to *his* proper place in the struggle for salvation of the human race. The motif of lieutenancy (place-holding) thus applies to the women characters as well as to Charles.

In his incarnation as an Allied soldier, Charles has the rank of lieutenant or, literally, "place-holder." His role is to act in the place of a higher authority, the Allied Command, at the head of which is the ultimate Commanding Officer, Churchill (p. 247). Acting in a hierarchical line of deputization, he receives from his local C.O. messages that have originated at the highest levels of the Allied Command, and then he carries these messages to subordinate powers such as Tito, and to the lowest echelons, the peasant guerillas in the Partisan group (pp. 247, 256, 260). Charles is important here not as an individual but as a link in a chain of being; he is one unit in the army struggling to create harmony. For the whole organization of delegated authority is designed to realize materially the ideal that Churchill and his war represent to the Partisan soldiers: "In those high mountains we fought against Evil, and were sure to win, for the stars in their courses were on our side, whose victory would be at last when the poor and meek and the humble had inherited the earth, and the lion would lie down with the lamb, and a loving harmony would prevail over the earth" (p. 259).

Just as Charles's women in the larger view all "hold the same place" in the greater story of Charles's spiritual progress, so Charles is simply a "place-holder," a lieutenant, in the greater story of human progress toward Harmony. In each one of his four stories, he is the deputy of a higher power with the job of transmitting the message of Harmony from that power to those below him in the hierarchy of Being. In the vignette of the gods, for example, the reigning power is called God, and the Sun is named "God's singing centre." From that center, rings of authority emanate, like planetary orbits. Mercury is the Sun's first messenger, "the carrier of news, or information from the Sun, the disseminator of laws from God's singing centre" (p. 117). There have been many substitutions, however: Mercury's "name was, also, Thoth, and Enoch, Buddha, Idris, and Hermes, and many other styles or titles in the earth's histories" (p. 117)[11] — among them, we might guess, Charles the lieutenant in Yugoslavia, Charles the discoverer of the City of the Crystal, Charlie the sailor and seeker of knowledge, and even Charles Watkins, the scholar who is trying to remember the task to which he has been appointed.

What Charles guesses about the system of Being surrounding him is true of the novel Lessing has designed to express it: "There is an idea of *doubleness* here, of *substitution*" (p. 126, my emphasis). Just as the soldier Charles undergoes a briefing by the Allies, descends from the sky by parachute, and transmits to the Partisans a message designed to further the cause of political harmony, so the Messenger attends a briefing by the gods, descends from the heavens to earth, and is programmed to transmit to other men the gods' message of the law of harmony. Again, Charles Watkins in his mental ward in London, 1969, seems the double of one of these Messengers, to whom Mercury had predicted: "You will each of you come to yourselves . . . with only a vague feeling of recognition, and probably disassociated, disoriented, ill. . . . There will be a period while you are waking which will be like the recovery from an illness" (p. 146). Finally, Charles the wanderer and explorer of the Crystal merely reverses the pattern of the Messengers and of Charles the Partisan; he is a man ascending, rather than descending, returning himself to the experience of harmony that he had forgotten while on earth.

There is a familiar Platonic structure to these stories and these images. The Crystal and the Sun are metaphors for the One, from which all beings emanate and toward which all long to return. We recognize, too, the notion of a hierarchy in which the spiritual One is ultimate good, and in which the beings that derive from it "descend" in orders of goodness — all reflective of the essential One, but becoming more and more inferior as the lowest degree, mere matter, is approached. (In fact, in Middle Platonism, a set of inferior gods is said to be interposed between the Divine Mind and men;[12] the similarity to Lessing's vignette about the petty gods who mediate between the Sun and men may be more than coincidental.) Further, the Platonic notion of "recollection" is also central to the novel. According to the Platonic doctrine of reminiscence or recollection, all apparent acquisition of knowledge is in fact only remembrance of knowledge pre-existent in the mind. (This doctrine is of course consistent with the idea that man emanates from the One; if he derives from the One, he in some sense echoes it — he retains a trace or "memory" of it and thus can recognize it. Since the One is the Truth, man is thus by his nature equipped to remember the Truth.)

"Remembrance" is also central to Sufism, which is the source through which Lessing may have become committed to the concept. Her Sufi master Idries Shah writes that remembrance is a basic step in

Sufi discipline,[13] and in a collection of Sufi writings, Shah offers this passage by Sheikh Ismail Hakki, which is used by Sufis as a group recital:

> Everything is dependent upon remembering. One does not begin by learning, one starts by remembrance. The distance of eternal existence and the difficulties of life cause one to forget.
>     It is for this reason God has commanded us:
>     "Remember!"[14]

The Western scholar Reynold Nicholson explains that "recollection," which he calls the keystone of practical Sufism, consists of concentrating on the idea of God with such intensity that the worshipper is absorbed in the Godhead.[15] The goal of remembrance, then, is reunion with the One, from which daily life tends to separate us.

When Charles Watkins enters Central Intake Hospital, his presenting symptom is that he has amnesia: he is in need of recollection. When the doctors assume that he needs to remember his outer existence in the daily world, Charles faces them shrewdly and insists, "That's not what I have to remember" (p. 156). A sense of urgency prompts him toward recollection in the Sufi or Platonic sense, but he is only vaguely aware of the object of this process. In frustration, he seeks a shortcut to recollection in shock therapy and thereby shortcircuits this round of his mind's promptings to recall a higher unity and a higher purpose to his life. His acquaintance Rosemary Baines ("Here's Rosemary, that's for remembrance") seems to be farther along on the journey toward the recollection of spiritual knowledge. She has the instinct of recognition when she comes upon a pointer toward the truth. When she hears Charles's lecture, she feels "recognition, as if I had been reminded of something I knew very well" (p. 182). What she experiences is the beginning of absorption into the harmony of the One: "But it was another flash of recognition, of joy, of 'yes, that's it,' and again, this quality of matching, of ringing together, of substances being in tune" (p. 183). The theme of universal harmony and of correspondences among the levels of being that emanate from the One is joined here with the motif of recollection, so as to demonstrate the interrelation of the concepts: recollection (recognition) consists in a return to knowledge of harmony (correspondence). This passage is echoed later by Charles's description of the Partisans' recognition that they were fighting so that "a loving harmony would prevail over the earth. We knew all this because — it was as if we remembered it" (p. 259).

Both passages in turn recall Merk Ury's speech to the gods and Messengers, in which he complains of how inept men are at remembering harmony. Although he sends a whole staff of special envoys "to keep alive, in any way possible, the knowledge that humanity, with its fellow creatures, the animals and plants, make up a whole, are a unity, have a function in the whole system as an organ or organism" (p. 141), he expects that, once on earth, even these envoys will have difficulty in placing the "vague feeling of recognition" (p. 146) that will be their only remnant of the truth. That, of course, is exactly Charles Watkins's fate. He frequently experiences the sensation of returning memory but he can't quite fix on the content of the memory; still, he remains convinced that "there's something else. Yes. There's something I *have* to remember" (p. 287). Lessing seems to urge the reader to seek connections such as these, which will in turn reveal the interrelation of the plots.

One way of reconciling all the narrative levels is to view the hospital plot as veridical, with all other narrative levels explained as Charles Watkins's fantasies. On the other hand, there is nothing in the text to disprove the theory that Watkins *is* an agent of the gods and that what we've been calling "the gods vignette" is really the determining level of plot. Carrying this logic further, it is possible that the man who sailed the oceans and the one who found the Crystal on land are one and the same, the former Charles, a man who found enlightenment and then was carried away in the Crystal to the place of the gods, where he received his Briefing for a Descent into Hell (Earth). If we are looking for the interpretation that least violates our sense of the probable, the hospital plot will certainly predominate, but it is significant that Lessing does not let us ever feel assured that this or any other of the plot levels takes precedence over the others. She simply encourages us to see the interrelationships, the essential unity among them all.

Lessing's handling of the several plot levels is described with startling aptess by David Richter, who defines one of the "signals" of the didactic fiction or apologue as

> a kind of organization which Barbara Herrnstein Smith [in *Poetic Closure*] terms "paratactic structure" (p. 98). In paratactic structure thematic repetition takes the place of narrative sequence (fictional "cause and effect") as the principle of coherence. Typically the novelist will present a series of incidents whose chronological sequence is more or less arbitrary and which set up no narrative lines. Though the minor characters who appear in the incident *may* recur, they more usually do not. What holds the various episodes together is simply a common theme, or thesis, or view of the world, and the reader, who by the end of this sequence is willing to grasp at any sort of coherence he can find (how avidly we try to make logical sense of what we read!) is forced willy-nilly into the rhetorical mode.[16]

Richter's statement neatly recapitulates the experience of the reader of
*Briefing*. At first the seeming unrelatedness of the scenes in the hospital,
on the voyage, in the Crystal, in Yugoslavia, etc., is vexing, but at last,
as outlined above, one begins to "grasp at" the coherence one can find in
the lesson concerning Harmony, Correspondence, and the importance
of Remembrance, which all the levels of plot conspire to teach, if not to
preach. Lessing's narrative strategy is, then, overdetermined. It is determined once by the need Richter describes, to signal the fiction's rhetorical motive; thus the multiple plots, frequently interrupted and
interlaced, frustrate interest in action and focus attention instead on
theme. The strategy is determined a second time by the content of that
theme; thus the correspondences among plots, characters, and motifs
express the metaphysical outlook Lessing espouses — the belief in a universal harmony that manifests itself continuously in correspondences
among the myriad aspects of existence.

The many allusions in the text seem to function similarly to break the
continuity of the narrative, thus minimizing the plot sequence, focusing
attention alternatively on the idea pervading the whole fiction. The references to Greek gods and heroes, for example, surface in Charles Watkins's thought stream as images through which he identifies himself as a
chosen servant of the divine principle, at times yearning to forget the divine call (Jonah, Odysseus), at other times stern in his determination to
follow it (Ulysses, Jason). Appropriate as these references are to the central theme of the novel, they are always made to be discordant with
their context. In the early part of the novel, Charles's claims to be Odysseus or Sinbad seem absurd and pretentious in the sterile hospital scene
with its impersonal doctors' reports and transcribed dialogues among
"Patient," "Doctor Y," and "Doctor X." Later in the novel, Lessing uses
the long section representing the Greek gods in conference regarding
the fate of earth to provide a platform for her views on cosmic harmony; yet she constantly undercuts the allusions to the gods by parodic
characterization (of Minerva and Jupiter, for example), trivialization of
the scenes by the use of mock-modern but unamusing names (Minna
Erve, Merk Ury), and rapid cuts between solemn prophecy in the biblical or classical mode and silly or banal conversations and scenes, which
Lessing herself deprecates with the narrator's (or is it Charles's) aside,
"Ah yes, all very whimsical" (p. 136). Lessing thus introduces a validating device — an appeal to ancient mythic tradition — to support her
theme, but then undercuts the authority of the validating device by
mocking it tonally. The aesthetic cost of this maneuver is very high, yet
Lessing seems to be working according to an overarching plan. The
"self-destructing" allusions parallel the "self-destructing" plots. To use

New Critical terms, Lessing seems at pains to destroy the "vehicle" once the "tenor" has been delivered, as if to better demonstrate the solidity and essential dignity of the underlying idea by showing the comparative evanescence and triviality of the conveyor of the idea.[17] As Minerva and Mercury agree in conversation, the deliverers of the Truth have been many, but "It is always the same Message, of course—. . . That there is a Harmony and that if they wish to prosper they must keep in step and obey its Laws" (p. 133).

It should be manifest by now that *Briefing for a Descent into Hell* is a didactic fiction of a special kind, designed to deliver a "Message" that is at once an admonition, a proposition about reality, and a way of seeing the world. Its means, moreover, are much more complex than the term "didactic" may suggest. We are dealing with no simple allegory with unity of plot and one-to-one symbolism, but rather with a highly complex series of signs designed to collapse in on themselves while leaving behind for the reader the sense of being in touch with the thing signified. Lessing has arranged her narrative so that the emotional energy generated by any single plot is left undischarged when that plotline terminates. This leftover emotional charge eventually has nothing to attach itself to except the abstract message that underlies all the action. The message, thus charged with the affective power of several plotlines, endures in the reader's mind as the one sure element in an otherwise elusive text.

In performing the maneuver, Lessing departs radically from the rhetorical strategies of her earlier novels, works written to help build the great age of literature that she called for in her essay-manifesto "The Small Personal Voice." They were realistic novels with social breadth and psychological depth, intended to project "the warmth, the compassion, the humanity, the love of people which illuminates the literature of the nineteenth century and which makes all these old novels a statement of faith in man himself."[18] They were novels that took seriously the author's stake in "strengthening a vision of a good which may defeat the evil" and yet which did so without becoming propaganda or utopian fantasy. Lessing herself repudiated the "simple demand for simple statements of faith [which] produces art so intolerably dull and false that one reads it yawning and returns to Tolstoy."[19] She wished her own art to reflect the difficult contradictions and frustrations of social and personal reality, and it did. While she built toward a vision of the ideal —a suggestion of what society and the individual might become under better conditions—she delivered a very full and tangible vision of the real, historical, and material conditions out of which the future good might be made to grow. One of the great gifts that Lessing demonstrated in those novels was her versatility in using the techniques of traditional realism (full depiction of setting and character, interesting development of conflict, and consequent changes in the character's and the reader's conception of reality) in tandem with the techniques of modernist realism (symbolic rendering of subconscious perceptions; distortion of time, memory, and present perception to reflect the limitation of individual consciousness; and at the same time innovations in form to express the author's and the protagonist's unconventional, creative, and potentially liberating reorganization of consciousness).

In *Briefing for a Descent into Hell*, Lessing departs from both the traditional and the modernist versions of realism and chooses the techniques of rhetorical fiction, or, in Sheldon Sacks's terms, the apologue.[20] Such fiction is not organized in order to convey the thick texture of lived experience, whether social or psychic. The text is not oriented primarily toward mimesis; rather, as Sacks so neatly puts it, everything in the text is "designed to alter our attitudes toward or opinions of the world we live in. The attitudes themselves are formulable critically as statements about the external world, though the aesthetic response required fully to appreciate the apologue need not go beyond an altered 'feeling'—a sentiment—about the external world."[21] Lessing clearly signals her rhetorical (rather than mimetic) intentions through the paratactic structure of the plots, through the constant presence of correspondences among elements of these plots, and through deaccentuation of character development.

This last alteration is perhaps the most disturbing of all to admirers of Lessing's earlier fiction, but it is essential to her success in the genre of rhetorical fiction. In order to focus on the production of a "formulable statement" about the external world, Lessing must—like any other writer of apologue—deny readers the pleasures associated with the novel of character. The close rendering of individual character, the building of an integral relation between a progressive action and growth in the character's personal consciousness, and the solicitation of the reader's concern for the character's fate—these most pleasurable tasks of the novelist must all be eschewed if the apologue is to achieve its aim. Sheldon Sacks uses the example of Johnson's *Rasselas* to make a point that David Richter extends to include rhetorical novels such as Twain's *The Mysterious Stranger*, Orwell's *Animal Farm*, Pynchon's *Gravity's Rainbow*, and even Forster's *A Passage to India*.[22] Sacks establishes the rule that considerations of character must not predominate in rhetorical fiction:

If we become more interested in Rasselas' emotional reaction to the Stoic's misery than we are in his recognition of the futility of achieving earthly happiness by the acquisition of "invulnerable patience," the apologue has failed: all elements of the fiction have not been subordinated to the creation of an example of the truth of a formulable statement. . . . To the extent that [Johnson] went one step over the line and made our interest in the relationship of characters in the episodes stronger than our interest in what the episode exemplifies, then, no matter how convincing the episode was "artistically," it could no longer convince us of the truth of the now-obscured statement.[23]

In the light of Sacks's dictum, Lessing's mode of characterizing Charles Watkins (and his various avatars) shows itself as highly appropriate to her rhetorical aims. Watkins is given minimal personal identity: a job title, a wife, and a few friends (more acquaintances than friends) who can describe how their lives have intersected with his. Nonetheless, he lacks substance in that identity: his work is described only generally; we know little of his wife beyond her name; both she and the friends describe Watkins as uncommunicative and lacking in feeling; and he himself demonstrates very little personal emotion during the course of his narrative. His rather blank identity parallels that of Rasselas, Candide, the Red Cross Knight, or Christian — and this personal emptiness leaves room for metaphysical meanings to gather where in another kind of novel individual character traits and feelings would develop. As David Richter puts it, "In apologues, in fact, even the element of 'thought' on the part of the personages of the fiction which is simply expressive of character will be subordinated to the 'thought' which is the ruling principle of the fiction as a whole."[24] The ends of the narrative are therefore well served when Watkins's thought stream dwells at length on the principle of Harmony or on a parable of spiritual growth such as his tale of the honeysuckle and the camellia rather than on his relationships with his wife, his mistress, or his work. If Watkins's characterization is "thin" with respect to personal traits, it is "thick" with the philosophical substance that the novel is primarily designed to convey.

Through this and other techniques of rhetorical fiction, Lessing elicits from the reader a quality and focus of attention different from the kind she sought in either the *Children of Violence* series or *The Golden Notebook*. There is no denying that when she wrote these earlier works, she adopted the role of teacher and even at times of preacher and prophet just as she does in *Briefing*. However, the themes so consistent throughout her work — the limitations of human consciousness, the threats posed to civilization by our blindness to the conditions of our being, and the painful heroism of those who attempt to break the bonds of consciousness for the sake of self and community — all were understood, envisioned, and fictionally enacted as problems of human character, first on the level of the individual, then on the level of the individual's relation to the collective. Therefore her techniques were those of the novel of character, the central tradition of the novel since *Clarissa*.

All Lessing's novels up to *Briefing* are essentially novels of character. The *Children of Violence* series adheres closely to the form of the *Bildungsroman*, the novel of character development in social context. Though *The Golden Notebook* breaks from the form of the *Bildungsroman*, it adopts (and splinters, to be sure) the form of *Clarissa*, the type of novel that renders changes in intimate personal consciousness through a series of first-person testimonies written over time. With *Briefing*, Lessing materially alters her technique and fundamentally shifts the situation of her theme. In *Briefing*, the theme of the woeful limitation of human consciousness is no longer a question of individual character or even of social consciousness; it is instead a metaphysical question—a matter of the relation of humanity to laws of the universe that simply (and radically) transcend individual personal existence. Lessing adopts the techniques of the apologue in order to lift her reader's attention from the personal to the metaphysical plane—or at least to that intermediate plane in which the two can coexist in brief moments of connection.

Although it would be instructive to learn what events in Lessing's personal, political, and spiritual life led to this change in her interests—and one hopes that a future biography of Lessing will provide us with this information—the issue here concerns the evolution of her narrative form. With the publication of *Briefing* Lessing nearly completely recasts her narrative technique, and one well might ask what she gains by the adoption of an almost totally new *modus operandi*. Probably the most important gain for her as a writer is the opening up of an arena in which "a statement of faith in man himself" is still possible. In 1957, in the midst of her writing of *Children of Violence*, she stated that goal for herself in "The Small Personal Voice." There too she bemoaned the fact that "the best and most vital works of Western literature"—the best works of the realist tradition, that is—"have been despairing statements of emotional anarchy," embodying no more emphatic moral feeling than "a tired pity for human beings."[25] She promised in her version of the realist novel to make a statement of hope and of moral commitment. Yet, as she attempted in her subsequent novels realistically to mirror and to extrapolate from social conditions and history, she found little scope for the expression of progressivist faith. History itself disclosed and predicted no public salvation from all the human ills from which Lessing sought collective deliverance. Only in the coda to *The Four-Gated City*, where she made an exception to her realistic technique and switched the rules of the text from those of realism to those of utopian fantasy, could she rescue herself and her readers from pessimism and despair.

The solution of the *Four-Gated City* coda became the solution of *Briefing* as a whole. In the realm of the fantastic, Lessing could and did find new scope for the imagination of salvation. As Roberta Rubenstein has pointed out, there is even in *Briefing* a glimpse at a utopian future which is an echo of the utopian vision in the *Four-Gated City* coda.[26] In the coda, children genetically affected by the poisoning of air and water in a nearly apocalyptic disaster develop extrasensory power and promise to become the saviors of the post-catastrophe civilization. Likewise, during his "briefing for a descent into hell," Watkins is shown a film that predicts a worldwide "emergency" in which most of the human race will perish, giving way to a small group of human mutants with "increased powers of perception, a different mental structure" which will allow humankind at last to see clearly that which the limited structures of their minds have heretofore obscured from them (pp. 139–140).

While the bulk of the novel does not directly deal with the utopian future predicted in the briefing sequence, there is much use of the fantastic in order to build a vision of a world order — even a theology — that would provide the metaphysical grounding for a utopian hope. In the briefing episode, for example, the gods are depicted (as in the Greek epics) as the bringers of supernatural aid to heroes in distress. In this case, however, the distress is no discrete danger — a Scylla or a Minotaur — but the inefficiency of all human brains. The heroes in distress are the Messengers who have been charged by the gods

> to keep alive, in any way possible, the knowledge that humanity, with its fellow creatures, the animals and plants, make up a whole, are a unity, have a function in the whole system as an organ or organism. . . . The main feature of these human beings as at present constituted [is] their inability to feel, or understand themselves, in any other way except through their own drives or functions. They have not yet evolved into an understanding of their individual selves as merely parts of a whole, first of all humanity, their own species, let alone achieving a conscious knowledge of humanity as part of Nature; plants, animals, birds, insects, reptiles, all these together making a small chord in the Cosmic Harmony. (p. 141)

It is in order to express the utopian hope of man's achieving such divine knowledge that Lessing departs from the realistic mode of her earlier fiction. Whether one calls Lessing's newly adopted genre apologue, rhetorical fiction, or "ethically controlled fantasy" (terms preferred by Sacks, Richter, and Scholes, respectively)[27] it clearly affords her an opportunity that realism finally denied — a field in which to develop "a vision of a good which may defeat the evil."[28]

There is a catch, however. Lessing's strong ethical impulse was combined in her previous fictions with commitment to the demands of full realist fiction-making. Having contracted, as a realist, to develop intriguing characters, compelling plot, fullness of situation, and thickness of emotional texture, she never allowed herself in any way to impoverish the *fiction* in favor of the lesson she would wish to teach. At the time of writing *Briefing*, Lessing's didactic impulse is not yet so well tempered by a deeply felt commitment to the demands of her new genre. Fabulation, too, has its imperatives. Responsive as it is to the didactic impulse, fantasy ultimately insists on its freedom to pursue its own dynamic, its will to play and to create delight for its own sake. The creative dynamics of the fable can operate even under the pressure of an overriding ethical, religious, philosophical, or political imperative — as is the case in apologues such as Aesop's fables, *Pilgrim's Progress*, *Candide*, and *Animal Farm*. The fabulous may be called upon to serve rhetorical ends, but once summoned it must be allowed free play within the rhetorical frame. If it is kept too closely within bounds, employed too willfully to make this or that point only, the danger is that the fabulous will not make itself at home in the narrative but will remain cramped and awkward in its context. That is what happens in *Briefing*.

The problem of the text is thus recast. The initial puzzle of *Briefing* is its narrative and stylistic discontinuity. That puzzle resolves itself when the theme of correspondences surfaces as the generating element of the novel, which is now seen to operate as an apologue rather than as a novel of character. The rhetorical task of the novel provides a rationale for multiple plot levels, premature attenuation of incidents, flatness of characterization, schematization of character relations, and stylistic excesses. The revelation of the secret harmony of the narrative elements in conspiracy to teach the lesson of the harmony of the universe satisfies the critic's drive to comprehend the text in its intellectual coherence, yet it leaves another problem unsolved. That is the issue of imaginative vitality. However well integrated the text is conceptually — an integration that is entirely necessary to its didactic purpose — it does not achieve imaginative integration, a quality necessary to its success as fiction.

# Chapter Six

# *The Summer Before the Dark*
## THE ACHIEVEMENT OF INTEGRATION

In *The Summer Before the Dark,* a novel about a mature woman's journey toward personal integration, Lessing appropriately regains for her art the imaginative integration that she failed to achieve in *Briefing for a Descent into Hell.* In *Briefing,* Lessing conjoined many layers of narrative to form a challenging puzzlebox for the nimble reader, but the solving of the puzzle affords a merely intellectual pleasure. For *The Summer Before the Dark,* Lessing takes essentially the same themes as those of *Briefing,* gives them music, and orchestrates them into a fugue that intrigues one's intelligence with the play of intricate motifs, mystifies one's spirit with hints of correspondences and conjunctions, and arouses one's emotions to a deeply felt engagement with Kate Brown's struggle to save her essential self from destruction.

The story of Kate Brown's recovery of selfhood and reintegration with the vital world is a successful version of Charles Watkins's failed quest for his forgotten "true" identity and community. In both novels, the middle-aged protagonist reaches a severe personal crisis. Years of social conditioning and performance of prescribed roles have so alienated the inner self that it has slipped away entirely, leaving only the empty shell of a social personality. Both Charles and Kate prolong the crisis, embracing the "illness" that affords special conditions conducive to the search for the forgotten self. The most obvious difference between the two stories is that Charles Watkins loses his grip on that powerful and knowing self which he had discovered beneath the personal ego and

111

thus loses his opportunity to be guided by it to integration with the harmonious universe, whereas Kate Brown establishes a firm connection with her once-neglected inner self and in caring for it discovers the way to thrive again in her proper element. Charles's example is a warning, whereas Kate's is a model. The premises of the quest that the two share are nonetheless the same.

Like *Briefing, The Summer Before the Dark* is an apologue — a fiction generated and closely controlled by a theme that in turn implies an ethical, spiritual, or philosophical imperative. Since the theme of *Briefing* was both conceived and rendered in esoteric terms, the didactic function is somewhat impaired, and many early readers were confused as to how to take the novel. Not so with *The Summer Before the Dark*. The reviews clearly reflect Lessing's success in signaling the didactic function of her novel. In a brief paragraph praising the novel as "stark, powerful, and economical," Dorothy Nyren perhaps unwittingly predicted the direction of the reviews to follow: "One cannot help reading it with avid interest, arguing its thesis every paragraph of the way."[1] While some reviewers chafed at the open didacticism of the novel, they often reversed themselves in the course of the same review, praising the novel's "disturbing and reverberating effect,"[2] its "openhanded simplicity and transparency,"[3] or its "intelligence and its profound understanding of the psychology and cultural dilemmas of modern women."[4] More tellingly, almost without exception the reviewers became entangled in passionate attacks on or defenses of the "lesson" of the novel, as they often termed it.[5]

Above all else, this novel *engages* its readers — with the main character, Kate, with the issues she confronts, and with the propositions concerning those issues that the action, dream-allegory, and narrative commentary all conspire to assert. To the apologue proper — a simple narrative vehicle for conveying an idea — Lessing has added the techniques of the psychological novel, to form a compelling amalgam. In thus moving from the relatively pure didactic form of *Briefing* to the syncretic form of *The Summer Before the Dark*, Lessing recapitulates a generic development traced by Sheldon Sacks in his essay "Golden Birds and Dying Generations." Sacks — the great apologist for moral suasion in fiction, as well as the best analyst of its narrative operation[6] — reminds critics that "since the time of Richardson, the Western world's most important writers of fiction had eschewed apologues and had begun to condemn even effective examples of the genre . . . as antiartistic, as utilitarian, as mere propaganda."[7] The development of the novel as a narrative form over the last two centuries has been largely in the opposite direction — an effort to refine techniques of character representation for the sake of greater fidelity in the depiction of individual personal experience. Along with this development has come the possibility of stronger identification between reader and character, a bonding which the author can use to intensify the emotional effects of the novel. Now, "in the most promising single development of contemporary fiction in the Western world,"[8] Sacks tells us, authors have begun to pursue the goals of apologue, using the techniques developed for the psychological novel.

> Using new techniques for representing characters, for revealing subtle states of awareness, for achieving complex emotional effects — techniques developed during two hundred years of experimenting with . . . represented actions [specifically, the psychological novel] — our new novelists have created new apologues with aesthetic and ethical effects far more subtle than those possible to Bunyan, or Voltaire, or Johnson. In Switzerland, Herman Hesse, in works like *Siddhartha* and *Steppenwolf;* in the United States, in Heller's *Catch-22,* or Pynchon's *V;* in England, in Golding's *Lord of the Flies;* and, above all, in France in Camus' *The Plague* and *The Stranger* — in all these places there is evidence that the Western novel is not dead. Its soul is merely transmigrating, possibly to reappear in the *Divine Comedy* of our day.[9]

While *The Summer Before the Dark* hardly aspires to the scope and spiritual grandeur of *The Divine Comedy,* Lessing's later novels of the *Canopus in Argos* series seriously do, and *The Summer Before the Dark* is an arena in which Lessing begins to prepare herself for that major effort. Her significant achievement in this earlier novel is the integration of techniques proper to previously distinct forms: the psychological novel and allegory. In *The Summer Before the Dark* these disparate elements are made to cooperate in serving the ends of apologue: In the words of Sacks, describing the apologue, everything conspires to "move us to some realization — implicit or formulated — about the world external to the literary creation itself."[10] Yet due to the rich powers of the elements derived from the psychological novel, that "realization" is as deeply and fully felt as it is clearly formulated — something that could not be said of *Briefing,* in contrast.

The difference lies largely in the characterization of Kate Brown. Charles Watkins, according to the conventions of apologue, has almost no personal character. For the bulk of the text he is simply a vehicle for dream visions that provide the allegorical substance of the novel. Lessing's revelations about Watkins's personal life are merely schematic, providing data for allegorical readings of his experience. Kate Brown, too, becomes the vehicle of dream-visions that allegorically express the novel's thesis. Kate herself asserts the ultimate primacy of her inner life in the archetypal dream world over her outer life in the world of personal and social experience: "All the things that went on outside, the job I did, and the travelling, and the affair—I had a love affair, if you can call it that, it was silly really—well all that simply . . . fed the dream. Yes. It was the dream that was . . . feeding off my daytime life. Like a foetus" (p. 230).[11] The analogy is telling: Kate's anxious struggle to complete and let go of her dream is like the efforts of a mother to bring a child to term and to a successful birth. (Lessing plays on the analogy by at least six references to Kate's "condition," several worded exactly as if they referred to a pregnancy.[12] At one point, in fact, she refers to her dream life and her emotional life as one entity, in language that could refer to the burden of an unwanted foetus: It "seemed like a traitor who had come to life inside her. What she was engaged in was the dream, which worked itself out in her" (p. 143). As in the inevitable processes of parturition, too, Kate finds herself unable to hurry or direct a sequence of events that is by its nature out of her willed control: "That was not how people changed; they didn't change themselves: you got changed by being made to live through something, and then you found yourself changed" (p. 106). If Kate is figured as a mother living through an uncomfortable pregnancy, the birth at the end is a joy to herself, and the story itself is always *her* story, the story of the mother rather than of the child. This analogy thus points to a major shift in rhetorical stress from *Briefing*. There, the visionary allegory was the primary value and Charles Watkins merely its deliverer. Here, the emphasis is on the process of deliverance as it feels to the individual who suffers it. In order to bring the reader into sympathy with that process, Lessing renders Kate Brown's psychology in such a way as to fully convey the stress and pain of her revolutionary inner experience.

There is some truth, of course, to the contention that Kate Brown is Everywoman. She is, as Lorelei Cederstrom points out, "an average middle-class, middle-aged British wife and mother with a limited imaginative range,"[13] a woman in a thoroughly banal situation. As Kate says herself, she has "become that well-documented and much-studied phenomenon, the woman with grown-up children and not enough to do" (p. 23). Lessing does give Kate Brown representative status. To conclude therefrom, as Cederstrom does, that "Kate's problem, moreover, is not a deeply psychological one" or that Lessing has given Kate the limitations of the average housewife "in order that the reader will not identify with her"[14] is to ignore Lessing's careful rendering of both Kate's daily life and her often painful emotional experience.

The novel's first sentence, in the openness of its reference, suggests

the typicality of Kate's position as housewife: "A woman stood on her
back step, arms folded, waiting." Yet the sentences that follow trace her
thoughts in such a way as to win the reader's interest in and respect for
the individual placed in this representative position.

> Thinking? She would not have said so. She was trying to catch hold of
> something, or to lay it bare so that she could look and define; for some time
> now she had been "trying on" ideas like so many dresses off a rack. She was
> letting words and phrases as worn as nursery rhymes slide around her
> tongue: for towards the crucial experiences custom allots certain attitudes,
> and they are pretty stereotyped. . . .
> The truth was, she was becoming more and more uncomfortably con-
> scious not only that the things she said, and a good many of the things she
> thought, had been taken down off a rack and put on, but that what she
> really felt was something else again. (pp. 3, 4)

Kate Brown is at this moment beginning a process of analysis that will
lead her to discern in her life a pattern of glaring discrepancies—
between her thoughts and her speech, between her "official memories"
and the past actuality, between her social roles and her private self.

While passages such as the one above have an essay-like generality,
many moments of private and very particularly rendered suffering follow to give experiential depth to Kate's more abstract speculations. For
example, in the first page of the novel, Kate reviews some of the stock
phrases that she has been using to sum up her crucial experiences. She
concludes that "the choice of one rather than another of these time-
honoured phrases has seldom to do with a personal feeling, but more
likely your social setting, or the people you are with on an occasion. You
have to deduce a person's real feelings about a thing by a smile she does
not know is on her face, by the way bitterness tightens muscles at a
mouth's corner" (p. 3). Kate poignantly demonstrates her own suscepti-
bility to these mechanical reactions when she thinks of the fact that not
only her four grown children but also her husband, Michael, will be
leaving her for the summer. She entertains the notion of accompanying
Michael on his trip to America but realizes, "there was the question
whether she would be cramping her husband's style . . . to go with this
thought there was an appropriate smile, almost a grimace, suitable perhaps for the words: *There has to be give and take in any marriage;* she
was quite aware that she was disinclined to examine this area too
closely" (p. 12). Whereas the first passage is simply a general speculation that might pique the reader's intellectual curiosity, the second passage elicits a sympathetic wince. Lessing prepares this response by de-
voting ten pages in between the two passages to Kate's thoughts about

her family and her present life. In these musings Kate reveals her deep attachment to her family, her attentiveness to their needs, her respect for their independence and for their more worldly judgments than her own, and most importantly her hurt at their indifference to her. With that preparation, the reader can imagine the pain that Kate must feel at the thought of her husband's preference for time alone in order to carry on casual affairs; as we have been shown implicitly and later are directly told, she still loves him and feels diminished by his unfaithfulness. Yet at this moment she corroborates her earlier comments, since the grimace in her smile reveals the ineffectiveness of the admonition to tolerance that she has chosen as a comment on her husband's philanderings. Later, the discrepancy between thought and feeling appears again. In the midst of a fantasy in which she proudly describes her marital arrangements to some younger women, she mentions again "this smile that was half a grimace" and suddenly realizes: "I'm telling myself the most dreadful lies! Awful! Why do I do it? There's something here that I simply will not let myself look at." On the spot, she resolves to "look at it all, try and get hold of it," rather than "making up all these attitudes, these stories" (p. 15).[15]

What becomes Kate's quest to liberate her inner self begins quite simply with this plan to strip away the phony facade that she has erected over the most meaningful (and most distressing) parts of her life. In one painful scene after another, she uncovers what she has really been feeling, separating the authentic emotion from "the dozen or so mental attitudes" that she has adopted as her habitual wardrobe—"garments taken down off a rack" (p. 25) to be thrown over the body of her feelings regardless of the fit. She discovers that she has been refusing to face up to her definite knowledge of Michael's affairs and has evaded dealing with her own resulting fury, hurt, and sexual diminishment. She realizes that her intelligent talks and joking with Michael about the stages of their marriage have been a travesty, as have her temperate discussions with her children about family tensions. None of these attempts at communication have tapped her actual emotions or touched her private self. As for her former view of these matters, Kate now "felt as if one pattern of memory was jostling another out of her mind; meanwhile she persevered with the one she was used to" (p. 70); however, "the official memories of all kinds were wearing thin, were almost transparent" (p. 91). What Kate now seeks is a clear view of the personal reality beneath these newly transparent lies.

Lessing creates a metaphor for Kate's quest in the description of her summer's work. Left behind by her family, Kate is fortuitously offered a job as a translator of Portuguese for an international conference. Just as in her personal life Kate seeks to break the codes of conventional thought and false memory in order to think about her experience truthfully, so at the Global Foods conference Kate's job is to break the code of a foreign language so that diplomats can communicate accurately. Especially when Kate herself leaves the conference and confronts a language unknown to her, the parallels in her efforts to understand the new language and her struggle to understand her own life become striking. She had earlier figured her attempt to dispel false memories as the thinning of some material to a state of transparency; now she imagines the Spanish language as a veil that her Portuguese can only partially help her penetrate: the language "was a veil between herself and Spain which she could not pull aside. But it was a semitransparent veil. . . . The conversation nagged, on the edge of meaning" (pp. 94 f.). As in Kate's emotional life, understanding stands maddeningly out of reach— but close enough to tantalize. Again, in parallel with her earlier experience, she finds that it is tempting to succumb to the easy route of listening only to the familiar code rather than straining to understand in new terms: "And her ears were still attempting to make amenable lumps of sound to which she did not have the key, while they absorbed other sequences of sound which sank easily into her brain" (p. 150; cf. p. 70).

Both in her private life and in her work, Kate is in search of what lies behind the veil — a once obscured meaning, a half-forgotten identity, a long-evaded truth. She is very much in the position of the questing knight; she seeks an equivalent of the Grail. As Tzvetan Todorov notes in his study of narrative forms, *The Poetics of Prose*, "The quest of the Grail is the quest of a code. To find the Grail is to learn how to decipher the divine language."[16] Kate Brown, whose employment is literally to decipher a foreign language, learns to pay attention to a higher language — the language of her dream world — and to aspire to grasp its message. One might say that her dreams are couched in divine language. It is at least a language beyond words, and it does at last deliver a message of salvation.

The quest structure of *The Summer Before the Dark* is one of the features that differentiates it formally from the psychological novel. Todorov distinguishes between two kinds of logic proper to fictional form— narrative and ritual logic.[17] Narrative logic, dominant in the traditional novel, propels the reader forward in a series of events that are interesting precisely because each development could have been otherwise; curiosity, suspense, the possibility of surprise are all key elements in the reader's orientation toward the plot. Ritual logic, in contrast, demands that everything unfold according to a plan that is known from the start; here the reader's interest focuses on the unfolding of the foreknown and on the implications of that unfolding for an understanding of the power that generates the whole ritual action. In *The Summer Before the Dark*, as in quest narratives generally, the two kinds of action are in constant counterpoint.

The quest begins with a prediction of its outcome. In the quest proper, this and other crucial announcements come from some sage kept apart from the action; here the narrator takes the place of commenting seer:

> Sometimes, if you are lucky, a process, or a stage, does get concentrated. It was going to turn out for Kate that that summer would be such a shortened, heightened, concentrated time.
>
> What was she going to experience? Nothing much more than, simply, she grew old. . . . Kate Brown was going to get the whole thing over with in a few months. Because while everything seemed so personal, and aimed at her — her patience, her good humour, her time — in fact it would be pressures from the other, the public, sphere pressing on her small life that would give what she experienced its urgency? However that might be, the summer's events were not going to be shaped through any virtues or capacities of her own. (pp. 8–9)

What is going to happen to Kate Brown will be dictated not by personality or individual circumstance (the stuff of the psychological novel) but by some power well beyond her individual self.[18] While in this passage the focus is on the force of "the public sphere," perhaps suggesting the social and political conditions of a particular time and place (the stuff of *Martha Quest*, for example), the phrase should be understood in a broader sense. Kate is going to experience archetypal pressures both as they well up from within her most impersonal self and as the collective forces them upon her from without. It will not be the personal traits that she has developed in forty-five years of living which will put her under trial; rather it will be the needs of her inner self at a certain universal stage of life, combined with the expectations that the collective brings to bear on women at that stage, which will determine the nature and extent of that ordeal.

The onset of her suffering has the inevitability of a coming storm: "She felt . . . as if suddenly a very cold wind had started to blow, straight towards her, from the future" (p. 20). In this case, however, the reader has been told how long the storm will last and what the result of it will be. Kate will "grow old" — whatever that means. There again, we have a parallel with quest narrative. We know who will obtain the Grail, but what does the Grail signify? In quest narrative the answer to that question is given allegorically in the hero's ordeals and visions and is stated explicitly in the commentary of the by-standing seer. Similarly, we learn what to "grow old" signifies in this text by interpreting Kate's ordeals, by decoding her dreams, and by attending to the commentary of the narrator.

In her summer's pilgrimage to old age, Kate journeys in a circle from her suburban home, to a London flat, to Turkey, to Spain, and back again to another London flat in preparation for a return home. The ritual form of the eternal return applies as well to the series of ordeals that earn her the prize of maturity. Her first suffering comes from the realization that both her children and her husband no longer need her — that after benefiting for twenty years from her selfless service and love, they find her stifling. Toward the end of her quest, she returns to these first wounds, searching her memory for clues as to how she lost her husband's sexual regard and her children's devotion. The experiences of the mid-time prepare her to find and to recognize the answer, just as the knight's ordeals prepare him to find and recognize the Grail.

Kate faces her first major challenge when she leaves her home to take a job. The material test — preparing her Portuguese and performing well in the translating booth — proves easy to pass. It is the accompanying spiritual test that gives her difficulty. Contrary to Kate's expectations, the worst part of leaving home is neither loneliness nor the stress of unfamiliar work. She finds herself in a state of panic, not from fear of the job but from fear of the thoughts that the job opportunity raises in her. The need to practice her Portuguese throws her back into memories of her girlhood year of reigning as a flirtatious belle in Portuguese-speaking Laurenço Marques, soon after which she decided to marry rather than pursue an academic career in Romance languages. Kate's fright comes to overwhelm her not when she thinks of the job itself but when she thinks of what it might have meant to have chosen a career twenty-five years ago: "If she had not married — but good God, she would have been mad not to marry, mad to choose Romance languages and literature. . . . What she was feeling was a kind of panic. Knowing this made it worse. It was stupid and irrational to feel frightened. What of?" (p. 19). As with her abortive thoughts about her husband's infidelities, Kate lets fear prevent her from answering her own question. The job is an opportunity to try out the option she had rejected in her youth — to find out what Kate Brown would be like if she were not a mother but a career woman. Afraid to find out, Kate rebuilds a maternal identity for herself on the job and is rewarded by her bosses with promotions and gratitude: "She had become what she was: a nurse, or a nanny . . . A mother. Never mind, in a few days she would be free of it all" (p. 33).

The knowledge of error that Kate consciously dismisses is pressed upon her from another realm. Like the errant knight who must be called back to the true path by a dream or vision, Kate receives her admonishment in a dream — the first of fifteen dreams that provide a running commentary on her quest. Just before sleeping she says to herself that she has made a mistake both in becoming a mother figure on the job and in agreeing to spend her time after the job acting as a part-time mother in a friend's home: "that was just cowardice." What she should do instead is to stay alone in her small London flat and think her way through to the recovery of her nonmaternal self: "Yes this is what she would choose, if she could choose . . . she dreamed" (p. 34). And the dream comes, like the knight's first vision, to instruct her as to the nature of her quest.

"She came down a hillside in a landscape that was northern, and unknown to her" (p. 34). The dream acknowledges, as Kate consciously has avoided doing, that she is in a new stage of life — in a dream-like pun, she is "over the hill" — feeling for the first time the cold of approaching old age. On the ground, she sees "something dark" — something mysterious and unknown — "a seal, stranded and helpless among dry rocks high on a cold hillside. It was moaning" (p. 34). In her habitually maternal way, Kate responds to the first moans by inquiring if she can help and by quickly accepting the seal's rescue as her own burden.

The seal, which appears in all fifteen of Kate's dreams, is rather obviously a symbol for some aspect of Kate's identity, though which aspect is a matter of dispute. Several major studies of the novel identify the seal as a symbol of Kate's submerged inner self, a personality that she dismissed at marriage in favor of the nurturing and accommodating personality of a wife and mother.[19] Helpful as that interpretation is during the reading of the bulk of the novel, it can force the critic into a self-contradictory or awkward assessment of the novel's ending. Barbara Lefcowitz, for example, consistently argues from the assumption that the seal is Kate's "abandoned private self."[20] Yet, at the end of her article, in explaining why Kate parts with the seal in returning it to the water, Lefcowitz suddenly must switch her symbolic definition of the seal: "Kate gets rid of the seal as a sign of her emerging freedom from maternal and wifely cares."[21] Josephine Hendin, on the other hand, puts all her weight behind the interpretation that Lefcowitz applies only locally: "The seal is Kate, *wife and mother,* a helpless, broken animal sealed in an alien world, a fish out of water, craving some clear northern sea. In her last dream, she sets the seal down safely in the sea, watching it disappear among other heedless beasts, and is lightened, finally delivered of this perpetual, damaged child after a lifetime labor."[22] Yet this interpretation proves problematic, because the happiness of the liberated seal is not mirrored at the end of the novel by Kate's happiness in her familial relations. Hendin is forced into the reductive conclusion that the novel offers dreams as mere escapist fantasies while demonstrating that actual, waking life is doomed to be unfulfilling. If we are to arrive at a more satisfying interpretation of the novel as a whole, we must acknowledge more fully than either Hendin or Lefcowitz the inherent ambiguity of the seal as symbol.

The physical description of the seal, for example, suggests several of Kate's aspects. Its dark eyes and Kate's are repeatedly mentioned. Kate's are always associated with "her need to love and give;" Kate rejects that need when she denigrates her warm brown eyes, calling them "the sympathetic eyes of a loving spaniel" (p. 48). In mirror image, the seal's dark eyes appeal to Kate's maternal side, silently pleading for assistance (p. 77) and reproaching Kate when she does not respond (p. 112). The dream image of the seal's eyes dually refers to Kate's responsiveness to the needs of others and — insofar as the seal represents herself — her own need to be nurtured in return. The description of the body of the seal, on the other hand, connects directly to Kate's identity on the job. Describing the hairdo that Kate adopts specifically in order to change her image from that of a proper matron to that of a liberated career woman, the narrator speaks of the "weight of heavy silk swinging against her cheeks" (p. 43), and Kate notices the "heavy curves" of the new hairdo (p. 53). In parallel language, Lessing repeatedly mentions the heavy weight of the seal, the slipperiness of its silken coat, and even the softness of its hide against her cheek (p. 145). Thus the description of the seal is symbolically ambiguous — referring at once to Kate's motherliness, her need to be mothered, and her desire to reject the motherly role in taking up a career identity. According to the context of each dream, one of these sides of Kate's nature is embodied in the seal image. In every case, however, Kate's care of the seal is a symbol of her attention to some part of her self, of her life: "She knew that walking into the winter that lay in front of her she was carrying her life as well as the seal's" (p. 145).

As Kate nurses the seal along on its journey to the sea, each dream episode constitutes a comment on her progress in waking life toward the grail of "old age." The first dream comes to assign Kate the task of finding a more hospitable climate for her inner self. Kate is "stranded and helpless" both in her home and in her summer job. Her deepest self is neglected in both environments, since in both places she acts only in response to others, hardly noticing any impulses that originate within herself. The only impulse of her own that is satisfied in these environments is the need to please, but this desire has bred in her a false character, "that person which was all warmth and charm, that personality which had nothing to do with her, nothing with what she really was" (p. 53). To shed that personality and find herself, she must set out on a journey, both physical and spiritual; to save the seal she has to willingly pick it up and carry it forward: "It moaned, and she knew she had to get it to water" (p. 35).

It would be misleading if we were to begin to speak as if *The Summer Before the Dark* consisted simply of two levels of narrative, Kate's action in her outward life and the dreams about the seal that interpret those actions. There is a third level of narrative development: the analytical and sometimes highly assertive commentary that the narrator delivers discursively throughout the novel. As noted earlier, the narrator initially acts the role of seer to Kate's knight and makes prophecies regarding the outcome of her quest (pp. 8–9). Later, as Kate becomes more aware of the imperatives of the journey, the narrator pulls back from direct commentary and conveys her judgments on Kate's progress largely through reflections of Kate's thought stream. This analytical commentary ought not to be dismissed as if it were simply undigested ideology;[23] it is not there inadvertently but intentionally, and it directly advances the aims of the novel. These sections of contemplative commentary serve to retard the narrative motion, giving the reader time and inclination to analyze the import of both action and dream. With the "openhanded simplicity" that impressed reviewer Walter Clemons,[24] Lessing moves in these sections of commentary to take a stand on the issues in play in her modern amalgam of quest narrative and psychological novel. In doing so, she violates the standard of moral disinterestedness that has been applied to the novel in modern times, but at the same time she joins company with all those writers who have ever employed elements of allegory or apologue in their fictions (and there is rather good company there).[25]

In each section of the novel, then, the action of the quest is interpreted by an allegorical dream and glossed by somewhat didactic commentary. In the second section, for example, Kate meets her next ordeal, the temptation to accept an administrative job at Global Foods—a job predicated on Kate's willingness to play the mother role, which would cut off her chances to explore other potentials in her personality. As with her first ordeal—the necessity to face the self she might have become without marriage—Kate makes the easy and mistaken choice. Having decided to accept the job, Kate vacillates between certainty that "she should have said *no* to Charlie Cooper and all the money and arranged to stay in London, in a room, quietly, by herself" (pp. 47–48) and the belief that it is only through such a job that she will be able to stave off the personal deterioration that she has felt herself prey to since her family stopped needing her (pp. 52–53). A dream comes to tell her that she has made the wrong decision (pp. 53–54). It is becoming clear that Kate is faltering in her care of her inner self; so, in the dream, the seal seems slippery in her arms, and she staggers under its weight. Likewise, just as Kate in waking life suspects that she has just made a decision injurious to her inner development, in the dream she panics from self-doubt and begins to carry the seal in the wrong direction. The dream tells her that she must go back to the original path (that is, return to the original intentions of her summer alone) and that if she applies salves to both the new and the old wounds of the seal, it will heal (that is, she herself will thrive if she repairs the damage that her soul has sustained both recently on the job and in the many long years of her marriage).

The narrator enlarges the significance of Kate's realization by means of an extended analogy. Calling a halt to the forward thrust of the plot, she introduces a four-page essay on the emotional costs of being an airline stewardess. This essay is couched as an observation that Kate had made a year before, when she travelled by airline to the States. However, there is no further reference to Kate in her position as observer of the stewardess, and the style is rather too rhetorical to pass as a record of Kate's informal impressions.

Such ambiguity in point of view is a frequent phenomenon in this novel, but in an effective way. Whereas at times the narrator speaks from a distanced perspective, frequently she speaks as if in consonance with Kate. Any large pronouncements, such as a comment on the managing function of women ("This is what women did in families — it was Kate's role in life," p. 52) are likely to come from the narrator, but with the suggestion that Kate shares the viewpoint either consciously or unconsciously. The effect of this maneuver is to soften the polemical air of the more highly didactic passages by suggesting that they echo the thoughts of Kate, whose emotionally stressful ordeals win her sympathy with the reader and give her warrant for some harsh social commentary. In this particular set piece of sociological reporting, a smiling young stewardess plays the role of "love supplier" to the public, only to find that the role has addicted her to the drugs of Love, Attention, and Flattery, without which she is unable to function. At the end of the self-contained essay, the narrator returns us to Kate, whom we see "smiling, smiling, in the beam of other people's appreciation, turning the beam of her own readiness outwards to warm everybody else" (p. 63). The comment is obvious: Kate's job, like the job of a stewardess, makes her too dependent on the reactions of others; she cannot become herself if she continues to occupy herself in seeking and giving love. By distancing herself almost to the level of essayist in order to make this point, the narrator suggests that the lesson applies generally to women who have accepted the nurturing role either in jobs or at home. Any such woman in the novel's audience is being exhorted to take up Kate's quest — to forego pleasing others in favoring of learning what will please herself.

Such a reordering of priorities is Kate's business in the course of her quest. The first sign of her success is her desertion of Jeffrey, her sick lover — an act that the former Kate would have judged as inconceivably heartless and irresponsible. The new Kate is able to realize, first, that she owes nothing to this young man, who has been a leech ever since he was fortunate enough to catch her in an emotionally needy moment and convince her to travel with him; second, that she can only give to him if she neglects herself; and, third, that her maternal ministrations would be useless to him. One of the most effective dream sequences foreshadows these realizations:

> She was looking at a film she had seen before, . . . watching that sequence of the poor turtle who, on the island in the Pacific which had been atom-bombed, had lost its sense of direction and instead of returning to the sea after it had laid its eggs, as nature ordinarily directed, was setting its course inwards into a waterless land where it would die. She sat in the dark of the cinema and watched the poor beast drag quietly away from the sea, towards death, and she thought: Oh the seal, my poor seal, that is my responsibility, that is what I have to do. . . . For while she could do nothing for the turtle, who was going to die, she must save the seal. (p. 77)

The symbols of the dream are nicely over-determined. The turtle with the poor sense of direction resembles Jeffrey, who feels irrationally compelled to travel inland by bus even though he is ill and should remain in his coastal hotel. In the dream, Kate realizes that she had better leave the moribund turtle to its doom and attend to the salvageable seal; likewise, Kate learns that since she cannot help Jeffrey, she should forget him and turn her attention to herself. On a second level of interpretation, both turtle and seal refer to parts of Kate. Like the turtle, Kate has lost her sense of direction after fulfilling her procreative role; instead of returning to her pre-maternal identity, here represented by the sea, she has mistakenly prolonged her stay in procreative territory and in fact has gone further into that territory than nature itself would have dictated — she has become a more-than-fulltime mother to a grown-up family who feel stifled by her care. The dream about the turtle suggests that she should not tinker with the maternal identity, attempting to change it to suit the present conditions; rather, she ought to recognize that her mothering instinct is so corrupted (as if by atomic radiation) that it is totally unreliable, doomed to self-destruction.[26] Therefore, her attention must be turned to what the seal here represents — her pre-maternal self, the self that she left behind when she became a wife. As the narrator tells us, "the future was not going to be a continuation of the immediate past" — she would not, like the turtle, continue inland; "No, the future would continue from where she had left off as a child," when adolescence had oriented her whole being toward the demands of procreation (p. 140). It is now time to return to what in the meantime had been neglected — her inner self.

The narrator here and elsewhere stresses the sad fact that family can rarely, if ever, help a mother repair her inner self after the stress of traditional child-rearing. Typically, both children and husband grow used to a woman's behavior in her mother role, and they consequently fail to see actions or hear statements that the woman makes from outside that role. Kate's case is representative: "All that time [of her marriage] she had been holding in her hands something else, the something precious, offering it in vain to her husband, to her children, to everyone she knew — but it had never been taken, had not been noticed. But this thing she had offered, without knowing she was doing it, which had been ignored by herself and by everyone else, was what was real in her" (p. 140). Children and husband are thus a threat to the woman's inner self, as is dramatically expressed in Kate's dream about an attack on her seal. In the dream, which comes just two pages after her realizations about her family's blindness to her inner self, Kate is with her seal in the circus of a Roman amphitheater. Like a Christian on trial for her religion, Kate must fight off the attacks of lions, leopards, wolves, and tigers. She must stick to the principles of her quest, fighting against the hostility that her children, her husband, and even perhaps her lover might show toward her new identity.

Since other people threaten her developing personality, Kate learns to desire solitude. In her isolation, she forces herself to relive the hurts of family life in order to fully absorb the emotions she had repressed — anger, bitterness, disgust, and grief. The experiencing of these emotions rapidly ages her face and her body, making them unrecognizable even to her best friend. Up till this time, Kate has been remarkably "well preserved," like a woman on ice — and the ice is frozen emotion.

A dream comes like a vision to tell her to unlock the frozen sea of feeling and to let salt tears flow. In the dream, the seal is nearly dead from the cold. "She should wet the seal's hide. But everything was frozen, and the seal needed to have on its dry hide some salt water" (p. 161).

Kate manages to make some salt water for the seal by breaking ice into salt crystals on a rock; similarly, in a new stage of her life, a stay in London with a young woman named Maureen, Kate learns to break down her reserves and express her grief over the inadequacies of her past relations to her husband, her children, and her self. The sadness of Kate's realizations is only deepened by her recognition that her sufferings have been part of a universal experience—the experience of motherhood—and that no other role that she might have chosen would have been without its own peculiar costs. The problem is wider than the woes of motherhood; the problem is the limitation of any role. Here Lessing returns to her perennial theme, the sadness of human consciousness—its strong propensity to give up its scope and freedom to the control of roles, habits, allegiances, and illusions.

In the last pages of the novel, Lessing shifts the reader's attention away from Kate, in order to widen the point. Through Maureen, Lessing demonstrates the myriad ways in which the playing of a role can limit one's capacities for thought and feeling. As Maureen tries on possible choices of feeling, she changes costumes, using clothes to label and fix her identity. The frequency and extremity of these changes make the very act of selecting a role seem ludicrous. Maureen's process of selecting a husband appears similarly artificial. In a husband she is obviously seeking the optimum way to limit herself, and each of the three men she considers is himself a case of extreme self-abridgement through the adoption of a publicly recognizable role—hippie, fascist, and aristocrat, respectively. The shame and folly of all self-limitation is demonstrated in a farcical scene at the zoo, a scene in which three human spectators, Maureen and a younger couple, act out a pitiable melodrama of romance and jealousy while simultaneously bemoaning the encagement of the animals in boxes no more constraining than their own human roles.

This disgusting demonstration of the human need to encage the self in a prescribed role finally convinces Kate to let go her maternal role and free her soul. The scene at the zoo prepares the way, then, for the final moment of vision toward which the whole action has been moving. All the stages of Kate's way have been marked by significant dreams; here, at the last step of her journey, a final dream delivers the climactic moment of vision. In its ambiguity—it has evoked completely contradictory interpretations from the critics—this last dream symbolically resolves the tension in the plot between Kate's identification with her maternal self and her need to discard it. The symbolic openness of the seal itself is the key to this effect.

The seal represents at once the burden of Kate's maternal role and the inner self that the maternal personality has imprisoned. In the dream, Kate herself appears as a maternal presence, nurturing the seal, as she has done in all the episodes of the serial dream. It is with pride in her maternal devotion that Kate performs her last sacrificial acts for the seal:

> Using the last of her strength, she lifted the seal well off the earth, so that its tail would not be made sore by dragging it, and she staggered down a little path that led to the sea's edge. There, on a flat rock, she let the seal slide into the water. It sank out of sight, then came up, and rested its head for the last time on the edge of the rock: its dark soft eyes looked at her, then it closed its nostrils and dived. The sea was full of seals swimming beside each other, turning over to swim on their backs, swerving and diving, playing. A seal swam past that had scars on its flanks and its back, and Kate thought that this must be her seal, whom she had carried through so many perils. But it did not look at her now.
> Her journey was over. (p. 266)

The reciprocal love of mother and child, suggested in the seal's parting gestures of affection toward Kate, support a positive view of motherhood and of family love; this scene helps to balance the impression of Kate's earlier thoughts about the stultifying effects of maternal love on both mother and children. At the same time, it is significant that this moment of mutual affection and peace occurs at the moment when the mother figure releases her charge to the freedom of a life without her. Thus the dream affirms the moment of relinquishing the maternal tie, without denying the importance and value of that tie at its proper time. In this reading, the seal represents Kate's children and all others whom she might nurture. In relinquishing the seal to the sea, Kate feels both pride in the accomplishment of her nurturing role ("she had carried [the seal] through so many perils. . . . Her journey was over") and certainty that an even more satisfying future lies beyond that role: "She saw that the sun was in front of her, not behind. . . . She looked at it, a large, light, brilliant, buoyant, tumultuous sun that seemed to sing" (p. 267).

Simultaneously, the seal stands for the inner, nonmaternal self that Kate has been nurturing back to life in the last few months. The returning of the seal to its natural element, the sea, and to a life with other playfully friendly seals, is an emblem for Kate's return to a society beyond the family—a society that offers the possibility of pleasurable interaction with other adults who do not threaten to become her dependents. The Kate who stands aside, viewing the release of the seal/inner self, is the conscious, objective ego that has managed Kate's struggle to put each part of her self in its proper place.[27] In either case, Kate "was no longer anxious about the seal, that it might be dead or dying: she knew that it was full of life, and, like her, of hope" (p. 266). Whether the seal is her family or her newfound identity, it can now thrive independently of her conscious nurturing effort. The warm breeze, the arrival at the sea, the spring grass and flowers, the sunlit sky—all are emblems of spring and rebirth.

How can these symbols be reconciled with the narrator's prophecy in the first pages of the novel? "What was she going to experience? Nothing much more than, simply, she grew old" (p. 8). Growing old in our culture generally means falling into disuse and becoming displaced—and in fact Kate feels herself in that condition: "I'm unemployed!" she says. "There's nothing for me to do" (p. 267). The significant fact is that she makes this statement immediately after waking from the joyous dream about the seal's deliverance, and the tone of her statement about her new situation is by no means despairing. Kate's relinquishment of her old place at home and her old job of mothering parallels her deliverance of the seal to the sea. There has been a loss, but the *sense* of loss is present neither in the dream nor in Kate's statements about her new stage in life. In both arenas, the accent is on the rightness of the new situation, and on the joyful feeling of possibility that accompanies it. Kate has undergone losses: "her face had aged. Noticeably. . . . The light that is the desire to please had gone out. And about time too . . . Her hair—well, no one could overlook that!" (p. 269). Yet there is a note of triumph in Kate's catalog of the visible signs of her bodily decay. She has infused these outward signs of the losses of old age with the joyful emotion that pertains to the gains of old age:

> Her experiences of the last months, her discoveries, her self-definition; what she hoped were now strengths, were concentrated here—that she would walk into her home with her hair undressed, with her hair tied straight back for utility; rough and streaky, and the widening grey band showing like a statement of intent. It was as if the rest of her—body, feet, even face, which was aging but amenable—belonged to everyone else. But her hair—no! No one was going to lay hands on that. (p. 269)

What Kate has gained is self-possession—that is the grail of old age toward which she has been moving. In this novel, "old age" means discovering and defining one's self, gaining the strength to act out of one's own needs, and developing the courage to make statements of intent. It is with the confidence of such an old age that Kate Brown, in the last line of the novel, picks up her suitcase and heads back home.

Both Kate's decision to return to her family and the state of her mind when she makes the decision have been much misunderstood by critics who do not give proper weight to the quest structure of the novel or to the dream sequences as cues to the stages of the quest. Three of the most intelligent critics of the novel — Roberta Rubenstein, Elizabeth Hardwick, and Doris Grumbach — object to what they consider a despairing ending and allude to the appropriateness of the title as a prediction of a dark future for Kate. Rubenstein understands Kate to have achieved acceptance of "the inevitable darkness of older age,"[28] Hardwick refers to Kate's "bleak journey, a drop into a funnel of depression and crucifying despair,"[29] and Grumbach states quite baldly that "it is 'the dark' to which she goes after the light of summer."[30] In order to make this assessment, these critics must ignore the central place of the dream sequences in interpreting both Kate's actions and the title of the novel. The culminating dream clearly instructs us that Kate was wrong in her assumption that this was her summer before the dark: "She saw that the sun was in front of her, not behind, not far far behind, under the curve of the earth, which was where it had been for so long" (p. 267). The reversal from dark to light in the dream requires a reversal in the reader's assessment of what Kate's aging means for her future. The aging process may have seemed all darkness and loss; here, at the end, it shows itself — surprisingly — to be light and gain instead.

Likewise, the critics' objections to Kate's return home[31] ignore both the context of that return and the appropriateness of a physical return at the end of a quest novel. The knight returns home, with his prize or without it, to contemplate the meaning of all he accomplished on his journey; we assume that his ordeals have changed him and given him wisdom that he will carry into episodes beyond the close of the tale. Similarly, at the end of *The Summer Before the Dark*, Kate returns home, with the wisdom of old age to guide her in the conduct of a battle beyond the scope of the novel — the struggle to maintain and expand her new identity as she fulfills (or divests herself of) the responsibilities that she inherits from her former self.

Kate's quest has a linear dimension; she moves from motherhood to the autonomy of old age. It also has a circular shape; in the process of her movement away from and then back toward home, Kate makes a full and rounded space for the inclusion of all parts of herself — the nurturer, the manager, the explorer, the lover, the recluse, the teacher — to the exclusion of nothing that her inner self recognizes as its own. By the end of the novel, the shape that contains all these parts feels satisfyingly rounded and whole.

In telling Kate's story, Lessing, too, has pulled disparate elements into unity. Whereas in *Briefing for a Descent into Hell*, the separate levels of the plot never flowed together to give power to the narrative line, in *The Summer Before the Dark*, Kate's actions, her dreams, and the thoughts shared by her and the narrator cooperate at every stage to give a single direction of feeling and movement to the novel. At the same time, Lessing has successfully combined the techniques and reaped the benefits of two different kinds of fiction. At the end of the novel, the reader is emotionally identified with Kate Brown as she makes "her way to the bus stop and so home" (p. 273). We feel the full psychological effect of her experiences and weigh, with her, their implications for her future. Yet, with another side of our reading self, we stand aside from her sufficiently to ponder the wider meaning of her quest — to define for ourselves the significance of her achievement of old age. Thus Lessing has induced the reader to integrate two styles of reading — the style appropriate to the psychological novel and the style appropriate to more rhetorical fictions, such as the allegory, the quest narrative, and the apologue. In the next novel, she will push her limits too far and overtax the reader's ability to balance two different kinds of narrative. For the moment, however, Lessing has, in this novel, achieved perfect imaginative poise.

# Chapter Seven

# *The Memoirs of a Survivor*
## CHANGING FRAMES

On June 4, 1978, Doris Lessing was honored by *The New York Times Book Review* as "the great realist writer of our time." Unfortunately, this generous piece of praise was likely to mislead the public as to the nature of Lessing's work in the previous twenty years. Starting with the publication of *The Golden Notebook* (1962), she began to move away from a strictly realistic mode. In *The Four-Gated City* (1969), *Briefing for a Descent into Hell* (1971), *The Summer Before the Dark* (1973), and *The Memoirs of a Survivor* (1974), Lessing experiments with techniques related to non-realistic modes such as expressionism, fantasy, science fiction, and allegory.

Especially since the publication of *The Memoirs of a Survivor*, Lessing critics have been engaged in a heated debate concerning this steady change in her techniques and in the vision that gives rise to them. However, this debate has occurred mostly behind the closed doors of conference sessions, issuing in very little public statement. Critics of Lessing's work, eager to see her recognized publicly, have allowed the popular press to praise her in terms that are by now anachronistic. Moreover, they have been reluctant publicly to find fault with the recent work of a novelist whom on the whole they greatly admire. If Lessing is to be treated seriously as a *contemporary* writer, this hesitancy must be over-

This chapter first appeared as "Changing Frames: Doris Lessing's *Memoirs of a Survivor*," *Studies in the Novel* 11 (Spring 1979): 51–62. © North Texas State University.

come, and critics must address themselves to the problems posed by her adoption of nonrealistic techniques in the novels of the 1970s and 1980s.

Two recent articles have attempted to take an evaluative stance towards the later Lessing, but each concentrates its attention on ideology, not form. Michael L. Magie, in his essay "Doris Lessing and Romanticism," faults Lessing for deserting rationalism and realism for irrationalism and mystical fantasy. His critique of the later Lessing is essentially a moral objection to the mystical content of the novels: "Lessing offers what is likely to be, culturally, for all of us, the least helpful model and exhortation imaginable, being not only delusive but indulgent and a spur to self-indulgence. She portrays our collective situation as hopeless, lightened only by the adoption of illusion."[1] What Magie deplores is precisely what Nancy Hardin praises, again on moral grounds, in "The Sufi Teaching Story and Doris Lessing." The fantasy realms of Lessing's later novels, she argues, are the locus of a saving vision that will teach us to "break out and away from contemporary conditioning" so that "we can awaken from the roles to which we have been so skillfully programmed."[2]

However, when we try to apply these arguments to the reading of a particular text such as *The Memoirs of a Survivor*, we find them of limited value. The debate on essentially ideological grounds both represents and provokes an automatic response: either "I believe in the rational approach to experience and therefore condemn the mystical fantasy in *The Memoirs of a Survivor*" or "I agree with Lessing that the world has extra dimensions open only to intuition, dream and fantasy, and thus I hail the mind-stretching vision in *Memoirs*." The critic's responsibility is to transcend such initial personal responses to the themes in the act of exploring how the novel itself operates, but with the later Lessing the task is not an easy one. While Lessing's first "nonrealistic" novels are much sparer than her earlier "realistic" work, they are more difficult to grasp as formal structures. Even Malcolm Cowley, astute critic that he is, admitted in an early review of *The Memoirs of a Survivor* that "it was all confusing to this reader."[3] Perhaps it would be sensible, then, to approach the problem of reading the later Lessing by admitting and seeking the reasons for our confusions with respect to this provocative text.

Relying heavily on unconventional techniques, *The Memoirs of a Survivor* has a most disorienting effect on the reader. Indeed, the most striking attribute of this novel is that it leaves the reader floating "out of frame," thus generating what sociologist Erving Goffman calls a "'negative experience'—negative in the sense that it takes its character from

what it is not, and what it is not is an organized and organizationally af-
firmed response."[4] In Goffman's terms, "primary framework" is that
perception of the pattern within an experience which allows the experiencer to answer the question "What is it that's going on here?"[5] Most
readers of *Memoirs* will have some difficulty in answering this question.

Presented with a fully realized world in which a social dilemma confronts the main characters, the reader begins to settle into a "realistic"
frame—the same kind that applied for the first four books of the *Children of Violence* series. However, no sooner is the reader settled there
than an alternative frame presents itself—a mystic or mythic dimension
in which the laws of time and space are suspended. Throughout the
novel, the narrator negotiates frequent shifts between these two radically incompatible universes. The problem is that the frame-shifting
mechanism falters as the reader develops resistance to being shifted
between frames; finally, in the last scene the machine breaks down
altogether.

In theory, the narrative strategy of making readers continually shift
primary frameworks is highly workable. William James long ago
pointed out that we all operate, more or less consciously, within a number of alternative "worlds," or meaning frames. While we live most of
the time within our preferred world (for most people, the world of sense
and of physical being), we are susceptible to temporary shifts into other
worlds, such as the world of abstract truth or the world of the supernatural. "The various worlds . . . appear . . . to most men's minds in no
very definitely conceived relation to each other, and our attention,
when it turns to one, is apt to drop the others for the time being out of its
account. Propositions concerning the different worlds are made from
'different points of view'; and in this more or less chaotic state the consciousness of most thinkers remains to the end. Each world *whilst it is
attended to* is real after its own fashion; only the reality lapses with the
attention."[6] Extrapolating from James we may conclude that as long as
an experiencer — the narrator or the reader of a novel, for example — has
a clear sense of "what it is that is going on" and in which "world" it is going on, the contradictions between conditions in the various worlds will
raises no barriers to belief or understanding.

Then, if a novelist wants the reader to accept shifts between worlds
with a sense of comfort, one of the novelist's crucial tasks is to mark
clearly the boundaries between worlds. At the outset of *The Memoirs of
a Survivor*, Lessing is particularly careful in this respect. The outer
world of the Catastrophe is fully established as a consistent world before the narrator's inner world is introduced. In presenting the first shift

into the inner world, moreover, the narrator creates a bridge of several
paragraphs explicitly addressing the issue of the different levels on
which she "knows" her several realities:

> The consciousness of that other life, developing there so close to me, hid-
> den from me, was a slow thing, coming precisely into the category of un-
> derstanding we describe in the word "realise," with its connotation of a
> gradual opening into comprehension. Such an opening, a growing, may be
> an affair of weeks, months, years. And of course one can "know" some-
> thing, and not "know" it. (One can also know something and then forget
> it!) . . .
>     Even at my dimmest and thickest, I did know that what I was becom-
> ing conscious of, what I was on the edge of *realising*, was different in qual-
> ity from what in fact went on around me. . . . (p. 7)[7]

Lessing then provides a spatial bracket for the inner world. It exists just
beyond the narrator's living room wall, "occupying the same space as —
or, rather, overlapping with — the corridor" (p. 8). The narrator never
enters this realm without providing a warning cue: She stands before
the wall and contemplates the flower-like pattern that is her entryway,
or she speaks of being "drawn in through the flowers" or of "moving
through the tall quiet white walls" (pp. 13, 63, 40). In this way she
keeps the two worlds distinct for both herself and the reader — at least
until the final pages of the novel.

At the beginning of *Memoirs*, the world of the senses appears as primary to the unnamed narrator. In concrete terms, she renders an account of her experience in the dying year of a great city somewhere in
England. Her "memoirs" record, in terms of a particular life, how the
institutions of a technological and bureaucratic society collapse from
inner corruption, and how humanity, in the midst of cultural rot, finds
itself faced with two alternatives — death or radical change. Situated in
the near future and in a characterless city easily identified with the
reader's own, this half of the novel fits into a fictional genre identified
by Robert Scholes: "Some of the strongest and most valuable of structural fabulations are direct projections of the present, which provide
concrete realizations of current trends in our political and social situations. . . . This form is marked by its emphasis on social questions.
Taken together these fictions of the near future represent a continuation
of the traditions of sociological and psychological fiction. . . . They are
projections of realism and naturalism into future time."[8] It is, of course,
as a realist and naturalist that Doris Lessing made her reputation as a
novelist, and sociological analysis has been the foundation of each one
of her novels. Continuing in the realist mode in her history of the Catas-

trophe in *The Memoirs of a Survivor*, Lessing merely moves from analysis of society after-the-fact to analysis before-the-fact. Operating under the rational constraints that pertain to realism and naturalism, she extrapolates from today to tomorrow and proceeds thus to demonstrate to her readers the grave implications of their present reality.

Indeed, the half of the novel that deals with the Catastrophe in the city is not only conventionally realistic but also determinedly materialist in its assumptions. There is plenty of evidence of the dialectical materialist vision that so dominated Lessing's early work. In the references to stages of social breakdown, to the culpability of industrial management in producing the Catastrophe, and to the widely held consciousness of something ending, we see illustrations of Engels's principle that the unjust mode of production will eventually bring about its own dissolution. And in the narrator's awed descriptions of the new social forms adopted by the children—the prevalence of squatter's rights, tribal organization, and the bartering of goods and skills—Lessing seems to follow Engels's admonition "to reveal, within the already dissolving economic form of motion, the elements of the future new organization of production and exchange which will put an end to those abuses."[9]

Furthermore, the main theme developed in this half of the novel is the limitation and outmodedness of the consciousness nurtured in the prerevolutionary society—a theme that Engels would have approved. For example, while the young people of the city recognize the totality of the chaos around them and take steps to cope with it, the narrator and her older friends have difficulty acknowledging what is really there. When they encounter children eating corpses, they refuse to admit to themselves what they have seen; as a result the adults fail to take elementary precautions against the coming attacks by the children.

Without directly addressing political issues, Lessing continues in her depiction of the Catastrophe to operate on the Marxist assumptions that guided her vision twenty years ago—the assumptions that consciousness is determined by the material conditions prevailing in society and that escape from the outmoded, limiting consciousness of the moribund society necessitates a great struggle to remain awake to new conditions and new influences. It is the task of the narrator's young friends Emily and Gerald to demonstrate this pioneering spirit to the adults in the everyday realm, where the battle for the physical survival of civilization takes place. Emily and Gerald become leaders in the post-Catastrophe society because they are able to shuck off old assumptions, decadent habits of behavior, and outmoded social relationships and assist a new social system to develop.

While Emily and Gerald take care of the physical survival of the race, the burden of spiritual salvation falls on the narrator. This she seeks in the second world of the novel, which she enters by concentrating on a submerged design on her "real-life" living room wall:

> Once there had been wallpaper. It had been painted over, but under the paint outlines of flowers, leaves, birds were still visible. When in the mornings sun did fall on part of that wall, the half-obliterated pattern showed so clearly that the mind followed suggestions of trees and a garden into a belief that the wash of light was making colour — greens, yellow, a certain shade of clear shell pink. (p. 11)

If the primary world of the novel is a material realm, this second world is a purely mental one, as emphasized by the narrator's admission that the world took form only when "the mind followed suggestions." While the first world, quite according to Marxist assumptions, is bound in history in a chain of cause and effect (which chain inexorably produces the Catastrophe), this world is set outside of time, space, and particular conditions. It is a world of archetypal figures (gardens, birds, leaves, flowers, magic carpets, goddesses) arranged so as to constitute a spiritual vision. This representation of an ideal Reality acts as a standard against which life in the everyday realm can be measured. In order to make this relation clear, the narrator consistently affirms the visionary function of the world behind the wall. In addition, while sojourning there, she comes upon a scene symbolizing the prophetic relation of this world to her daily life. She sees a six-sided room with a dulled tapestry on the floor; this carpet can be brought to life if she can find somewhere a piece of material that matches part of the carpet pattern. Piles of potentially saving pieces are bunched haphazardly on tables set against two sides of the room. The swatches are clearly a figure for the sometimes jumbled visions of this imaginary world, which, properly arranged and understood, can illuminate the patterns of waking life.

In moving from the world of material reality to the world of imagination and vision, Lessing has moved from Marx to Jung. The six-sided room, for example, comes straight out of the Jungian symbol-horde that Lessing knows so well: For Jung the six-pointed or six-sided figure represents "the union of the personal, temporal world of the ego with the non-personal timeless world of the non-ego." Because the figure is at base formed from two intersecting triangles, it signifies for Jung "a process — the creation, or coming into being, of wholeness."[10] Similarly, in her fictional construction, Lessing is trying to create a dynamic tension between the so-called real world of temporal experience and the timeless world of inner experience—which, interpenetrating, should produce wholeness for the narrator, and perhaps for the culture of which she is a representative.

The narrator, in fact, seems to seek in the imaginary world what Anna Wulf of *The Golden Notebook* sought in Jungian therapy (and later in madness)—a reintegration of the psyche through close attention to dream and fantasy. Lessing has made the narrator's journey into the dream world correspond exactly to Jung's description of the stages of significant dreaming. In the fantasy world (as, according to Jung, in significant dreams) the narrator discovers first an etiology of suffering, then "a suggestion as to the course of treatment," and finally "a prognosis or anticipation of the future."[11] The visions of the origins of suffering come in what the narrator calls the "personal" scenes. These are vignettes from Emily's childhood, so ridden with the clichés of depth psychology that they could be packaged for educational television and labeled: Sibling Rivalry; Oral-Anal Regression; Sexual Tension Between Father and Daughter. Lessing uses these scenes, over-obviously, to demonstrate that cultural and political patterns begin in the family and in childhood. If in the new social units of the city "the old patterns kept repeating themselves, re-forming themselves" (p. 133), so in the lives of individual adults, the old patterns established in childhood keep repeating themselves. Tendentiously, Lessing counters this deterministic vision of human neurosis with the second stage of the dream-vision: the recommendation of a cure. Again Lessing paints with a broad brush and produces a propaganda poster, this time in favor of spiritual regeneration. Her narrator enters rooms "behind the wall," cluttered rooms filled with strangely familiar furniture—old, grimy, and stuffy: "The whole place should be cleared out, I kept saying to myself. . . . Bare rooms would be better than this infinitely genteel shabbiness, the gimcrackery" (pp. 24–25). Even if one were not familiar with the psychiatric slang in which "furniture" is used (like "baggage") to refer to old, dispensable psychological patterns, it would be apparent that the narrator is metaphorically enjoining herself to reorder her mental life by completely discarding some patterns and radically modifying others: "Everything I looked at would have to be replaced or mended or cleaned, for nothing was whole or fresh" (p. 24). Finally the narrator is given a portent of transformation and wholeness—a moment of mystic transcendence, in which she and her young friends cross over from the world of daily reality into the inner realms behind the wall and finally "out of this collapsed little world into another order of world altogether" (p. 213). The narrator at last receives a face-to-face vision of the goddess-like figure whom she had occasionally glimpsed moving through para-

disical rooms "all open to the leaves and the sky, floored with the unpoi-
soned grasses and flowers of the old world" (p. 99). In the last moments of
the novel, Eden is at last recovered and the characters euphorically submit themselves to the long-lost protection of the mother-goddess. At that
moment, several principal characters have left what was previously con-
strued as the primary world of the novel and have entered the world "beyond the wall," a world that at this point symbolizes mystical union.

The intention of the final passage is to fuse the two worlds into one
new and different universe. But something is amiss in the construction
of the scene. Until this final scene we have been able to separate the outward life of the narrator from her inner world, depicted in the scenes
beyond the wall. Although there have been symbolic indications that
the two worlds will interpenetrate (the six-sided room, the magic carpet), from the beginning we understand the outer world of the crisis to
be primary and the inner world of the narrator to be an imaginative off-
shoot of it. Then suddenly in the last paragraphs of the book the narrator attempts a shift in the hierarchy of worlds. She says that the characters from the "real" world have approached the border of her inner
world, the patterned wall, and have climbed through it. With that action, the initial frame of the novel is broken, and in this case, the house
of fiction falls with it. The reader, unwilling to accept the new frame as
primary and unable to retreat into the old one (which has just disap-
peared) is forced to step outside both frames and disengage from the act
of participation in the novel as world. This is experienced as a repudiation of the text as a whole.

That is a phenomenon to account for, since the frame-breaking technique is one of the great successes of post-modern fiction (one thinks of
stories by Borges, Cortázar, Barthelme) as well as a key element in count-
less works of pre-modern fantasy. Moreover, Lessing herself used the
frame-breaking technique brilliantly, if more conservatively, in the structuring of *The Golden Notebook*. Why doesn't the device succeed here?

In his pioneering study *Frame Analysis: An Essay on the Organization of Experience*, sociologist Erving Goffman examines the reactions
of individuals to frame-breaking in ordinary life. What he says applies
as well to fiction as to fact. "In general," he asserts, "when an astounding event occurs [and the walk through the wall in *Memoirs* certainly
qualifies as an astounding event], individuals in our society expect that
a 'simple' or 'natural' explanation will soon be discovered, one that will
clear up the mystery and restore them to the range of forces and agents
that they are accustomed to and to the line they ordinarily draw between natural phenomena and guided doings. Certainly individuals
exhibit considerable resistance to changing their framework of frame-

works."[12] In order to make readers overcome that resistance, not only must a writer offer the reader an event that contradicts the primary frame and makes sense in terms of a newly offered frame but she must also make the contradictory event — what Goffman calls the "astounding event" — completely compelling.

William James lists a number of characteristics necessary to make the astounding event believable. Among the most important are sensible vividness, emotional interest, and a "stimulating effect upon the will, i.e., capacity to arouse active impulses."[13] In all these respects, Lessing's "world behind the wall" is wanting. Although the "personal" scenes have particularity and a good deal of emotional charge, these factors are vitiated by the diagrammatic nature of the incidents. As soon as one recognizes the scenes as demonstrations of Jungian or Freudian principles, one distances oneself from them and is reluctant to let them maintain their autonomy as "real" scenes. Similarly, the other two thirds of the world — the narrator's wanderings through rooms and gardens and the apparitions of the female Presence — is a mélange of symbols associated with ancient religions and the experience of mystic ecstasy: the Edenic gardens, the primeval forest, rooms to be ordered or abandoned, columns and ruins suggesting the ruined Greek temples of the gods, and finally the nature goddess herself, with her inexpressible beauty, her glowing light, and her calm smile. Particularly at the end of the novel, where the strain on credulity is greatest, the components of the scene are so schematic, in the fashion of allegory, that they fail to constitute a world for the reader.

It might be reasonable to maintain that the cardboard qualities of the goddess and her world are appropriate to their allegorical functions. But Lessing seems to be working at cross-purposes, trying to produce a world that will be viable both as allegory and as fantasy. If readers are supposed to recognize the goddess as a symbol for the strength, beauty, and reliability of Oneness and at the same time be able to accept her as a guide into a marvelous other-world — the trick is doomed to failure. As Tzvetan Todorov points out in his study of fantasy fiction, "the fantastic is effaced by allegory"; if the narrative illustrates an idea, "the fantastic receives a fatal blow."[14]

With this structural impediment, Lessing compounds the problem by giving the narrator a most unpersuasive prose style. Her laconic musings are often toneless and unaffecting, and by the end her inarticulate gropings and repetitions have become thoroughly tiresome:

> Emily took Gerald by the hand, and with Hugo walked through the screen of the forest into . . . and now it is hard to say exactly what happened. . . .

But the one person I had been looking for all this time was there: there she was.

No. I am not able to say clearly what she was like. She was beautiful: it is a word that will do. I only saw her for a moment, in a time like the fading of a spark on dark air — a glimpse: she turned her face just once to me, and all I can say is . . . nothing at all. (pp. 212–213)

Even if it is conventional in mystical literature to retreat before the beauty of the One, an artist nevertheless has to *earn* such a retreat from the task of rendering the reality taken as subject matter. The suggestiveness of compelling images or of full, intense characterization might have helped to compensate for evasiveness at the crucial moment. Neither is provided.

As a result of Lessing's treatment, then, the second world of the novel does not meet three of James's criteria for commanding belief. It is neither vivid to the senses nor compelling to the emotions; furthermore, it fails to have a "stimulating effect upon the will." While the world of the Catastrophe arouses our sympathies, angers, and frustrations, prompting us to imagine some way of averting disaster, the world behind the wall attempts to pacify us with visions of tranquility in peaceful gardens. Nowhere in the second world of the novel is there an indication of how the active impulses aroused in the first world are to be discharged either by the characters or by the reader. The world that demands an active response is simply abutted to the world that counsels passivity, with an enchanted wall set between. That wall is the wall between Marx and Jung, between a Western, materialist vision of reality and an Eastern, spiritualist vision of it. There is nothing in the text that would convince the reader that a true bridge can exist between these worlds. Naturally, then, many readers are reluctant to accept the trick that magically turns the wall into a drawbridge.

For most readers, moreover, the Catastrophe world — its conditions, its characters, its dilemmas, and the active emotions it raises — is the primary framework in terms of which the plot and themes require resolution. But there is no resolution for the tensions developed in the "real world." In the last scenes of the novel, that framework is suddenly and totally negated. "This collapsed little world" is no more. At this point the reader is in the predicament that Borges calls "vertigo" and that Goffman describes as "negative experience": "Expecting to take up a position in a well-framed realm, [the reader] finds that no particular frame is immediately applicable, or the frame that he thought was applicable no longer seems to be, or [as in the case in *Memoirs*] he cannot bind himself within the frame that does apparently apply. He loses command over the formulation of viable response. He flounders."[15]

In any case of literary frame-breaking, the crucial question is whether the reader stays with the experience of disorientation and finds profit in it or rejects it as unproductive. The reader who holds on — whether to experience the disorientation as a pleasure in itself or to inquire further into the nature and significance of the dilemma — thereby expresses confidence that the fiction has been competently managed by the writer and, thus, that the moment of frame-breaking is part of the intended structure of the story. Borges is a writer who inspires such confidence in his readers, manipulating the contradictory elements of his baffling fictions with such finesse that readers are left not only reeling but delighted to have been sent reeling. More importantly, perhaps, his readers are also left prepared to contemplate their own futile attempts to build a consistent frame for the story and thus they are able to realize the ironic relation of reality and human perception.

But with Lessing's novel, irony is out of the question. As Nancy Hardin so well demonstrates in her account of the Sufi themes in *The Memoirs of a Survivor*, this novel, like the Sufi teaching story, attempts to "'teach' a shift in perspective from a more logical linear mode of thought process, which we of the Western world have been taught to hold in the highest esteem, to a more intuitive perception."[16] In *Memoirs* the rational perspective is embodied in the world of the Catastrophe (thereby suggesting where Lessing believes rational thinking will lead us) and the intuitive perception is embodied in the world behind the wall. When Lessing's readers refuse to walk into that world, therefore, they are refusing to adopt the vision of reality toward which Lessing has so obviously intended to lead them.[17] The breaking of frame here consists of a breakdown in the apparatus by which the novel was intended to convey its vision; it is not, as with Borges, an event designed to break, in turn, the reader's misconceptions about the nature of frames.

At the conclusion of *The Rhetoric of Fiction*, Wayne Booth sets a rigorous standard for judging the works of our contemporaries: "The author makes his readers. If he makes them badly — that is, if he simply waits, in all purity, for the occasional reader whose perceptions and norms happen to match his own, then his conception must be lofty indeed if we are to forgive him for his bad craftsmanship. But if he makes them well — that is, makes them see what they have never seen before, moves them into a new order of perception and experience altogether — he finds his reward in the peers he has created."[18] It may seem harsh to bring this standard to bear on *The Memoirs of a Survivor*, since so clearly it fails the test. But the harshness is certainly softened by the fact that in terms of her total oeuvre Lessing, perhaps more than any other living writer, has succeeded in moving her readers from one order of perception to another. Certainly in *The Golden Notebook* and *The Four-Gated City*, Lessing created successful strategies for suggesting an order of experience beyond the merely rational. There she found a way to demonstrate the Sufi wisdom of Omar Khayyam:

> Do you know what a man of earth may be, Khayyam?
> A lantern of imaginings, and inside a lamp.[19]

She grounded the novels firmly in the primary framework of material existence, from which "lamp" she could then cast the aura of a timeless and intangible reality.

In *Memoirs* she tries to use another Sufi metaphor — that of the two worlds — to embody the wisdom of the mystic in ecstasy, who says at the end of his spiritual journey: "I have put duality away, I have seen that the two worlds are one."[20] However, those readers who can say that have already undergone a complete change of frame. They are ready to read *Memoirs* with total sympathy; they are the readers of whom Booth speaks — the "occasional reader[s] whose perceptions and norms happen to match [the author's] own." In this unregenerate time, we can assume that the majority of the readers of *Memoirs* remain in need of being transformed — by Lessing's craftsmanship — into the peers she seeks.

No longer content to be "the great realist writer of our time," Lessing desires as well the mantle of spiritual seer. In the one role, she uses the familiar techniques of the realistic novel — copious material detail, discursive comment, intensive characterization and carefully concretized settings; in the other she experiments with the techniques of fable, allegory, and myth. In *The Memoirs of a Survivor* Lessing demonstrates the will but not the means to unify her vision. She herself may feel the continuity between one vision and the other; unfortunately, her narrative techniques do not yet effect for the reader the desired transformation of frame.

# Chapter Eight

# *Canopus in Argos*
## THE TRIUMPH OF THE PLURAL?

Lessing has always produced her most exciting work when struggling to integrate seemingly incompatible perceptions, ideologies, and styles. The works in which she most comfortably rests in a single attitude and genre (for example, the socialist realism of *Retreat to Innocence* or "Hunger") are literary pygmies by comparison with the giant works (*The Four-Gated City*, for example, or *The Golden Notebook*), in which competing attitudes, warring styles, wage a fierce battle, first to last.[1] The *Canopus in Argos* series promises to be another of those giants — a work at odds with itself philosophically, stylistically, generically.

In *Shikasta* (1979), the first volume of the series, one can clearly trace what Roland Barthes calls the "braid of codes," the stereophony, the "triumphant plural" of the rich text.[2] On the one hand, Lessing uses many of the tropes of science fiction (flights to the stars, "the rivalries and interactions of great galactic Empires,"[3] extraterrestrial visitors to and influences on earth, the report of the alien to superiors in a higher galaxy) and generates her narrative according to the basic rules of the genre: First, one extrapolates from present earthly conditions to a scientifically plausible future, or para-reality, and, second, one estranges one's readers from their former view of earth's place in the universe so that they may be tutored to evaluate history from an alien perspective. On the other hand, in the same novel Lessing violates utterly some of the essential elements of the science fiction code. She downplays the scientific and technological aspects of her story, while emphasizing magi-

143

cal and supernatural elements; she overlays the more fantastic sections of the narrative with allegorical significance; she bases the whole of the fiction on a mystical vision of the cosmos and often stops the narrative in order to sermonize on the necessity to accept and live by mystic knowledge. Each of these narrative maneuvers has been identified in the past as a cardinal sin against the integrity of science fiction. Lessing commits these "sins," moreover, in order better to perform some of the functions of sacred literature, a genre that many writers of science fiction declare to be diametrically opposed to their own. In *Shikasta*, the code of extrapolative logic is confronted by the code of belief—and against all predictions, they coexist without destroying each other. Nonetheless, the reader continually feels a sense of scandal at the incursion of religious imperatives onto essentially agnostic ground, the territory of science fiction. The resulting threat of the reader's disaffection gives a special tension to the narrative, which ultimately is positive, because it involves the reader in a constant evaluation of an initial reaction to the narrative and the premises behind it.

If *Shikasta* triumphs through a pluralism of styles and attitudes, its sequel, *The Marriages Between Zones Three, Four, and Five*[4] (1980), succeeds on an altogether different basis. Where *Shikasta* is all turmoil and variation, *Marriages* is all calm and unity. It is generically a single thing—a legend, as Lessing herself terms it.[5] The contrast in the experience of the reader is striking. *Shikasta*, corresponding closely to Roland Barthes's description of the "writerly text," excites the reader, providing material for the production of imaginative satisfaction, but leaving to the reader the task of "writing" the constituent elements into a whole. "In this ideal text, the networks are many and intersect, without any one of them being able to surpass the rest; . . . the systems of meaning can take over this absolutely plural text, but their number is never closed."[6] As Barthes grants, no actual novel is completely writerly or plural, in his sense of the terms; if one were, it would be totally without narrative structure or logic. Yet he holds up an ideal of openness that corresponds to Lessing's practice in *Shikasta*: There the reader finds much scope in which to perform the synthetic work of interpretation. Barthes's counter-term is the "readerly text," a term of disapprobation applied to works so tightly controlled toward the goal of a definitive meaning or emotional reaction that the reader is left no room for active participation in the process of creating (or, as Barthes terms it, writing) the fictional experience.[7] Again, no text can be completely "readerly" without giving up its status as literature; Barthes seems to be directing his critique especially at works that are closed formally and rhetorically. Lessing's *Marriages* is just that. It has been recognized as thinly veiled allegory by nearly all the reviewers. Surprisingly—against the pattern of Lessing's work to date—this wholly unambiguous work succeeds brilliantly. It has a light and often comic charm that is wholly new to Lessing's work, and the plot moves more quickly, clearly, and engagingly than any before. Lessing here avoids the pitfalls of the "readerly text"—the mindlessness, the condescension, the boredom, of the obvious—by placing her simple fable in the context of a whole series of more complicated texts which provide for it a complex philosophical and imaginative frame. *Marriages* becomes one strand in the "braid of codes" that *Shikasta* establishes and that the *Canopus in Argos* series may be expected to complete.

Lessing opens the series with "Some Remarks" that suggest the plural nature of her project:

> *Shikasta* was started in the belief that it would be a single self-contained book, and that when it was finished I would be done with the subject. But as I wrote I was invaded with ideas for other books, other stories, and the exhilaration that comes from being set free into a larger scope, with more capacious possibilities and themes. It was clear I had made—or found—a new world for myself, a realm where the petty fates of planets, let alone individuals, are only aspects of cosmic evolution expressed in the rivalries and interactions of great galactic Empires: Canopus, Sirius, and their enemy, the Empire Puttiora, with its criminal planet Shammat. I feel as if I have been set free both to be as experimental as I like, and as traditional: the next volume in this series, *The Marriages Between Zones Three, Four, and Five*, has turned out to be a fable, or myth. Also, oddly enough, to be more realistic. (p. ix)

Lessing here identifies the experimental with science fiction, the traditional with myth, fable, and realism (itself an odd combination, as she notes). These several impulses converge in *Shikasta*.

In her pluralism of conception and technique, Lessing feels herself to be in the mainstream of science fiction. However, she claims for science fiction a scope much wider than many of its own practitioners and theoreticians would grant. She praises not only the predictive accuracy of much early science fiction but also the eclecticism of those science fiction writers who "have also explored the sacred literatures of the world in the same bold way they take scientific and social possibilities to their logical conclusions so that we may examine them" (p. x). For her, predictions that science fiction writers make about "scientific and social possibilities" are on a par with the prophecies of sacred literatures concerning man's spiritual destiny—and the two kinds of future-projection may be mixed in a single work. Most writers on science fiction vigorously oppose this view and exclude from the canons of science fiction those works which give prominent place to mystical or spiritual concerns.[8]

For all those critics who have attempted to set limits between science fiction and surrounding genres, a fundamental distinction is that science fiction, as its name implies, grounds itself in *science*. All forms of fantasy posit conditions that the reader recognizes as untrue to present-day reality. Science fiction is that form of fantasy which extrapolates logically from accepted *scientific* facts and theories to hitherto unknown but plausible conditions as the basis for a narrative. The demands of scientific logic control the conditions and give direction to the incidents in science fiction; in other forms of fantasy, narrative premises and their development are controlled by the demands of religious or philosophical belief or by the pressure of irrational fears or desires. Science fiction is at pains to be natural, not supernatural; secular, not sacred; rational, not irrational; empirical, not philosophical, religious, or mystical; turned outward to the tangible realities of the cosmos, not turned inward toward the personal psyche or "upward" toward God or any other spiritual reality. As the novelist Michel Butor points out, science fiction is "a fantasy framed by a realism." It is the realism, the "scientific guarantee" of plausibility, that "constitutes the specificity of SF which we can define [as] a literature which explores the range of the possible, as science permits us to envision it."[9]

Lessing therefore strikes a special kind of reading contract with her audience when, in the preface to the first volume of *Canopus in Argos*, she so prominently identifies herself with science fiction and with a specific subgenre, the tales of the galactic empires. The epic of galactic civilization has its roots in early works of space travel, such as Jules Verne's *From the Earth to the Moon* (1865) or H. G. Wells's *The War of the Worlds* (1897) and *The First Men in the Moon* (1901), but it did not achieve its own integrity until 1929 when Edmond Hamilton's stories began to appear in the American magazine *Weird Tales*. Hamilton imagined an Interstellar Patrol, headquartered "on a planet of the mighty sun *Canopus*."[10] The task of the Canopean patrol was to rescue stars from destruction and to protect the civilizations of the Canopean galaxy from hostile invaders. The parallels with Lessing's *Canopus in Argos* series are extraordinary. The first volume, *Shikasta*, is offered as a compilation of documents relating to the missions of Johor, who calls himself an emissary in the Colonial Service of the Canopean galactic empire. Johor, like the members of Hamilton's Interstellar Patrol, reports to his superiors on the astronomical threats to stars and planets; his main function, however, is to help human beings on the planet Shikasta overcome the pernicious influences of the invading "Empire Puttiora, with its criminal planet Shammat" (p. *ix*). With these parallels of plot and the borrowing of the name Canopus, Lessing situates her narrative in the context of not only Hamilton's stories but also the running saga by many hands which it helped to generate — the story of the rise, decline, fall, and restoration of the Galactic Empire.[11]

## SHIKASTA (1979)

In her preface to *Shikasta*, Lessing speaks of her admiration for Olaf Stapledon's *Last and First Men* (1930), the first major chronicle of the Galactic Empire. *Shikasta* is in many ways an extension of Stapledon's novel. His is a future history, beginning with his own time and extending two thousand years to the destruction of our galaxy. Lessing's is a retrospective history, moving from the founding of the human race to just a few years beyond our own time. Together, Lessing's and Stapledon's works trace the evolution of human consciousness from the first stirrings of practical intelligence to the achievement of a universal overmind and cosmic harmony. To Stapledon's "cosmogony of the future,"[12] Lessing appends her cosmogony of the past and present.

Science fiction in the form of cosmic history developed at the point of convergence of several prerequisite cultural factors: first, public interest in science and the scientific method; second, the secularization of knowledge that followed; third, acceptance of the theory of evolution; and finally, the development of astronomy and public interest in the question of whether life exists beyond Earth. It is thus a modern and secularized cosmogony.

To a large extent, Lessing's *Shikasta* fits comfortably within the genre. The novel chronicles a crisis in the affairs of the Canopean Empire. The reports by the Canopean Johor, diary entries by humans, and letters between the officials of the evil Puttioran Empire all refer to Colonised Planet 5, Shikasta (obviously our Earth). Having the conditions for rapid evolution of species, Shikasta is a key location in the Galactic Empire and, as Johor notes, always an important item on "the cosmic agenda" (p. 4). As in other fiction of the Galactic Empire, the force of evolution is a prime mover of plot and theme. The whole genre is built on the belief that life in the cosmos is in a constant process of change according to the dictates of the "cosmic agenda" — and predominantly this is a progressive movement. A basic supposition is that just as we have developed from primitive tool-using animals into intelligent beings capable of philosophic inquiry and complex technological accomplishment, so we shall further develop into beings capable of establishing contact with forces and with lives situated beyond Earth. Lessing has always held a progressivist faith, even at the darkest moments of her vision of apocalypse. In *The Four-Gated City*, in *The Summer Before the Dark*, and in *The Memoirs of a Survivor*, the sting of the predicted world catastrophe is lessened by the knowledge that a few people have developed the spiritual and psychic powers to survive or help others survive into a better future. In *Shikasta*, Lessing's faith in the beneficent power of evolution is emphasized more definitely than ever before. The mission of Johor is to assist in the evolutionary progress of life on Shikasta:

> The planet was for millions of years one of a category of hundreds that we kept a watch on. It was regarded as having potential because its history has always been one of sudden changes, rapid developments, as rapid degradations, periods of stagnation. Anything could be expected of it. . . . We wanted the northern hemisphere, because it was chiefly here that a subgroup of the former "monkeys" had established themselves and were developing. . . . They showed rapid increases in intelligence. Our experts told us that these creatures would continue a fast evolution and could be expected to become a Grade A species in, probably, fifty thousand years. (Provided of course there were no more accidents of the cosmic type.) (pp. 14, 15)

It is in terms of the science of genetic management (of our race by Canopus) that Lessing explains the extraordinary evolution of human life. The faults of the human race — its stubbornness, selfishness, arrogance, and ultimately disastrous belligerence — she renders in terms of the effects of one of those dreaded "accidents of the cosmic type," a "shift in stellar alignments" (p. 21) that leads to disruptions of the lines of force between Canopus and its colonial charges. In the tradition of science fiction, she re-imagines human history from a cosmic, rather than an earth-centered, perspective. In so doing, Lessing rewrites both the secular Darwinian history of evolution and the sacred history of the Fall.

As is typical in science fiction, a de-mythologizing impulse runs through the text, at the same time as the narrative itself establishes a new mythology. We might call this a process of re-mythologizing, except that the constant reinterpretation of old myths points the reader toward the conclusion that all myths are provisionary models of understanding and that none is to be taken literally. This highly modern attitude toward myth is frequently stressed by the messenger Johor, who continually admits the partial nature of his own perceptions and the inadequacies of his images and fables to the depiction of the reality he is trying to express. Nonetheless, Johor's overturning of our past scientific theories and, more especially, his wrenching of Biblical history and Western myth into Canopean perspective constitute the major sources of interest in that part of the narrative which operates under the science fiction code. For example, the giants and "little people" of Celtic and European legend prove (after "scientific" blood, tissue and bone tests) to be species from planets of faraway galaxies, placed on earth by the Canopeans to tutor the rather slow-thinking natives in arts, sciences, and "Higher Powers" (which seem to be equivalent to what science fiction writers call "psi powers" — e.g., mental telepathy and precognition). The dual image of these beings in our myths — their benevolence in some tales and their malevolence in others — is explained by the story of their degeneration after the break in the lines of communication with Canopus. Like all other creatures of the once-Edenic planet, the giants and little people could not remain good after they were deprived of Canopean energy, the *sine qua non* of right perception and moral judgment.

While the positing of such a universal force for good smacks of the fanciful and the mystic, Lessing does attempt to legitimize the concept in scientific terms. As in *The Four-Gated City* she uses the language of electronic communication to describe the working of this supreme psychic power: One "tunes in" to Canopean "vibrations" or "broadcasts"; each geometrically formed city is a "mathematical entity created and maintained" as a "transmitter" of the "Canopean strength [that] was beamed continually into" the planet (p. 34). At the end of the text, the reader is referred to the "Physics section" of the Canopean Archive to find information on the "properties of, densities of, variations in effects on different species" of the "Canopean Bond," called SOWF on Shikasta. In Johor's descriptions of the patterns of stones set up to conduct the power through the earth's natural lines of force, the reader recognizes the ruins of Stonehenge, Avebury, and Carnac. The explanation that giants constructed these stone configurations and that they were instruments in the literally astronomical enterprise of the Canopean Empire echoes folklore and amateur speculation, while setting them in novel perspective.[13]

*Shikasta* is full of such readjustments of context. We are made to see the Biblical Flood and the inundation of Atlantis as results of a shift in Earth's axis — one of the many misalignments of a confused time in our galaxy. The rescue of Noah and his crew is carried out by a Canopean messenger, mistaken as a god by the ignorant patriarch. Likewise the covenant of the ark, the songs of King David, the wanderings of Moses, the delivery of the Commandments, the fall of the tower of Babel, the destruction of the cities of the plain, the birth of Ishmael and Isaac to the elderly Abraham — even the modern worship of the Infant of Prague — all make "scientific" sense in the story of Canopean interference in human history for the purpose of fostering a stronger line of communication (called "the Lock") between the sun Canopus, source of health, and the morally weak inhabitants of Shikasta. In the course of these revisions of Biblical history, the messenger Johor often indulges in antireligious diatribes worthy of the purest science fiction, which always works to secularize knowledge. Johor declares woefully primitive the humans' tendency to speak of the messengers as Lords, Gods, and Masters. He bitterly decries the organized religions, which "distorted what was left of our envoys' instruction" (p. 111) and which often acted as the agents of the evil planet Shammat, encouraging militarism, self-righteousness, and bigotry.

At the heart of Lessing's reconception of earth's history and destiny is a Golden Age myth, made fit for science fiction by the supposition that all human good depends on a physical force which is not native to earth, but which must be supplied by a beneficent power beyond us. The messenger Johor stumbles in his efforts to describe this substance: It is "a rich and vigorous air, which kept everyone safe and healthy, and above all made them love one another." Again, it is the "substance-of-life" or "SOWF — the substance-of-we-feeling" (p. 73). The poignance of the Shikastan dependence on this foreign substance and the horror of their degeneration when the supply of the substance dwindles are powerfully rendered from the alien perspective of the Canopean Johor.

Lessing's aim is to startle her readers into a fresh recognition of human weakness, as they temporarily adopt Johor's point of view. Some of the most moving passages depend for their effect on our evaluating human emotions and tendencies from cosmic perspective while at the same time we recognize those emotions and tendencies as our own.

The alien perspective enormously facilitates the reader's participation in a simultaneous act of self-distancing and self-understanding. In the opinion of Darko Suvin, the chief academic critic of science fiction, such an estranging device is essential to successful science fiction. The attitude of estrangement creates the opportunity for a fresh and penetrating consideration of subjects that are normally approached with the glazed eye of habitual perception. "SF, then, is a literary genre whose necessary and sufficient conditions are the presence and interaction of *estrangement* and *cognition*, and whose main formal device is an imaginative framework alternative to the author's empirical environment."[14]

The estranging device in this case is built into the narrative structure of the work. *Shikasta* is a compilation of documents from the Canopus in Argos Archives, "selected to offer a very general picture of Shikasta for the use of first-year students of Canopean Colonial Rule" (p. 2). Apparently in order that the selections may be readily comprehensible, the documents all relate to the visits of emissary Johor, although there have been thousands of other emissaries over the centuries. The majority of the documents are his own reports to his superiors, but the authorities also have included reports by emissaries whose work relates to Johor's, relevant selections from the official *History of Shikasta*, letters written by Johor in human incarnation as George Sherban, letters and diary entries by Sherban's friends and relatives, and communications between world leaders whose actions impinge on Sherban's fate. Thus the reader experiences not only Johor's compassionate viewpoint, but also a variety of other extraterrestrial and human perspectives.

Johor himself varies in his degree of empathy with human beings. While he seems deeply and even painfully moved by those people with whom he forms relationships, he gives terse, distanced reports of a large number of individuals who are due to play parts in the Canopean plan for Shikasta's salvation. These reports read like a sociologist's case histories: We have reports titled "Individual Three (Worker's Leader)," "Individual Four (Terrorist Type 3)," etc. These reports differ tonally from Johor's more personal responses, but in their own way they too serve both to estrange the reader from familiar material (one recognizes some of the models for these reports—Patty Hearst, the Baader-Meinhof gang, even Doris Lessing herself) and to encourage a more original and probing consideration of the depicted sociological phenomena than a contemporary familiarity with the data would tend to promote.

Although the reports on key individuals do swiftly and tellingly sketch characters who are wonderfully memorable, they do not offer us character treatment in the usual novelistic form. Of the twenty or more individuals who are sketched in the middle of the book, only one (or possibly two) reappear. The only character who appears continually in the narrative is Johor; however, because he focuses his attention outward on his assignment (the development of Shikastan potential from prehistoric times to a near future), we never have the sense of following a single character's story through the narrative. Certainly very little attention is given to Johor's personal psychology and none at all to his development—he is a static character. *Shikasta* does not really have a central character, though it does have in Johor a presiding presence.

In this respect, again, the novel operates according to the code of science fiction. Concerned as it is with the fate not only of a world but of a cosmos, the literature of the Galactic Empire focuses its attention on the grand sweep of history, not on individual experience. Science fiction

writers are concerned with those conditions of existence which transcend, while determining, the individual case. Their task is a difficult
one—to expand the reader's consciousness so that it can grasp events
from the alien perspective of huge vistas of time and space. (Here we see
surfacing Lessing's consistent theme, the attempt to transcend the limits
placed on consciousness by the thought conventions of a particular historical moment and situation.) This has been the conscious agenda of
Galactic Empire fiction since Olaf Stapledon's *Last and First Men*, one
of Lessing's acknowledged models. In the "Introduction" to Stapledon's
book, an extraterrestrial narrator similar to Johor justifies the cursory
treatment of character that has become conventional in space fiction:

> I must help you to feel not only the vastness of time and space, but also
> the vast duality of the mind's possible modes. . . . I have to present in one
> book the essence not of centuries but of aeons. Clearly we cannot walk at
> leisure through such a tract, in which a million terrestrial years are but as a
> year is to your historians. We must fly. We must travel as you do in your
> aeroplanes, observing only the broad features of the continent. But since
> the flier sees nothing of the minute inhabitants below him, and since it is
> they who make history, we must also punctuate our flight with many de-
> scents, skimming as it were over the house-tops, and even alighting at criti-
> cal points to speak face to face with individuals.[15]

Just so, Johor and the impersonal historical documents give a bird's-eye
view of Shikasta's history—the genetic experiments that led to human
life, the establishment of the Canopean Bond, the leaking of the SOWF
line, the interference of Shammat with even "the little trickle of SOWF
that reached this place" (p. 73), the gradual decline of the human race,
and finally, the history of "The Century of Destruction," our own. The
*History of Shikasta* disposes of this century in eleven succinct pages,
noting our wars, our ideologies, our living conditions, and our disas-
ters, which include chemical poisioning, epidemics, famine, and finally
nuclear war.

By contrast, the journals and letters of the Sherban family (relatives
of Johor, incarnate as George Sherban) provide a more detailed and
emotionally charged account, from the human angle—from the viewpoint of those who, lacking Canopean perspective, are astonished by
both the calamities of the apocalyptic decade and the marvels of their
last-minute deliverance into peace and harmony. In the last pages of the
novel, Kassim, the stepson of George Sherban, writes to Suzannah,
George's wife:

> The first houses are already up, and the central circular place is paved,
> and the basin of the fountain is made. As we build, wonderful patterns ap-

pear as if our hands were being taught in a way we know nothing about.
. . . George left after a few days. I walked with him a little way. I said to
him, What is happening, why are things so different?

So he told me.

George says he is going into Europe with a team. He says that you knew
he would be going, but not that he would be going now, and that I should
tell you that when his task in Europe is finished, his work will be finished. I
did not understand until he had left that it meant he would die then and
we would not see him again. . . .

How did we live then [before the restoration of harmony]? How did we
bear it? We were all stumbling about in a thick dark, a thick ugly hot darkness, full of enemies and dangers, we were blind in a heavy hot weight of
suspicion and doubt and fear. (pp. 363–364)

In these last paragraphs of the novel we hear Roland Barthes's "stereophony," the music of two very different instruments—science fiction
and scripture—intertwining in melody.

Everything in this passage is explicable in terms of the science fiction
motifs developed throughout the novel. For example, Kassim's description of the newly built town echoes Johor's descriptions of the geometric
cities that he visited many thousands of years before, at the time of the
first threat to the SOWF line. The geometric town, with a fountain and
circular plaza at its center, is Lessing's architectural ideal (present also
in the utopian fantasies of *The Four-Gated City, The Memoirs of a Survivor,* and *Briefing for a Descent into Hell*). Johor's early reports prepared us to understand that this architectural imperative is physically
(that is, empirically, scientifically) determined by lines of Canopean
force in the earth, a grid structure no more mysterious than a magnetic
field. Scientists of our century have learned that birds are "taught in a
way we know nothing about" (that is, by instinct) to follow the earth's
lines of magnetic force in their seasonal migrations; the physical properties that enable the birds to "tune in on" the "vibrations" of the magnetic field are as yet not understood by scientists, yet we do not doubt
that the phenomenon of the birds' knowledge of the correct path of
their migration is ultimately explicable in purely empirical terms. We
may speak of it as a marvel—just as Kassim speaks of the new capacities
of his friends as "wonderful"—but we do not feel ourselves to be denying the laws of physical science when we do so. Likewise, there is nothing in this passage that is not comprehensible under the rubric of science
fiction, as we have so far defined it. In positing the Canopean force and
its control of the human building of cities, Lessing has extrapolated
from known scientific fact to an "estranged" but plausible human
future.

Yet Kassim's awe-struck tone creates an atmosphere more appropri-

ate to religious legend than to science fiction, and the passage is thick
with allusions to messianic literature. Kassim walks a little way with
George, in the same cadences as many a Christian hymn has asked the
faithful to walk a little way with Jesus, in imitation of the Apostles.[16]
This allusion is only the culmination of a whole string of passages that
equate George Sherban (Johor) with the redeemer-god of the New Testament, Gnostic legend, and ancient myth. George is the keeper of the
esoteric knowledge toward which parables may hint but which must be
kept protected from the prying eyes of the populace. Here we have the
first statement in the novel suggesting that Johor ever shared his Canopean vision of earthly history with any human being, and it is passed
over quickly, as if to keep "the veil" over the ultimate Truth. As if this
were a Gnostic text, we next read that the savior must die when his work
— the spreading of the divine Knowledge — is finished. Finally, Kassim's
words suggest that humankind has been released from limitations of
spiritual vision, as the New Testament has predicted: Before our deliverance we saw as through a glass, darkly — "all stumbling about in a
thick dark" — but now we begin to see the Canopean truth face to face;
then we, like David and Sais, knew that truth only in part, but now we
begin to know that truth even as also Johor and Canopus knew us (see I
Cor. 13:12). "And this will go on for us," Kassim predicts, "as if we were
being slowly lifted and filled and washed by a soft singing wind that
clears our sad muddled minds and holds us safe and heals us and feeds
us with lessons we never imagined" (p. 364). Like divine grace, the
Canopean substance-of-life washes away the human tendency toward
error and provides the strength for conduct and belief in harmony with
Canopean law. The Fall is redeemed.

The compatibility of the scientific and the spiritual perspectives in
this passage may offend the arbiters of the science fiction genre, but it is
there to be accounted for. Moreover, this intertwining — or as Barthes
calls it, this "braiding" — of codes is a constant feature of the text. The
set piece of this braiding is the treatment of Johor's mission from Canopus to Earth. On the one hand, Johor is little different in conception
from the many benevolent messengers in science fiction who are sent
from a superior to a lesser civilization in order to teach the skills of survival and the rules of galactic cooperation: LeGuin's Genly Ai (*The Left
Hand of Darkness*), Arthur C. Clarke's Karellan (*Childhood's End*), or
even Stapledon's Last Man (*Last and First Men*). On the other hand,
rarely, if ever, has an extraterrestrial messenger been depicted with such
consistently messianic overtones. Just as the Messiah is the servant of
God, Johor is the servant of Canopus; Canopus, as a star, is one of the
gods, the creators and sustainers of life (p. 40). Johor's mission to earth

also parallels Christ's, both in intention and in practice. He comes to "save" (p. 107) or to "redeem" (pp. 107, 113, 168) human beings from the consequences of their fall into "disobedience to the Master Plan" (p. 47). It will be his work to re-establish the flow of the substance-of-we-feeling (SOWF), a gift from Canopus that is constantly equated with the grace of Christian theology. In order to perform the act of redemption, Johor must, like Christ, become incarnate; although his essence is incorporeal, he must take on bodily form, being born to human parents selected, like Joseph and Mary, for their saintly attributes.

Much of the interest in the messianic parallel comes from contrasting the story of Johor's redemptive mission with the version of Christian scripture and tradition. The first departure is that Johor's incarnation is a multiple event. He records three visits before his embodiment as George Sherban — one about 35,000 years ago when the fall from grace had just begun and Earth was beginning to decline from its Edenic state, one at the time of Abraham, and one in the recent past (perhaps in the 1970s) when he scouted around for proper parents for his most important incarnation, as George Sherban. Moreover, these manifestations on Earth are not Johor's only missions; in between visits to Earth, he undertakes missions on other planets. Unlike the coming of the Messiah in Judeo-Christian tradition, Johor's incarnation is not the unique and all-important event in salvation-history. Indeed, Earth is by no means the center of the Canopean "Master Plan"; here, Lessing's braiding of the messianic story with the cosmic viewpoint of science fiction has salutary effects on the implied theology. Humanity may no longer see itself as the only child of an alternately doting and punitive Father; now human beings must democratically share their position with myriad brothers and sisters, the planets of all the galaxies: "We are *all* creatures of the stars and their forces, they make us, we make them, we are part of a dance from which we by no means and not ever may consider ourselves separate" (p. 40). This attitude involves a radical departure from Judeo-Christian cosmology, and in turn a major alteration in the role of the messiah.

As one among many Canopean emissaries, Johor must be much more independent and enterprising than his Biblical counterpart. Unlike Christ, Johor must negotiate his own entryway into the flesh, choosing his parents and arranging his passageway through the dangerous Zone Six, the waystation of souls seeking reincarnation. The constant counterpointing with the Biblical version provides a wry sort of humor, as we watch Johor struggling, scheming, and sweating his way to a messianic incarnation. No doubt, such touches of light irony are largely responsible for Lessing's success in combining the interests of science fiction and sacred literature in her representation of Johor's mission to Shikasta.

With the depiction of Zone Six, however, Lessing sorely tests the reader's confidence in her delicate generic balance. For Zone Six is a truly fantastic invention—expressive of spiritual realities, but wholly unconnected to the empirical code of the space fiction. With the exception of Zone Six, every amazement in the Shikastan/Canopean world is made to "make sense" in terms of extrapolation from present-day scientific fact; the existence of giants and dwarves, the wonders of ancient stone monuments, the workings of SOWF, the fall from its grace, the existence of satanic and divine forces in the universe—all are given physical explanation. Zone Six stands alone, nearly completely sealed off from the rest of the fiction, as the sanctuary of the purely fantastic imagination.

The structure of six Zones, each lying concentric to earth's surface in an ordered hierarchy of levels, is established in the first pages of *Shikasta* and then largely forgotten—except for the important Zone Six. However, the next novel explores at length the allegorical and fantastic implications of these Zones. Shikasta itself, the earthly level of existence at the center of the Zones, is depicted as both geographically and spiritually the lowest level of existence. As in dualistic Christian heresies and Sufi mystical tradition, the earth itself is a dangerous snare, a "drag and pull" (p. 6) on the soul aspiring to Canopean harmony. As in some Sufi lore, "the world" is a "place to be visited only in case of need," like a latrine.[17] For human beings, the common necessity is the obligation to earn deliverance into a higher order of being—or Zone—by living one good life in "the world" of Shikasta. If one fails, one is returned to Zone Six, the first level of spiritual existence.

In *The Marriages Between Zones Three, Four, and Five,* Zone Six takes its place in a spiritual allegory, based on the mystical tradition of "stages" or "stations"[18] of enlightenment. In Sufism, the mystic tradition that Lessing knows best, various Sufi masters count the number of stages differently, but all lists start with the stage of repentance, called *tawbat.* The scholar Reynold Nicholson tells us that "this is the Moslem term for 'conversion' and marks the beginning of a new life."[19] The genuineness of one's entry into this first stage is tested by whether one does in the new life abandon one's sins. Likewise, the soul who enters Zone Six expresses the repentance proper to this "station" by recognizing the failures in a past life in Shikasta and repentantly getting in line for a new life in which to prove a sincere resolve to sin no more.

When, in *Marriages,* the six ascending orders of being are developed in the context of a fabulous fantasy, complete with kingdoms, queens, magic wishes, and talking animals, the allegory (elaborated much more fully than in *Shikasta*) succeeds brilliantly, largely because it never arouses and thus never violates the expectations proper to realism. Here, in *Shikasta*, realism and fantasy meet in a major confrontation. In the depiction of Zone Six, there is no attempt to use extrapolative logic to justify affronts to the reader's sense of the plausible. Most outrageously, there is no discussion of how six layers of being, each with an earthly geography, can be said to be "in concentric shells around the planet" (p. 5). Obviously, if she were writing this section in the science fiction mode, Lessing would have to answer such elementary questions as how people on Shikasta see the stars, if there are six physical shells of matter between the earth and the universe beyond. Lessing does not address the issue. If the six zones were to be viewed as wholly immaterial and yet somehow existent, a science fiction writer would feel obligated to suggest a scientific or pseudoscientific theory under which such an anomalous state could obtain. Lessing supplies such a theory, for example, in regard to SOWF, and again in regard to Shammat's interference with SOWF (see the description of the invention Effluon 3 and its SOWF-deflecting properties, p. 66). Yet in her trips into Zone Six, Lessing seems to feel no such obligation. For these sections, she wholly abandons the rules of extrapolation and adopts the much looser rules of analogy. As in allegory, conditions and episodes are invented in *parallel* to the author's perceived reality, without the need for the parallel world to be tied to the "real world" by any logic but analogic.

It requires the most skillful sleight of hand for Lessing to convince her reader to accept the coexistence — indeed, the interrelationship — of two fictional worlds that operate on such different principles. First, she makes sure that the short and infrequent visits to Zone Six, the sections that are most out of alignment with the science fiction mode, are the most brilliantly conceived and stylishly written passages in the book. The Zone Six sections are thick with metaphor and alive with startling descriptions of the wondrous phenomena of the special locale. In these descriptions, too, Lessing's sentence style is conspicuously more direct and her vocabulary more emphatic than in the rest of the novel. For example, the brief, intense description of Johor's descent into throbbing, fermenting flesh contrasts sharply with the prolixity of the sections dealing with Shikasta — Johor's prosaic reports on social conditions, the historians' flat summaries of aeons, or Rachel Sherban's adolescently chatty diary. The Zone Six sections are, simply, both beautiful and gripping. As such they gain a special status with the reader that no amount of conceptual or generic incongruity can undo.

Second, Lessing provides compelling characters who bridge the distance between Zone Six and Shikasta. At about the middle of the book, not only Johor himself, but also two lost souls named Rilla and Ben, pass from Zone Six into human flesh — as George, Rachel, and Ben Sherban, respectively. By this point in the narrative, we are starved for characters to follow consistently. Ben and Rilla in their new incarnations feed this hunger. We are ready to grasp at Rachel's diaries and Ben's letters for a sense of the personal texture of Shikastan life. As we become attached to their stories, which fill the second half of the book, we become seduced into accepting the linkage of Zone Six and Shikasta — for at every turn of Ben's and Rachel's narratives we are made to recall the terms under which they have entered Shikasta and confront the question of whether either is passing the test of true repentance that passage from Zone Six into Shikasta represents.

The third way in which Lessing allows for a plural text — a text that accommodates separate and very different systems of meaning — is by using typography, headings, and spacing to signal shifts from one kind of narrative to another. For example, the sections of the book that most boldly represent the extraterrestrial perspective of the space fiction — the official Canopean histories — are set in a boldface version of Electra type. The sections written by Johor, an ordinary emissary of Canopus, are set in normal Electra type. His sections are further divided by headings and line spaces that demarcate his reports on Shikasta from his reports on the fantastical Zone Six. The letters written by Johor, Rilla, and Ben in their Shikastan incarnations are distinguished by an italic version of the Electra that had described them in Zone Six. Finally, the very few documents written by officials of the power that rivals Canopus and all its emissaries are set in a completely distinct, Spartan type; this emphasizes the likeness in difference of all Canopean perspectives (normal, boldface, and italic Electra) as against the radically opposed perspective of Shammat (Spartan).

Most important, the fact that the novel is a compilation of documents from different sources gives the reader an early signal that the reading of this text will involve frequent shifts of perspective. The most significant of these shifts is perhaps the most subtly handled. In the secular mode of science fiction, the bulk of the text makes a brief for cooperation among the races, laying down of arms, respect for the environment, for animals, for human life — all under the rubric of harmony with the rule of the great star Canopus. Threaded through this basically secular fabulation is a spiritual message which finds its greatest concentration in the allegory of the six Zones: the belief that a divine Master Plan, not individual will, directs the course of this planet and its inhabitants and that submission to that will is the swiftest — indeed, the only —

road to deliverance from worldly suffering. In the Edenic period before the diminution of contact between Canopus and Shikasta, "everybody accepted that their very existence depended on voluntary submission to the great Whole, and that this submission, this obedience, was not serfdom or slavery . . . but the source of their health and their future and their progress" (p. 26). Individual human will becomes irrelevant under these conditions: "There could not be disharmony, because they *were* harmony" (p. 288). In Johor's spiritual vision of the cosmos, all earthly creatures, all nations, all planets in the universe are the "ever-evolving Sons and Daughters of the Purpose" (p. 35). But, Johor admits, even the Gods err in their service to the Purpose, and when they do — when stars explode or wander in their courses — then sickness of spirit occurs, the Degenerative Disease becomes epidemic, and creatures lose the ability to act in accordance with the Master Plan. That is what happened to the creatures of Shikasta, when "the misalignment" sapped their supply of SOWF, the substance designed to keep the inhabitants aware of "how they stood in relations to stars, planets, the dance of the heavens, the forces of the earth, the moon, our sun" (p. 288). Johor bemoans the fate of the Shikastans, which he depicts both as an accident of the stars (the secular version) and as an error of the Gods (the sacred version) — but in neither case as a fault of the doomed themselves:

> Creatures infinitely damaged, reduced and dwindled from their origins, degenerate, almost lost — animals far removed from what was first envisaged for them by their designers, they are being driven back and away from everything they had and held and now can take a stand nowhere but in the most outrageous extremities of — patience. . . . Shikastans are, in their awful and ignoble end, . . . reaching out with their minds to heights of courage and . . . I am putting the word *faith* here. After thought. With caution. With an exact and hopeful respect. (p. 203)

In this passage, we see how even the spiritual vision of the novel is itself a mediation between two seemingly contradictory views — the Christian myth and a more fatalistic cosmic vision. On the one hand, the story of Shikasta echoes continually the essentials of Christian belief — the existence of one omnipotent, benevolent Creator, the fall of his creatures from grace, their redemption from sin by a messiah, and finally their individual salvation by means of an act of faith in that redemption. Yet, in fact, Johor's story subtracts from the Christian system two of its essential elements. First, the God of Shikasta is neither unique nor omnipotent. According to Johor there are many Gods — the stars — and they are neither faultless nor eternal. The divine liability to error is, in fact, the key to the plot, since the fall of Shikasta directly results from an error in Canopean alignment with other celestial bodies. With that error, the second essential element of Christian theology goes by the board; there is no free will for creatures who are designed to depend on grace (SOWF) for their moral health but who, through no fault of their own — indeed through the fault of their God — are denied it.

Still, Johor in awestruck tones praises the Shikastans' courage and faith, as if the thoroughly fated human beings could somehow be credited with strength of personal will in "reaching out with their minds to heights" of courage and faith. Johor makes this illogical judgment "with caution," for it contradicts everything he has said about the absolute dependence of human moral judgment on SOWF. This passage is not an anomaly. It is typical of the logically inconsistent but imaginatively potent plurality of the text as a whole. The voice that denies free will is countered by a voice that affirms it. Likewise, the terse voice that respects the empirical bias of science fiction at times is overtaken by the impassioned voice that speaks in wildly fantastic or reverently spiritual tones. No matter that the contrary voices often issue from the same person, Johor — they are voices of different moods, different moments, different sections of the book. As Roland Barthes says of the ideal plural text, in *Shikasta* we find that "everything signifies ceaselessly and several times, but without being delegated to a great final ensemble, to an ultimate structure. . . . This text is a galaxy of signifiers, not a structure of signifieds."[20]

The text traces a movement without end, an action without climax. There *is* tension in the narrative, most notably between the science fiction and spiritual strands of the work. In fact, the reader is often curious, puzzled, even at times frustrated, because of the refusal of the terms of the text to resolve into unity. However, we come to realize that the terms that create the tension are in a continual process of being pulled and twisted into the form of an endless braid. The viewer of this braid focuses on the twistings of the separate strands against each other and wonders at the long line of strength that they build together, without ever losing their separate identities in the "gestalt" of a fully transcendent form.

Arranged as an archive, a respository of diverse perspectives, *Shikasta* is both open to multiple interpretations and readable in various modes. As the book drifts to an end, with an instruction to consult other volumes of the archive, the reader is implicitly asked not to conclude, not to settle on a single perspective, but to sustain tentatively and simultaneously the appreciation of both the science fiction saga still in progress and the spiritual fable that has only begun to be developed. The former will be continued in *The Sirian Experiments*,[21] while the latter is the business of volumes that precede and follow it. At the same time, the reader is asked to have the patience of the Shikastans in awaiting a time when apparent contradictions of theme, such as the conflict between free will and determinism in Johor's cosmic vision, will become comprehensible to our cleared and expanded imaginations. For the mid-time, the closing speech of Kassim applies not only to his own experiences but also to the reader's experience of the first volume of *Canopus in Argos*:

> And this will go on for us, as if we were being slowly lifted and filled and washed by a soft singing wind that clears our sad muddled minds and holds us safe and heals us and feeds us with lessons we never imagined.
> And here we all are together, here we are. . . . (p. 364)

## THE MARRIAGES BETWEEN ZONES THREE, FOUR, AND FIVE (1980)

Whereas *Shikasta* is a plural text, even at the end promising illumination in the form of *multiple* lessons rather than a single truth, its sequel *The Marriages Between Zones Three, Four, and Five* moves continually to bring multiplicity into unity, difference into affinity, separateness into consolidation. The title itself, echoing Blake's *The Marriage of Heaven and Hell*, promises to argue along with Blake that "Opposition is true friendship" and that the marriage of "Contraries" is not only possible but necessary to human progress.[22] In fact, Lessing extends Blake's vision of ultimate integration to the dialectical level: She imagines not only the transformation of two enemies into a companionable couple, but also a continual stepping outward of the transformed mate to meet and embrace a new opposite. The movement is always toward unity, but the unity of a steadily advancing evolutionary line, not of a single and fixed entity. There is therefore no permanent marriage in this novel; instead there is a process of loving and learning—in this case, learning to ally oneself with the communal progress toward Gnosis.

The form of the novel mirrors this single-minded purpose. Upon publishing *Marriages*, Lessing granted an interview in which she distinguished between *Shikasta*, which she sees as "a series of queries" to which she did not yet have answers, and *Marriages* which she considers "a sort of legend."[23] The archive format perfectly suited Lessing's purpose in *Shikasta;* in the various documents of the archive, she could offer many perspectives on the issues she introduced, without being obligated to arrive at a definite solution to any of them. In contrast, Lessing's "legend," *Marriages,* is as obviously rooted in belief as the legend of the Holy Grail, and its form, too, is the form of belief. It is an allegory of spiritual progress, loudly signalling its affinities with the grail legend and the Arthurian cycle by its medieval romance trappings — king and queens, courts and palaces, magic shields, a noble steed, warriors in armor, women in long flowing dresses, and, most importantly, a call to adventure issued by supernatural beings who use the adventure to instruct the protagonists in the ways of the spirit.

Through the form of an allegorical romance, Lessing at last gives full definition to the theme of "stages of consciousness" which she has been developing since her earliest works. In the first half of her career, at least until 1962, Lessing's novels focused on the ways in which an individual's perception of experience is necessarily limited by the intellectual, social, and material conditions of a particular time and place. The progress through stages of consciousness which she envisioned for a Martha Quest, for example, was tied inexorably to the history of her culture and its evolution (in broadly Marxist terms) toward an apocalyptic political and social transformation. Increasingly, since *The Golden Notebook,* Lessing has shifted the burden of the evolution of consciousness to the individual — to be sure, without ever giving up the notion that individual progress is tied to social progress. The difference is that in the early books the individual can progress only so far as cultural factors permit (the limits of vision are determined by material conditions), whereas in the later books, the culture can evolve materially and socially only in response to the evolution that occurs in the consciousness of its people (the limits of material progress are determined by the limits of vision).

The zones of *Marriages* are obviously figures for stages of consciousness. Arranged from depths to heights, from earth to air, the zones mark the stages of cultural, personal, and spiritual development. The ghostly Zone Six, closest to the hellish planet where torture and murder prevail, is hardly mentioned, having been pictured for us in *Shikasta* as a stage of repentance from earthly error. Zone Five, dominated by the wild queen Vahshi, knows "no limits to deception, treachery, guile, dishonour" (p. 215), except within the tribal unit, where honor and generosity are fiercely guarded standards. Zone Five is the essence of barbarism, with all its severities and its vigors. As such it represents the attainment of a rudimentary, childlike morality, moving beyond self-interest only to the stage of loyalty to kin. Its neighbor, Zone Four, ruled by the soldier-king Ben Ata, is orderly, disciplined, and socially coherent; yet its virtues have an underside — the repression and austerity of a heavily militarized society. Zone Four achieves the virtues of adolescence — self-control, cooperativeness, and a limited altruism — while suffering as well the adolescent's crudeness, rigidity, and arrogance. Zone Four is woefully underdeveloped when compared to Zone Three, a model of maturity; here, the lovely queen Al·Ith presides over a land of peace, plenty, and accomplishment, a utopia where personal freedom is complete because right intuition of the communal good informs all actions. Yet even this stage of mature fulfillment is susceptible to error — to the complacency and stagnation of self-satisfaction. The inhabitants of Zone Three are so contented with their pleasures that they fail to notice the existence of higher realms, the mountains of Zone Two. In those unearthly mountains, the lone traveler Al·Ith discovers that the brilliant blue light, flame-colored clouds, and crystalline ground have blinded her vision, yet she senses that this "high delicate place" (p. 196) is full of beings she had previously known only in folk tales and songs. What lies within and beyond Zone Two is ineffable. No one in our story has heard even a hint of what Zone One might contain.

Having developed this topography of consciousness, Lessing proceeds to use it to explore a theme that has dominated her career — the evolution of consciousness, now figured as proceeding along a mystical pathway. The image of the Path enters Lessing's work late in her career, after the influence of Sufism has been brought to bear on her writing. Although Martha Quest and Anna Wulf go through stages of development leading toward moments of illumination, these stages tend to be loosely demarcated and to be keyed to historical or personal developments rather than to a universal plan of spiritual progress. It is in *Briefing for a Descent into Hell* that Lessing first represents a schema of spiritual progress in the metaphor of a journey from the depths (in this case, a turbulent and confused sea) to the heights (the gods' crystalline station in the heavens). In *The Memoirs of a Survivor,* the emphasis is on the barrier between the worldly state and the spiritual stages; the wall in the narrator's apartment represents the initial obstacle to the spiritual journey, while various rooms, gardens, and landscapes situated beyond the wall represent the several stages of spiritual growth. *The Marriages Between Zones Three, Four, and Five* is the first work in which Lessing develops the metaphor of the mystical path — seemingly, too, without any desire to disguise the sources of her thinking in the literature and lore of Sufi, Gnostic, and Christian mysticism. In all three of these traditions, the way to enlightenment is figured as a path, divided into anywhere from three to ten stages or stations. Again in all three forms of mysticism, the progress is represented as an ascent from depths to heights, from darkness to blinding light, from flesh to spirit. In all, too,

the progress upward toward ultimate union with the principle of Light
is often preceded by a necessary descent into the dangers of flesh and the
despair of darkness. Finally, in all, love—often, in fact, erotic ecstasy—
educates the lower faculties, turning them toward spiritual ends.[24] The
plot of *Marriages* exploits each one of these elements of the mystic
allegory.

In this novel, Al•Ith, the queen of Zone Three, is the unwilling pilgrim from one spiritual state to another. She illustrates the spiritual rule
formulated by William Blake in *Jerusalem:* "As the Pilgrim passes while
the Country permanent remains, / So men pass on, but States remain
permanent for ever." The burden of her story is that the countries of the
mind are eternal and stable in themselves but that none should be a permanent dwelling place, whether for individual or nation. Thus the
novel opens with the puzzlement of Al•Ith over two phenomena that
she cannot relate to one another—the diminishing fertility of her land
and a call from the Providers that she descend to Zone Four and marry
its crude king. Her chroniclers protest, "But the Zones could not min-
gle, were inimical by nature" (p. 4). Each zone has, in its own way,
closed off the path of the pilgrim. Zone Three in its passive fashion has
simply forgotten the other zones and attended happily to business in the
high plain of the country, so that no one bothers to look up to the mountain peaks of Zone Two or down to the valleys of Zone Four. Zone Four
in its aggressive way has strictly forbidden even looking toward Zone
Three and has fought to keep intruders from crossing its borders with
Zone Five.

Somewhat heavy-handedly, Lessing focuses the reader's attention on
the question of why the Providers (obviously, the forces of Providence,
whether sacred or secular) have acted to force intercourse between the
zones. At least a dozen times Al•Ith dramatically questions herself and
the heavens as to what the marriage means, what has gone wrong in the
realms, and what her people "had not only forgotten but now forbade"
(p. 140). The allegory is so transparent that the questions often seem
melodramatic if not simpleminded, but Lessing makes up for this
breach of literary tact by the charm, even the poignancy, of Al•Ith's reluctant mating, flowering passion, tender motherhood, and brutal
parting from her husband and child. It is through the delicate handling
of the love-fable that Lessing touches the reader's emotions and metaphorically conveys the stresses, the confusions, the joys, and the terrible
deprivations of the mystical experience.

"Love is, for the Sufis, the only legitimate way to educate the base
faculties," says Annemarie Schimmel in her discussion of the Path of the
Sufi mystic.[25] The relationship of Al•Ith and Ben Ata is presented as a

process of mutual education of the senses and the spirit. Each discommodes the other, yet duty to their ailing realms and obedience to the Providers forces them to learn each other's ways and empathize with each other's feelings. The painful yet often amusing process of their coming to a sexual understanding represents nicely the difficulties of any individual who seeks to move from one level of spiritual consciousness to another: Inexperience, suspicion of difference, incomprehension, pride, stubbornness — all threaten to thwart the approach to a new state. Finally, as the two succumb to mutual need and submit to each other's instructions, Lessing offers her readers one of her rare depictions of positive sexuality, a lyrical description of the process by which the lovers become "thoroughly wedded" and mutually satisfied. Lessing is so precise in these and later descriptions of the lovers' sexual rhythm that she attains a wonderful complexity of narrative levels — advancing at once the spiritual allegory, the plot of the fable, and a critique of the sexual cycle in married love. To give only one example, Lessing with great delicacy depicts the aftermath of fulfilled passion: "They lay in each other's arms as if in the shallows of a sea they had drowned in. But now began the slow and tactful withdrawals of the flesh, thigh from thigh, knee from knee" (p. 69). This first benign moment of necessary withdrawal is more than a physical event; it is, indeed, a portent of the hardest lessons of love and of spiritual progress. For after the stages that the Sufis describe as the approach to divine Love — after the development of closeness, longing, and intimacy[26] — and even after the attainment of blissful contact with the divine, comes the Dark Night of the Soul, "the most terrible of all the experiences of the Mystic Way: the last and most complete purification of the Self, . . . the intense sense of the Divine Absence."[27] For Al•Ith, this means the relinquishment of both her lover and her infant son, as she learns the last lesson of the mystic: "The human instinct for personal happiness must be killed."[28] Some of the most powerful parts of the fable involve the depiction of Al•Ith's grief and at the same time the expansion of her visionary capabilities. It is only in her double isolation from the passion upon which she had come to depend in Zone Four and from the contentment of Zone Three, which she now sees as a fatuous refusal of aspiration, that Al•Ith breaks through the limitations of vision proper to each zone and opens her eyes to a higher possibility — a pilgrimage to the eternal light of Zone Two.

The marriage, like the attainment of Love in the Sufi Path, is not itself an end, but only a means to enlightenment. Thus in the last pages of the novel Al•Ith still suffers from the pain of disengagement from Ben Ata and jealousy of his love for the queen of Zone Five but is consoled by the knowledge that "they were still married, for all that they were so

finally separated" (p. 244). Al•Ith's journey to Zone Two would never
have been started if her passion for Ben Ata had not shaken her evaluation of herself and of her realm. Similarly, Ben Ata would not have
known how to tame Vahshi or teach her the ways of reflection and control if Al•Ith had not taught him these ways in love. Neither would any
of her people have sought the difficult passage to Zone Two, as the spiritually gifted among them now begin to do. The marriage is a spur to
movement among the zones, just as, to the mystics, spiritual love is an
encitement to exploration of all the states of conscious being.

To the Persian mystics the end of the Path brings the realization that
"Everything is He"[29]; Blake's last line in *The Marriage of Heaven and
Hell* reveals that "everything that lives is Holy"; the ultimate wisdom
that the chronicler of Lessing's *Marriages* learns from his story is that
"We are the visible and evident aspects of a whole we all share, that we
all go to form" (p. 196), and this whole is clearly a good.

The knowledge of the mystic Path is present in every zone — in every
stage of spiritual development — and in every person. The last pages of
the novel make clear, moreover, that the Path will be followed — that
the predominant movement in the Zones will lead upward, progressing
toward full enlightenment: "There was a continuous movement now,
from Zone Five to Zone Four. And from Zone Four to Zone Three — and
from us, up the pass" — to the Light (pp. 244–245).

The last words of the novel concede that "the movement is not all one
way" (p. 245), as witnessed by the fact that songs of the higher zones are
sung in the camps of the lowest. (Still, this is simply to say that the spiritual feats of the earliest pilgrims to the Light serve as inspiration to
those who must eventually follow in their footsteps.) The chronicler of
Lessing's spiritual fable does admit along the way that goodness cannot
thrive without its shadow side. Al•Ith, for example, cannot become a
pilgrim to Zone Two until she has learned to suffer from passion, jealousy, and loss. Goodness is not unalloyed, one observes. Nonetheless,
nowhere in the novel is there even a hint of a true counterforce to
goodness. Temporary errors are committed by the poorly trained and
ill-informed — yes. But no one is evil; no one even struggles with evil impulses from within the self. Consequential degrees of rapacity, vengeance, hatred, or cruelty are never registered in the precincts of the
Five Zones.

*The Marriages Between Zones Three, Four, and Five* is a *charming*
fable in large part because it does not confront the problem of evil at all.
In fact, the marked stylistic superiority of *Marriages* may depend rather
heavily on Lessing's evasion of the problem, which preoccupies so much
of her narrative attention in other novels.

Lessing clearly has the ability to control her prose—to achieve a shapely plot, a compelling conflict, and a style both economical and evocative, but she does not often in her career exercise that control for the duration of a whole novel. *The Grass Is Singing*, her first novel, is perhaps the only one before *Marriages* in which the demands of narrative form continually take precedence over a conscience that wants to have its say in essay form. In every other of Lessing's novels — even those organized as romance or parable, Lessing succumbs to the temptation to preach whenever she feels the burden of evil to be just too heavy to be borne in silence. In *The Summer Before the Dark*, for example, Lessing feels moved at last to "speak out" on world hunger and on woman's imprisonment by sex roles; in *Briefing for a Descent into Hell*, the human imperviousness to a mystical view of the universe moves Lessing finally to diatribe. In both cases, happily, she soon recovers herself and returns to the narrative. The strength of Lessing's plots, thematic design, and characterization is attested to by the fact that readers are willing to endure the boredom of such occasional lectures as a payment for the pleasures of the text "proper," which are considerable.

In *Marriages*, Lessing has withdrawn from the novel the very thing that usually tempts her away from the pure delights of fiction. She has set aside the problem of evil, freeing herself to concentrate on fabulation around a more benign theme, one which has continually fascinated her — the possibility of spiritual evolution.

Interestingly, both *Shikasta* and *The Sirian Experiments*, the novels that provide the context for *Marriages*, give Lessing enormous scope for her moralizing urge. Moreover, in both, evil is not only recognized as a component of the human situation; it is also isolated and objectified in the person of Tafta, emissary of the criminal planet Shammat. Both novels suffer a good deal on account of Lessing's assault on the principle of evil. Lectures on the foulness of "soft living" and the horrors of greed become tiresome before very long. Moreover, the fable of the war between Good (Canopus) and Evil (Shammat) for dominance over Earth (Shikasta) often strikes the reader as an irresponsible and even childish formulation of the human moral situation, since human beings are depicted as mere pawns of Good and Evil, so thoroughly manipulated by these great abstract powers that human actions have no moral import at all. We are oddly buffeted, in these novels, between a prophet's aggressive wrath against evil itself and the depressive passivity of characters convinced that life will get better or worse regardless of their personal effort. Finally, the "uplifting" endings to both novels fail to dispel the atmosphere of gloom and fatigue generated in the course of the prophet's and the characters' struggles with evil. Both books leave the reader in a state of tension — tempted by the easy optimism of the fable's ending, but held back by the pessimism of the narrator's earlier commentary. *The Marriages Between Zones Three, Four, and Five* gives the reader of the series release from this tension, by removing evil, the source of the pessimism. There good and evil are not at war; the reader is not torn between idealistic and realistic views of experience; and there is consequently no tonal struggle between the comic and the tragic. Because of its simplicity of moral vision, *Marriages* is able to be a singular, a readerly, and a pleasurable text — the classically well-made novel.

Yet it does not stand alone. As only one volume of the *Canopus in Argos* series, it becomes itself an element in a larger tension — between the optimism generated through the fable (the vehicle of desire, imagination, and belief) and the pessimism generated in the science fiction (the vehicle of observation, extrapolation, and hypothesis). In *Shikasta* and *The Sirian Experiments*, the fabulous is brought into relief — and into doubt — by the more realistic, prosaic, and speculative elements of the science-fiction saga. Likewise, the singularly fabulous quality of *Marriages* as a whole is brought into relief — and into question — by the plural quality of the texts that precede and follow it in the series.


## THE SIRIAN EXPERIMENTS (1981)

This is not to say that *Shikasta* and *The Sirian Experiments*, in their generic difference from *Marriages*, are themselves identical in narrative strategies. *Shikasta* is an archive — a highly discursive history of events, recorded by observers who aim to be true to the facts of their experience. *The Sirian Experiments*, in contrast, is a report from a single and limited perspective — a comparatively focused account of one woman's encounter with Shikasta. The woman, Ambien II, aims to be true to the spirit, rather than the facts, of her experience. As if to complement *Shikasta*, she tries "to write a history of the heart, rather than of events" (p. 286).

In the preface to the novel, Lessing tells us that Ambien II is "deluded about her own nature." She is the ideal first-person narrator: earnest, observant, ruminative, articulate, but lacking — at the beginning of the narrative — in instinct and imagination. As she recounts her millennia-long involvement with the planet Shikasta, she gives evidence of her growing sympathy with Canopean values and her consequent alienation from the perspective of Sirius — a pragmatic, amoral, technologically advanced, and philosophically bankrupt culture painfully like our own. Because the reader has a single protagonist to identify with—moreover, one whose moral development is continually at risk—*The Sirian Experiments* is a much more engaging fiction than *Shikasta*. Although the strategy of multiple narration has its advantages in *Shikasta* (and I have enumerated these above), there are drawbacks to the strategy, and they become obvious when the novel is contrasted with *The Sirian Experiments*. In *Shikasta*, the narrative line is fragmented by the shifts from one narrator to another. In *The Sirian Experiments*, the drama of an individual consciousness caught between two cultures and learning the necessity of shifting loyalties is told in one continuous line—in one increasingly intimate and compelling voice. Because the most frequent narrators of *Shikasta* (Johor and the anonymous archivists of Canopus) are all-knowing, all-virtuous, and never-changing, they fail to arouse psychological or dramatic interest. The reader's attention remains at the less compelling—if loftier—level of metaphysical principle and moral law.

Caught between Sirian wrong-headedness and personal intelligence, Ambien II is, in contrast, a vital and involving narrator whose struggles to understand her concrete experience in fresh terms become the reader's own. She is also a much better vehicle than Johor or his cohorts for the exploration of Lessing's favorite theme, "the nature of the group mind, the collective minds we are all part of, though we are seldom prepared to acknowledge this" (p. *ix*). Since the "group mind" that Johor belongs to—that of Canopus—is the arbiter of truth in the cosmology of the series, it hardly counts as a "group mind" in Lessing's usual sense. (The phrase usually means to her a temporary, historically conditioned complex of attitudes which prevails in a culture and prevents its members from observing facts or drawing inferences inconsistent with group values.) Much of the drama of *The Sirian Experiments* hinges on the question of whether and how Ambien II will be able to break through her Sirian mindset and construct "a reinterpretation of history"—that is, a version of history that takes into account the benevolence and wisdom of Canopus, the rival of her own Sirian Empire.

While the task of Ambien II is basically the same as Martha Quest's—to free herself from historically-determined conventions of vision—the intergalactic setting gives Lessing special opportunities for exploiting the narrative situation established by that task. The confrontation of the heroine with strange races and alien terrains over aeons of time provides the premise for some striking passages of description. The birth-throes of Shikasta, the upheavals that attend its shift of axis, the space-lift of the Lombis (an alien culture whom *our* histories have mistaken as one of the evolutionary links between ape and man) to Rohanda and their racial degeneration under the "care" of Sirius, the confrontation of Ambien II with the silvery-grey insect-people of Planet 11 — these extraordinary scenes evoke from Lessing a stark, intense prose. This, for example, is how Ambien II sets the scene for her meeting with Klorathy, representative of Canopus:

> What I could see from the windows was a flat featureless landscape, greyish in colour, under a greyish sky. The sun was pale and large. As I looked, the sun plunged out of sight. A reddish disc appeared over the opposite horizon. A moment later, close to it, came a smaller bilious green disc. These two moved fast across a lurid sky, giving me a sensation of whirling rotation. Looking out made me feel queasy, so I read the information sheet on the wall. (p. 100)

The paragraph brilliantly mediates between the bizarre and the prosaic, expressing precisely both the actual disorientation of Ambien II and her typically Syrian insistence on maintaining equilibrium. While the startling images evoke in the reader a sympathetic reaction of nausea and recoil, the plain diction and exclusive focus on fact warn the reader that this narrator has firmly repressed such "weak" reactions. The most successful passages in the novel capitalize on this peculiar nexus of qualities in the narrator and her situation. A "dry, just, dutiful, efficient, deluded" bureaucrat (p. *ix*) meets a disconcertingly rich, various, chaotic, dangerous, and magnificent universe. The possibilities for irony and drama abound.

Oddly, however, Lessing misses many obvious opportunities to exploit the potential of the narrative situation she has established. A case in point is the interaction of Ambien II and Klorathy, the closest thing in the novel to a protagonist-antagonist pairing. Consonant with her plan to reveal the inadequacies of the Sirian mindset, Lessing counters Ambien II's habitual hostility to Canopus with an unaccountable personal attraction to Klorathy, its representative. Dramatic convention dictates that Lessing develop the implications of this conflicted relationship. One expects, at the least, that the attraction between Klorathy and Ambien II will produce sexual and romantic tensions and that those tensions will be resolved only when each of them changes — necessarily in a manner representative of the changes required in the empires they represent. After arousing such expectations, Lessing neither fulfills them nor countermands them; she simply forgets them. That is certainly a literary error. The reader senses (very much as in *The Memoirs of a Survivor*) that Lessing is not in full control of her fiction — in fact, that her mind is on other things. The distraction (again, as in *Memoirs*) is mysticism. In her haste to establish Klorathy as a spokesman for Canopean wisdom, Lessing neglects to give him a personal character. In her eagerness to grant Ambien II access to Canopean knowledge, Lessing fails to dramatize effectively the process of her development into a fit companion for Klorathy. Their relation could have been depicted as an unwilling mutual seduction, which, though it might appear illicit and shameful from the Sirian's perspective, plunging Ambien II into despair and self-reproach, would eventually reveal itself as one of the many necessary "marriages" in the Canopean plan for cosmic evolution. Instead the relation between Klorathy and Ambien II is distant, wooden, and dramatically ineffective.

In one of the more vivid scenes in the novel, Ambien II mourns the fact that the uncivilized Lombis are so easily bedazzled into mindlessness. "Awe is a great inhibitor of intelligent questioning," she wisely observes. Her statement can easily be turned back on the novel that provides its context. Lessing's own awe before the grand principles of which Canopus and Klorathy are symbols both inhibits the intelligent questioning which might enable her to conceive her metaphysic in more subtle terms and restrains the imaginative vitality that might lead to a richer representation of that metaphysic, especially in the characterization of Klorathy. In a spirit of religious awe, Lessing apotheosizes her notion of the good into the Canopean Empire, an entity too purely virtuous, too inexorably correct, to be of interest to unregenerate mortals. As herein depicted, Canopus and its citizens are about as likely candidates for compelling novelistic treatment as God and His saints. In fact, the few novelists who have attempted to treat the latter have inevitably given the heavenly crew a strong admixture of earthly failings; that may not make theological sense, but it makes literary sense. Lessing, in contrast, is too true by half to her basically Manichean metaphysic. The battle of the Good (Canopus) and the Evil (Shammat) for control of the Ignorant (Sirius, Shikasta) is conducted here in such absolute terms that a novelistic treatment—rather than, for example, a mythic or purely fabulous approach—is inappropriate.

Yet the rhetoric of the narration is essentially novelistic: The first-person narrator has depth of personality and limits of perception; we are more interested in her inner development than in her outer adventures; the entire plot is enacted in and through a complex social structure; and the operation of social forces on the perceptions of the protagonist is one of the main issues in the story. *The Sirian Experiments* is structured as a novel of character and thus is committed to a degree of realism. Yet Klorathy, the major antagonist of the story, is a figure from a prose romance, and he represents one side of a duality that is conceived in fabulous—not realistic—terms.

"Awe is a great inhibitor of intelligent questioning." It keeps Lessing
from modifying her dualistic metaphysic to fit the narrative strategy of
*The Sirian Experiments.* It also inhibits any serious examination of the
metaphysic within the bounds of the novel. The disquisitions by Klorathy and Ambien II on the principles of Canopean Wisdom are just
that — firm and dogmatic statements of a Higher Law to which Lessing
fairly obviously ascribes, not propositions to be brought into question
either by plot developments or by counterarguments from other characters. When Klorathy informs Ambien II that "Health [is] being in balance with the natural forces — of the Galaxy" (p. 226), she does not
probe him for more concrete definition of the terms of his proposition or
challenge its accuracy. (Indeed, the statements of Canopean Wisdom
are so broadly platitudinous that they hardly *can* be disputed.) When
Ambien II, at the end of the novel, has become the chief spokesman of
Canopean Wisdom in the Sirian Empire, she turns away the questions
of her peers, claiming that her knowledge is beyond logic or verbal explanation (pp. 260–261). It is, therefore, unquestionable. While such a
presentation of Canopean Wisdom may accurately represent Lessing's
attitude toward the principles of a wisdom to which she herself has attained and toward which she feels reverence, it is a failure as either a
persuasive device or a fictional strategy. The novel threatens to founder,
at its very climax, in a haze of mystic rhapsody.

At the last moment, Lessing restores the balance of her fictional enterprise by reintroducing irony as a counterforce to awe. Ambien II
finds her faith in Canopean destiny tested by the rapid deterioration of
Shikasta and by her punitive exile from Sirius. These last-minute developments allow the reader to face at last those emotional and intellectual
misgivings which the Canopean enterprise early raised in the mind of
Ambien II but which were shunted aside as the narrative progressed to
a climax. In the last seven pages of the book, the Ambien II who was so
recently a mere mouthpiece for Canopean ideals, confesses that she
feels "undermined by the familiar dry sorrow at the waste of" Shikastan
riches, in the course of the struggle between Shammat and Canopus for
ascendency there (p. 282). She remembers one of the more effective and
subtle characters in the first half of her story, Nasar, who "had learned
to contain his pain on behalf of this sad place" (p. 283). Nasar, in fact,
supplants Klorathy as the wisdom figure of these last pages of the book.
It is he who gives Ambien II the strength to go on, and he does so without recourse to the kinds of abstract idealism so characteristic of Klorathy. In contrast to Klorathy, Nasar is a full and subtle character. He
responds richly to the contradictions of the thwarted utopia for which
he is a worker. His parting words stress the physical reality of Canopus,

not its principles. He counsels Ambien II to remain loyal to Canopus because the facts demonstrate that the Canopean Empire does not "deal in failure" (p. 284). It is that *tangible* basis for hope that comforts Ambien II when she feels pain over the suffering of her dear Rohanda. She ends her "history of the heart" on a dissonant but arresting note of ironical faith in the Canopean enterprise. While she declares her confidence that Canopus will soon move its utopian plans forward, she realizes — wincingly — that the next step in the plan involves the dismantling of the Sirian oligarchy, which she still considers "the most valuable regulator of our Empire" (pp. 286, 288). *The Sirian Experiments* thus ends back on track as a work of "realistic" science fiction, but one must admit that it has been too often sidetracked into the field of mystical apologetics.

## THE MAKING OF THE REPRESENTATIVE FOR PLANET 8 (1982)

Lessing "saves" *The Sirian Experiments* by allowing the narrator, Ambien II, to express honorably her very rational doubts (the reader's own) about the ultimate wisdom of either Canopus or Necessity — even as she pledges her faith to both. *The Making of the Representative for Planet 8* leaves less scope for honorable doubt. Not that the narrator, Doeg, does not voice some misgivings. On the contrary, his repeated questionings are wearingly ubiquitous. Rather, these doubts, in fact all Doeg's speeches, are clearly tagged as the misapprehensions of a spiritual infant, while Johor's replies always have the old familiar paternal authority — however pained — of Canopean Wisdom. Insofar as doubt is human, the reader is being patronized throughout this text.

As is true of the whole series, the questions propelling the narrative are those that accompany "the problem of evil": If God is all-powerful, why does He allow so much suffering? Why doesn't God come to save His chosen people? If we are asked to believe that we must endure evil because God knows that it is necessary to some Higher Purpose — then how are we to talk of moral responsibility? (If evil is *necessary*, who is to blame for it?) Finally, if, under Necessity, we must endure suffering, be forced by privation into crime, and ultimately face death — how are we to endure it? This last question is the one for which Lessing has an answer, and she gives it at the end of *The Making of the Representative for Planet 8:* We endure it by believing that after our suffering, crimes, and death, our atoms will cross over into Light and a higher, painless form of existence.

It is very difficult to make an "answer" into a good novel. With great care and skill it can be done, as Lessing demonstrates in *The Summer Before the Dark* and *Marriages*. Here, however, Lessing is not so successful. The most recuperative stance one can take toward this book is that it offers itself, like *Marriages*, as only one strand in the braid of the series. There is much to be said for that position. Both *Shikasta* (vol. I) and *The Sirian Experiments* (vol. III) are long, sober, and complex novels that balance within them many points of view on the problem of evil, represented in both books in the decline of the planet Rohanda from its golden age. In contrast, *Marriages* (vol. II) is a short, light-hearted, and simple fable with a single purpose—to proclaim the beauties of the mystical "stages of consciousness," which are shown to lead the earnest seeker to mystical knowledge and bliss (with only slight discomfiture along the way). In the second book of the series, the problem of evil is wholly ignored; the text is all pleasure, as it offers the reader a taste of the joys of right striving and right belief. *The Making of the Representative for Planet 8* (vol. IV) offers itself as a counterbalance to *Marriages*. Like its sister volume, it is a short and single-minded fable. Yet while *Marriages* celebrates the joys of the individual's spiritual quest, *The Making* mourns the pains of spiritual evolution on a cosmic scale. While the plot of *Marriages* unfolds under the supervision of an all-powerful, all-knowing, and wholly benevolent Providence, the situation of *The Making* develops under the wincing regard of a relatively powerless, fallible, and disobliging—if apologetic—servant of Canopus (which up to this point in the series has been equated with Providence). Whereas *Marriages* is (nearly) all light, warmth, and optimism, *The Making* is (nearly) all dark, cold, and pessimism. *The Making* gives us, with admirable honesty, a good hard look at that underside of the philosophy of Necessity which *Marriages* was at pains to hold out of the reader's sight.

In this light, *The Making of the Representative for Planet 8* is a brave and forthright attempt to grapple with the *felt* problem of evil, in the context of a metaphysical system that disallows evil as a category. Johor, representative of Canopus, repeats to Doeg, the representative of Planet 8, the message that he had brought many a time to Rohanda/Shikasta: "The hardest thing for any one of us to realise—every one of us, no matter how high in the levels of functioning—is that we are all subject to an overall plan. A general Necessity" (p. 16).[30] For Doeg's once-paradisiacal Planet 8, the Necessity decrees an Ice Age which produces a degree of suffering that in itself seems an evil—since there has been no sin, no crime, by which to justify the suffering as a punishment. Worse yet, the hardships of the Ice Age are of such severity that they absolutely force the inhabitants into crime. Doeg reports: "It had been, before The Ice, a rare thing to have a killing. Now we expected murder. We had not thieved from each other: now it was common" (p. 21). Over and over, the Representatives remind themselves: "No crime has been committed! You are not at fault!" (p. 36). Moreover, Johor assures Doeg that the apparent crimes of the populace — the murders, for example — are only inevitable results of the pressures now exerted on a race that was bred, by Canopean design, from a number of species, one of which was "easily roused to killing" (p. 61). In the grand scheme of things, there is no room for guilt nor reason for woe. The sufferings of Planet 8 are all part of the (Necessary) evolution of the cosmos.

What is dogma to Johor, however, is a source of doubt and anguish to Doeg. He desperately wants to believe that Planet 8 "had been taking part, under their [Canopus's] provision, in a long, slow progress upwards in civilisation" (p. 5). In the face of his people's sufferings, Doeg asks himself: "If we are not channels for the future, and if this future is not to be better than we are, better than the present, then what are we?" (p. 39). Nonetheless he reports, "we felt grief, we were struck and slowed with grief, for at last we had become enabled to feel, really feel, in our substance, in our deepest selves, that our world, our way of living, everything we had been — was done, was over. Finished" (pp. 8–9).

The most convincing portions of the narrative are Doeg's detailed descriptions of those times of grief. The first such moment occurs when Doeg and some other representatives tour a valley that once supported thick vegetation "and light, quick, playful animals." Now, instead,

> there were hillsides covered with short, rough greyish plants and rocks growing new species of lichen, grey and thick, like fur — and there was a herd of heavy-shouldered, heavy-jawed cattle, all facing us, their horns lowered, great hooves planted solidly. And, as we stood, trying not to be dismayed, because we had learned to fear our grief, the greyish-brown of their shaggy hides lightened to silvery grey. The air was shedding greyish crumbs. We put out our hands and saw them fill with this rough grey substance. A grey sky seemed to lower itself, pulled down by the weight of itself. We stood there, shivering, pulling close the new clothes Canopus had told us to use, thick and warm and not easy to move about in, and we were there a long time, despite the cold, knowing that we needed such moments of sharp revelation so that we might change inwardly, to match our outward changes. (pp. 9–10)

On a later occasion, Doeg describes a journey into the ice region, where caves filled with fresh animal droppings furnish the best shelter for sleep. He and his companions keep a night-long vigil in the mouth of a cave. They hear the stirrings of small animals in the back of the cave, and they find their hearts going out in sympathy to these ice-creatures: "Did the little snow rodents mass in what caves still were free of the ice packs? . . . It was with feelings of loss, even of anguish, that we left those creatures behind: this was because, of course, we identified with them. How could we not, pressed in upon as we were, so that our lives became ever smaller and narrower? We could feel for these poor animals, whatever they were, surviving in an icebound cave" (pp. 28–29). Through Doeg, the reader is made to confront the pathetic and tragic aspects of "the grand plan" of evolution.

Unfortunately, Doeg is all too quickly pressed into service as the "representative" student of Canopean wisdom. Especially at this point in the series, when the Canopean doctrines have been more than sufficiently elaborated in three previous volumes, it is superfluous to submit readers one more time to the lessons. We already know that there is no permanence in the galaxy; that all matter is "a dance and a flow" (p. 15); that Canopus is a nurturing force in the Universe (p. 34); that our dreams, like our identities, are communal (p. 60); that the many and the One are interchangeable (pp. 62–63). We have lost the patience that attends lovingly to each moment of the initiate's struggles to respond to "the announcement deep in myself of something I should be understanding" (p. 65).

There are not one but many passages purporting to represent mystical wisdom, and they echo—in fact, they practically parody—speeches in *Marriages, Shikasta, Briefing for a Descent into Hell,* and *The Memoirs of a Survivor*:

> There is a core—of something. Yet that dissolves and dissolves again. And around it some sort of dance of—pulsations? But the spaces between this—core, and the oscillations are so vast, so vast . . . that I know this solidity I feel is nothing. A shape of mist, I am, a smear of tinted light, as when we see—or *saw*, for we see only snow now, filling the spaces of sunlight—a spread of light with motes floating there. I am, from a perspective of vision very far from my own proper eyes, not dense or solid at all . . . (p. 66)

Or, somewhat more histrionically:

> I, a smear or haze of particles on which light shines, I, a nothing, a conglomerate of vast spaces defined by a dance my mind cannot comprehend, am running forward into—nothing, for if I saw this summer land as Johor does, with his Canopus eyes, I would see a universe of space in which faint shapes drift and form and dissolve—I, nothing, run forward towards nothing, weeping as I run—and where live the emotions that make these tears, Johor? Where in the great spaces in the faint mist that I am, where in

the fluid flowing structure of the dance of atoms, where . . . and how
. . . and what, Johor? (pp. 72–73)

The reader has limited tolerance for such gasping exclamations and can
only be relieved when, finally, these statements of inner conviction become outward reality, as Doeg and his companions die in the flesh but
pass on into ghostly shapes that "went floating onwards, free and light"
— passing right over "the carcasses we had inhabited" and up into the
crystalline atmosphere. "Ghosts among the ghostly worlds," they de-
part Planet 8, to rejoin Canopus and to "represent" the dead popula-
tions in the future evolution of the cosmos (pp. 117, 119–21).

Dreary to the last, and constantly attentive to human dismay at the
present level of earthly suffering (for surely the Ice Age of Planet 8 is a
metaphor for the myriad degeneracies of earthly existence today), *The
Making of the Representative for Planet 8* nonetheless insists, like its
companion volumes, on the redemptive power of Necessity. One would
wish that, for the sake of truly balancing *Marriages*, this volume had eschewed the "deus ex machina" deliverance at the end. Moreover, one
begins to feel bullied by the heavy insistence that this is the best of all
possible worlds, in spite of murder and suffering, in spite of the annihilation of whole races and worlds. Here, Lessing's adherence to the
doctrine of Necessity seems to derive less from principle or conviction
than from compulsion. The shape of the series of narratives suffers as a
result.

Although more seriously flawed than most of Lessing's fiction, *The
Making of the Representative for Planet 8* nonetheless can be said to
typify her work. Here, as throughout her career, Lessing struggles to accommodate her progressivist faith with her observations of human failing and earthly squalor. As in each of her other novels, the narrative
strategy — here, the chronicle by an initiate to Canopean wisdom — is
the carefully chosen weapon that Lessing wields in her effort to defeat
despair on new fictional ground.

From the first, Lessing has been experimenting with her choice of
weapons, but the issues at stake in the battle remain the same throughout her career. Will humanity succumb to despair? Is despair justified? Is the path of human events preordained by a supra-human destiny? Is that path leading the human race to destruction? Or, is the
prevailing feeling of dark inevitability simply the underside of a coming
deliverance?

These are the puzzles that nagged at Martha Quest from her childhood to the last pages of *The Four-Gated City. Children of Violence*

ends with her climactic realization that the answers she has been seeking, the understanding for which she has been questing, the happiness for which she has been longing, are all imminent in the present moment.[31] Concentrating on that moment, Martha learns the wisdom that is finally codified as Canopean Law in the Canopus in Argos series — that the forces guiding evolution toward greater manifestation of the good are continually provident, because both the good and the program for its gradual realization are inherent in everything that lives (just as are the necessary "terrible energies of the underside").

Reviewing the *Children of Violence* novels in the light of that final revelation, one can see that they are philosophically thoroughly congruent with Lessing's latest novel, thus suggesting a stability of belief and theme in Lessing's work at least from 1952, when *Martha Quest* was published, to the winter of 1982, the date of the publication of *The Making of the Representative for Planet 8.* What Martha Quest must learn to perceive in the textures of daily life in Africa and London, Doeg discovers in his chronicle of the death of Planet 8: that there is a Necessity operating in all human events, but that it is no cause for despair; that we all are part of the evolution of the cosmos and that, with care, we can soothe, if not hasten, the process of that evolution; that Necessity has appointed certain human representatives whose duty is to be aware of the evolutionary goal and to lead others to it; that such representatives must be open to the necessary progressions through "stages of consciousness" leading to blissful understanding. In fact, we could make the case that Anna Wulf learns these lessons as well as Martha Quest, that this is the lesson that Mary Turner cannot perceive in her blindness, or that Charles Watkins fails to remember, or that Kate Brown lives through without formulating, or that the narrator of *Memoirs* learns without being able to fulfill personally.

Yet the differences in form among Lessing's novels give evidence of essential differences in conception and effect which *situate* the theme differently in each case. In *The Grass Is Singing*, the limited and retrospective point of view, the concentration on prevailing material conditions and social forces, and the tragic form of the action all militate toward a basically deterministic view of human consciousness and its potential movements. In choosing for her novel the fit genre (a mix of tragedy and Marxist realism) and technique (a modernist ploy in which the controlled point of view dictates that all realistic detail is potentially symbolic), Lessing determined her *stance* toward the theme of the stages of consciousness. That stance was to be the darkest of her career: a shocked and helpless acceptance of the violence encumbent on changes of perception within a racist society.

With each succeeding novel, Lessing's choices of genre and technique make the telling difference in the handling of her perennial theme — the potentialities and limitations of consciousness. In the *Children of Violence* series, for example, the pattern of the *Bildungsroman* on its face dictates a radical departure from the harsh determinism of *The Grass Is Singing*. *Bildung* is development, and in the history of the German and British novel of development, the word is understood to mean change that is positive for both the individual and the society. The choice of genre thus necessitates (or reflects) a given attitude toward the stages of consciousness: The novelist of development assumes the possibility of progress from lower to higher stages, ending ultimately in the achievement of a kind of maturity. Moreover, that form also dictates a certain openness of effect; since the heroine does not achieve fullness of wisdom until near the end of the text, the feeling of search, of quest, dominates the story, and the reader is allowed the freedom to speculate on and anticipate the content of the illumination to come. Choosing to present Martha Quest's history of development in a five-part series, Lessing further builds into the reading process a long period of uncertainty for the reader, as well as a high likelihood of identification with the heroine in her search for meaning. Lessing's formal choices here involve the reader in an assumption of a progressive potential in personal and social consciousness, while encouraging the reader to view that potential as constantly at risk in history, where the individual must struggle in order to understand and fulfill that potential.

In contrast, *The Golden Notebook*, written while Lessing was in the midst of pursuing the positive agenda that her formal choices set for *Children of Violence*, firmly disallows a progressivist reading. Rather than recording a heroine's progress toward a specific wisdom (as she does in the Martha Quest series), in *The Golden Notebook* Lessing creates a space that will reveal the simultaneous value and fallibility of the many kinds of consciousness open to the narrator, Anna Wulf. The constantly revolving format of Anna's five notebooks and novel reflects Lessing's new stress on the relativity of perception, while tending to commit her narrative to definitions of progress and meaning that would seem to be at odds with the *Children of Violence* series' confidence in revelation. The notebook structure itself stresses the organizing activity of the individual mind, throwing into doubt (or at least out of conscious account) the existence of a provided order or the possibility of its being revealed to the heroine. The fragmentary fashion in which the notebooks are presented also suggests the partial nature of any single "fix" on the world and frustrates the reader's search for meaning by continually shifting the terms of the discourse. Finally, Lessing's choice to present one notebook as a culmination of the others, and to present it whole, indicates her faith that the courageous thinker may yet arrive at a provisional state of awareness that can stand, at least for a time, as a distinctive achievement. Still, by framing this Golden Notebook with the last section of the splintered and inadequate novel "Free Women," Lessing reminds her readers of the precarious and doubtful nature of any achievement of consciousness. The whole construct in which the Golden Notebook is enclosed was chosen "to shape a book which would make its own comment, a wordless statement: to talk through the way it was shaped."[32] As in all Lessing's novels, the form situates the novel's exploration of the potentials and limits of consciousness. In this case, the form necessitates a focus on epistemological questions: How do we know? Can language be adequate to describe our experience? If not, how valid are our verbal statements of meaning? If our verbal formulations are necessarily only relatively meaningful, is it at all worthwhile to pursue the search for stable meanings? If not, where and how does one ground one's existence?

In *The Golden Notebook*, Lessing seems to have exorcised her most radical epistemological doubts. When she returns to the *Children of Violence* series, she strengthens the strain of mysticism incipient in Martha Quest's early moments of illumination, integrating the mystic development of Martha Quest with the imperatives of the *Bildungsroman* — the protagonist's growth in worldly wisdom, moral insight, and social awareness. At the same time, again adhering to the dictates of the *Bildungsroman* format, Lessing makes her heroine's personal development — mystical and otherwise — both representative of, and instrumental in, promoting an analogous advance for her society.

In the novels that follow *The Four-Gated City*, Lessing's formal choices suggest that, although she still has hope that key individuals may act a useful part in the spiritual education of others in their society, she now sees the individual's personal spiritual development as the paramount concern. In *The Grass Is Singing* and *Children of Violence*, the consciousness of the individual was constantly depicted as dependent on the state of development of her society, with moments of personal breakthrough a rare and evanescent phenomenon. In *Briefing for a Descent into Hell*, *The Summer Before the Dark*, and *The Memoirs of a Survivor*, Lessing's attention turns to the internal spiritual journey of individuals who are not strategically or representatively placed in a social context in the way of Mary Turner or Martha Quest. She traces their personal encounters with spiritual possibility in such a way as to convey a hidden lesson about the ways of spiritual quest — rather than using their stories to comment on the social ramifications of a character's achievement of spiritual enlightenment. All three novels end before any social consequences of the protagonist's story can be explored, and this fact has caused some consternation to critics who have tried to fit these novels into the frame of Lessing's earlier works.

These later novels are not unfinished on their own terms, however. Each is arranged like a Sufi teaching-story or a medieval allegory to suggest the outlines of an approach to a transformative knowledge, while leaving the veil over the ineffable essence of the ultimate experience. Framed from the first as rhetorical fictions, these novels rarely arouse in the reader the expectations of social realism or highly individualized treatment of character that were proper to the formats of Lessing's previous novels. (When they do, as when the narrator of *Memoirs* dwells on conditions in the world of the Catastrophe and speculates on the historical reasons for their development, the reader immediately senses a contradiction in the narrative structure.) Lessing's generic choices in these three novels — her adoption of apologue, allegory, or teaching-story to her fictional purpose — commit her to the role of spiritual guide and imply the existence of a correct, or at least a desirable, state of consciousness toward which the rhetorical fiction would move the reader. The relativity of vision signalled in the dizzying structure of *The Golden Notebook* is replaced by a deliberate progression through a series of stages of consciousness, the order of which is external to the individual, determined in the pre-existent order and harmony of the universe itself. In *Briefing*, *Summer*, and *Memoirs*, the point of view is that of a novice to the journey in consciousness, so that the reader is drawn into the process of spiritual exploration, experiencing with the protagonist the ignorance, fears, doubts, gropings, and leaps of faith essential to the process. Both the limited point of view and the allegorical mode of these three novels keep the veil over the final experience of heightened consciousness.

The science-fiction format of the *Canopus in Argos* series implies the seeking and the finding of a knowledge — a science. In the chronicle structure of *Shikasta* Lessing allows for the widest possible perspective to be brought to bear on the nature of human consciousness, its natural stages of development, and its ultimate goal. The primary narrator, Johor, is an emissary of the God-like Canopus, endowed with the knowledge that comes directly from the divine source itself. His history of one planet's spiritual evolution and his statements about its meaning are provided without a hint of doubt as to his dependability as a spokesman for the ultimate Truth that underlies the organization of our galaxy, if not the universe as a whole. His gradual revelation of this truth, chronicled in his reports as Johor and in the transcriptions of his messi-

anic statements as George Sherban, deliver to the reader at least a
glimpse of the ultimate knowledge—the plan of the universe—and a
statement of those moral and spiritual obligations which the master
plan implies for humankind.

*The Marriages Between Zones Three, Four, and Five,* written from
the perspective of the initiate who has as yet not attained the highest
knowledge, allows Lessing to draw back from the sober stance of the
prophet and use all the charm, color, and playful fantasy open to romance and allegory. The effect is to feed, exercise, and educate the
emotions of the reader, adjusting them to the challenges of the stages of
mystical consciousness. As readers experience with Al•Ith the stress of
contact with fleshly lusts or, on the other hand, the strain of a visionary
experience that discounts the flesh, they learn with her the necessity to
accept both poles of experience as stages on the way to an indescribable
joy. The training of the emotions that this allegory provides comple-
ments the appeal to the intellect made by *Shikasta.*

By employing first-person narration in *The Sirian Experiments,*
Lessing gives a personal dimension to the saga of spiritual initiation.
Like Al•Ith, Ambien II is a ruler of an empire complacent in its wealth
and power, yet arrested in its moral development. Again, like her fairy-
tale counterpart Al•Ith, the realistically-drawn Ambien II must set
aside her pride and submit herself to tutelage by a man who rules a
country for which she has no small measure of disdain. Both women
evolve, under this tutelage, into prophets of a Providence which they
had previously grossly misunderstood. In both novels, the reader observes the process of the woman ruler's spiritual transformation. We
meet her just as she has begun to experience unease about her self and
her empire; we leave her as she moves so far beyond her people in spiritual understanding that they make her an exile and brand her a criminal. One might assume, therefore, that *The Sirian Experiments,* sharing with *The Marriages Between Zones Three, Four, and Five* a plot
and key mythic elements, is likewise an allegory—a spiritual fable.

Though *The Sirian Experiments* is, in its deepest structure, just that
—an allegory of cosmic evolution—it is on its surface and in its major
fictional strategies a novel of character. The first-person point of view
allows a full psychological portrait of Ambien II, who comes to seem no
fairy-tale figure but a flesh-and-blood woman of considerable moral
depth. We follow her through the mundane decisions of her office, discover the complex motives, misgivings, and misperceptions that lie behind her errors, empathize with her in her periods of depression, and finally take measured satisfaction as she achieves a partial understanding
of Canopean Wisdom. The world of Ambien II is more complex and

more compromised than the world of Al•Ith. Her moral task for example, requires not only direct confrontation with evil (as Al•Ith's does not) but also a continual struggle to overcome the thousand resistances to the good that she discovers within herself and the Sirian colonies on Shikasta. If her world is relatively prosaic, her voice is fittingly flat — the voice of a bureaucrat, reporting the small successes and major disappointments of her mission to an imperfect world. (In contrast, Al•Ith, the queen, is spoken for by a chronicler who maintains the honorific tones of the court historian, recording the glories of a sacred reign.) The prosaic voice of *The Sirian Experiments*, the in-depth characterization of its main character, and the inclusion of the principle of evil (even if its conception is sometimes more fabulous than seems quite proper to the prosaic context) — all prepare the way for a conclusion that contrasts sharply with the ending of the prior volume. While the chronicler leaves Al•Ith in a haze of earthly love and spiritual glory, Ambien II ends her tale still suffering grief over Rohanda and regret at her own unwitting contributions to its decline. The calmness of her tone, even as she writes from exile to her jailers, gives evidence of her progress toward acceptance of Canopean Providence — but the pain of temporary defeat is never wholly absent from her voice.

Each volume of *Canopus in Argos* is structured to explore a different aspect of that spiritual evolution which is Lessing's primary concern in this period of her career. The braid of science fiction and fantasy in the first volume, *Shikasta*, provokes the reader to question the adequacy of logic, on the one hand, and imagination, on the other, as guides to our future as a race. Lessing there employs a plural, archival structure and multi-generic approach to arouse in the reader curiosity about the ultimate questions and desire to entertain those questions earnestly. *Shikasta* appeals to the speculative faculty and to the hunger for a revealed truth, with minimal attention to the personal emotions. *The Marriages Between Zones Three, Four, and Five*, with its omniscient point of view and its fabulous aura, brings readers' emotions back into play and confronts us squarely with a call to belief. Lessing does not let us rest in the comfort of spiritual certainty, however. The fallible, first-person narrator of *The Sirian Experiments* reminds us of the realities of day-to-day spiritual struggle in a universe as yet far from its evolutionary goal.

At the end of *The Sirian Experiments*, then, the reader still experiences the free play of multiple perspectives on the puzzle of cosmic evolution. The series, for all its apparent moral earnestness, has affinities with the plural text that Roland Barthes so admires. In replaying the archives of *Canopus in Argos*, the reader must undergo "a serial movement of dislocations, overlappings, and variations." What seems in rad-

ical question *here*, will (scandalously) appear as dogma *there*. What
Barthes says of his ideal Text is largely, if oddly, true of *Canopus in
Argos:* "The logic that governs the Text is not comprehensive (seeking to
define 'what the work means') but metonymic; and the activity of associations, contiguities, and cross-references coincides with a liberation
of symbolic energy." [33]

If *The Making of the Representative for Planet 8* threatens to become
an anomalous "Work" (in Barthes's terms, a writing that limits itself by
insisting on one meaning), in the context of a series as "Text" (writing in
which a fixed meaning is continually deferred in favor of the play of
meanings), it does so by virtue of neither its singularity of theme nor its
unity of narrative structure. *Marriages*, with a singular theme and
structure, offered itself to the plurality of the textual series by indicat-
ing, in the playfulness of its discourse, that its symbolic surface, however open to exegesis, nonetheless maintains its metonymic status as
only one (very pleasurable) system of figures in a multilayered construction that itself resists definitive interpretation. *The Making of the Representative for Planet 8*—with its bleak and forbidding landscape, its
blank characters who offer neither the interest of psychological depth
nor the pleasure of vivid archetypal figuration, its attenuation of plot,
and its disproportionate emphasis on the discursive presentation of a
cosmic philosophy—calls the reader away from narrative play to the
*serious* business of defining and affirming a moral imperative, the one
figured in the series as Canopean Wisdom. This reader rebels when re-
called so abruptly from the pleasures of the space-fiction saga—with all
its variety of settings, characters, and points of view—to the harsh discipline of instruction in the *one* right way. Whether the next volume of
the series will throw the reluctant reader's rebellion and the author's didactic pose into an ironic or otherwise expanded light is now an open
question. It would be quite like Lessing to surprise her readers by an altogether unexpected alteration of her stance.

From the pessimism of *The Grass Is Singing*, with its vision of an awful doom developing inexorably from a fated construct of material conditions, to the optimism of *Canopus in Argos*, with its projection of the
evolution of human consciousness toward harmony with the rest of the
ever-evolving universe, Doris Lessing's novels have passed through an
astonishing tonal transformation. Yet her core concerns and even her
ideas are essentially the same throughout her career. If it is valid to trace
the historical influences on these changes of mood—the breakdown of
Lessing's Marxist faith after the Hungarian revolution and the Prague
trials, her Jungian analysis, her reported friendship with R. D. Laing,
her study of Sufism under Idries Shah—it is equally important to notice

that a series of formal choices in the structuring of her novels has led her to explore to the limit the implications of the attitudes implicit in each form. Lessing's own conception of the stages of consciousness suggests that any one way of thinking and feeling, once taken to the limit, leads almost by dialectical reaction to the necessity of exploring another stage. Similarly, in her novels Lessing seems to have been driven to exhaust the implications of a given genre or arrangement of point of view — implications that dictated as much as they reflected an attitude toward her material — only to find that she felt drawn to explore in another novel the opposite technical choices and their ramifications for her feelings about her stable theme, the limitations and possibilities of human consciousness.

While there are those who tie their evaluation of Lessing's novels to her choice of technique — some reserve their praise for the earlier, "realistic" novels, while others claim that only the "visionary" novels succeed artistically — it seems to me that the telling factor is not *which* technical choices Lessing made in each work, but how bold and distinctive those choices are. For example, the choice of a tragic structure for *The Grass Is Singing*, a novel based on a Marxist understanding of history, is an aggressive, a contentious, and ultimately, a liberating fictional strategy. The tragic form channels the action and feeling of the novel in such a way as to reveal aspects of Lessing's theme to which a more conventional socialist realist format would not give scope. Similarly, the highly crafted architectonics of *The Golden Notebook* condition — in a sense, create — Lessing's reading of the epistemological issues that dominate that work. Finally, the creative tension of the science fiction and scriptural codes of *Shikasta* and the wonderfully effective anachronism of the medieval romance format of *Marriages* are assertive, even defiant choices that give great vitality to these first volumes of *Canopus in Argos*. The novels that fade into the background while these masterpieces take precedence, are those which are crafted in a conventional, predictable way or those in which the technique is muddied. The middle books of the *Children of Violence* series, for example, constitute the drabbest portions of Lessing's oeuvre, precisely because in them the tandem development of the *Bildingsroman* pattern and the socialist realism is so very predictable. On the other extreme, the attempted amalgam of realism and fantasy in *The Memoirs of a Survivor* fails in effect because the two genres are made neither to cohere nor to clash significantly; there is instead a simplistic division in the text.

A well-defined and arresting structure — no matter how complex or simple — liberates the energy inherent in the matter on which it impinges. When Lessing succeeds in finding such a structure, she em-

powers herself to write, in the words of Anna Wulf, "the only kind of
novel which interests me: a book powered with an intellectual or moral
passion strong enough to create order, to create a new way of looking at
life." [34] It is a tribute to Lessing's intellectual, moral, and artistic passion that in her career of thirty years she has written such varied and
such powerful examples of the kind of novel that she has set as her own
ideal. *The Grass Is Singing, The Four-Gated City, The Golden Notebook, Canopus in Argos* — these at least will stand as novels that "create
a new way of looking at life" precisely because they "talk through the
way [they are] shaped," channeling, intensifying, and realizing the
power of consciousness, which is their constant subject.

NOTES

SELECTED BIBLIOGRAPHY

INDEX

# Notes

## INTRODUCTION

1 Doris Lessing, *Re: Colonized Planet 5, Shikasta* (New York: Alfred A. Knopf, 1979), p. 3.
2 Doris Lessing, *The Sirian Experiments* (New York: Alfred A. Knopf, 1981), p. 14.
3 Mary Ann Singleton, *The City and the Veld: The Fiction of Doris Lessing* (Lewisburg, Pa.: Bucknell Univ. Press, 1977), pp. 19, 20.
4 Roberta Rubenstein, *The Novelistic Vision of Doris Lessing: Breaking the Forms of Consciousness* (Urbana: Univ. of Illinois Press, 1979), p. 11.
5 "Testimony to Mysticism: Interview with Doris Lessing," conducted by Nissa Torrents, trans. Paul Schlueter, *Doris Lessing Newsletter* 4 (Winter 1980): 1. Originally published in the Spanish journal *La Calle* 106 (April 1–7, 1980): 42–44.
6 Doris Lessing, "The Small Personal Voice," reprinted in *A Small Personal Voice*, ed. Paul Schlueter (New York: Alfred A. Knopf, 1974), p. 14. Originally published in *Declaration*, ed. Tom Maschler (London: MacGibbon and Kee, 1957), pp. 11–27.
7 "Testimony to Mysticism," p. 1.
8 "Doris Lessing at Stony Brook: An Interview by Jonah Raskin," May 1969, reprinted in *A Small Personal Voice*, pp. 65, 66. Originally published in *New American Review* 8 (New York: New American Library, 1970), pp. 116–179.
9 Doris Lessing, *The Sirian Experiments*, p. 14.

## CHAPTER ONE: *THE GRASS IS SINGING*

1 Quotes are from the following sources, respectively: Walter Allen, *The Modern Novel in Britain and the United States* (New York: E. P. Dutton, 1964), p.

276; Antonia White, "New Novel," *The New Statesman and Nation*, April 1, 1950, p. 378; Joanna Spenser, *New York Herald Tribune Book Review*, Sept. 10, 1950, p. 8; *Times Literary Supplement*, April 14, 1950, p. 255; John Barkham, *The New York Times*, Sept. 10, 1950, p. 4.

2  Currently there are only three articles devoted exclusively to *The Grass Is Singing* and two that discuss it in tandem with other novels. In contrast, all but one of Lessing's other novels have been given scholarly treatment in six or more articles; there are twenty-nine articles on *The Golden Notebook* alone.

   The one work that has not been treated in article form is *Retreat to Innocence*, the programmatically Marxist novel that Lessing published in 1956 and later repudiated as part of her canon. The book has been long out of print and has been given serious consideration only twice. Roberta Rubenstein treats it briefly as an introduction to her more extensive study of *A Ripple from the Storm*, in *The Novelistic Vision of Doris Lessing*, pp. 49–56. David Smith gives the novel qualified praise in the few pages he devotes to it in his book *Socialist Propaganda in the Twentieth Century British Novel* (New York: Macmillan Press, 1978), pp. 148–151. I follow Lessing's wish in omitting discussion of the novel, which is untypical of Lessing's work in its simplistic political rhetoric.

3  In an "Interview with Doris Lessing" by Roy Newquist (1963), Lessing reports that she was twenty-six or twenty-seven when she began to write *The Grass Is Singing;* that would place the date at about 1945. In Doris Lessing, *A Small Personal Voice*, p. 46. Originally published in Roy Newquist, *Counterpoint* (Chicago: Rand McNally Co., 1964), pp. 413–424.

4  See Dee Seligman's biographical article "The Four-Faced Novelist," *Modern Fiction Studies* 26 (Spring 1980): 15; and Doris Lessing, *Going Home* (New York: Ballantine Books, 1968).

5  See Doris Lessing, "The Small Personal Voice," p. 20.

6  Doris Lessing, *The Golden Notebook* (New York: Simon and Schuster, 1962), p. 58.

7  Ibid., p. 61.

8  In a private communication regarding this statement of mine, Dee Seligman rightly points out that our "tragic terror" is focused on the fear that what happened to Mary Turner (as a *result* of her ignorant malice) might happen to us.

9  Aristotle, *Poetics*, trans. S. H. Butcher (New York: Hill and Wang, 1961), XIII, 2, p. 75.

10 Doris Lessing, *The Golden Notebook*, p. 61.

11 For references to Lessing's participation in one or more communist-leaning study groups in Rhodesia, see Seligman's "The Four-Faced Novelist," pp. 9, 13, and several sources in Schlueter's *A Small Personal Voice:* "The Small Personal Voice," p. 20; "Doris Lessing at Stony Brook: An Interview by Jonah Raskin," (May 1969), p. 74; and "A Talk with Doris Lessing by Florence Howe" (Oct. 1966), pp. 79–80.

12 Bertolt Brecht, from *On Experimental Theatre* (1935–1940), in John Willett, ed., *Brecht on Theatre* (London: Methuen, 1964), p. 135.

13  Bertolt Brecht, from *Theatre for Pleasure or Theatre for Instruction* (c. 1935), in *Brecht on Theatre*, pp. 70–71.

14  See Geoffrey Brereton, *Principles of Tragedy: A Rational Examination of the Tragic Concept in Life and Literature* (Coral Gables, Fla.: Univ. of Miami Press, 1968), pp. 123–124.

15  Page numbers in this chapter refer to the following edition: Doris Lessing, *The Grass Is Singing* (New York: Popular Library, 1976). The novel was originally published in London by Michael Joseph and in New York by T. Y. Crowell, both in 1950.

16  Raymond Williams, *Keywords: A Vocabulary of Culture and Society* (New York: Oxford Univ. Press, 1976), pp. 87–91.

17  Ibid., p. 90.

18  It is in "Beyond the Pleasure Principle" that Freud discusses repetition as a fundamental principle of psychic life.

19  Dorothy Brewster, *Doris Lessing* (New York: Twayne, 1965), p. 40.

20  Antonio Labriola, *Essays on the Materialistic Conception of History*, trans. Charles H. Kerr (Chicago: C. H. Kerr & Co., 1908), pp. 109–113.

21  Karl Marx, Preface, *A Contribution to the Critique of Political Economy* (1859), trans. S. W. Ryazanskaya (New York: International Publishers, 1970), p. 21.

22  Frederick Engels, *Anti-Dühring: Herr Eugen Dühring's Revolution in Science*, 3d ed. (1894; Moscow: Foreign Languages Publishing House, 1962), p. 36.

23  Kenneth Burke, *A Grammar of Motives* (Berkeley: Univ. of California Press, 1945), p. 38.

24  Karl Marx, *Capital: A Critical Analysis of Capitalist Production* (London: S. Sonnenschein, 1889), Vol. I, pp. 660–661.

25  See especially Robert B. Heilman, "Tragedy and Melodrama: Speculations on Generic Form," in Robert W. Corrigan, ed., *Tragedy: Vision and Form* (San Francisco: Chandler Publishing, 1965), pp. 246–248. The essay was originally published in *The Texas Quarterly*, Summer 1960, pp. 36–50.

26  Doris Lessing, "The Small Personal Voice," pp. 11–12.


## CHAPTER TWO: *CHILDREN OF VIOLENCE*

1  Anon., Review of *Martha Quest* and *A Proper Marriage*, *The New Yorker*, Jan. 30, 1965, pp. 122–123.

2  Marvin Mudrick, "All that Prose!" *Hudson Review* 18 (Spring 1965): 110. Italics added.

3  Frederick P. W. McDowell, "The Fiction of Doris Lessing: An Interim View," *Arizona Quarterly* 21 (Winter 1965): 330.

4  Elizabeth Dalton, "The Saving Graces of Prose," *The Kenyon Review* 17 (Summer 1965): 573.

5  Ibid., p. 572.

6  Frederick P. W. McDowell, "The Fiction of Doris Lessing," p. 330.

7  Walter Allen, *The Modern Novel in Britain and the United States*, p. 276.

Although McDowell was the first to give Lessing full consideration in an article and the first to argue vigorously that she had earned an honorable place in contemporary British letters, Walter Allen preceded him in making some succinct and central observations about Lessing's *Children of Violence*. In the three paragraphs he devotes to Lessing in the omnibus volume cited above, he notes that the *Children of Violence* series is a feminine variation on Bennett's *Clayhanger* or Lawrence's *Sons and Lovers*, that it is steeped in irony, and that this "portrait of a young woman has become a study of a society in a process of disintegration." These observations are developed in McDowell's analysis and form the basis of my discussion as well.

 8 Doris Lessing, quoted by Barbara A. Bannon, "Authors and Editors," *Publishers Weekly*, June 2, 1969, p. 52.

 9 Robert K. Morris, *Continuance and Change: The Contemporary British Novel Sequence* (Carbondale: Southern Illinois Univ. Press, 1972), p. 2.

10 Doris Lessing, "The Small Personal Voice," p. 14. Some critics who take this statement as central are: Selma Burkom, "'Only Connect': Form and Content in the Works of Doris Lessing," *Critique* 11, no. 1 (1969): 51–68; Lois Marchino, "The Search for Self in the Novels of Doris Lessing," *Studies in the Novel* 4 (Summer 1972): 254; Mary Ann Singleton, *The City and the Veld: The Fiction of Doris Lessing*, p. 18; Michael Thorpe, *Doris Lessing: Writers and Their Work*, no. 230 (London: Longman for British Council, 1974).

11 Doris Lessing, "The Small Personal Voice," pp. 12, 14.

12 Frederick P. W. McDowell, "The Fiction of Doris Lessing," p. 334; Frederick R. Karl, "Doris Lessing in the Sixties: The New Anatomy of Melancholy," *Contemporary Literature* 13 (Winter 1972): 15–33; Annis Pratt, "Women and Nature in Modern Fiction," *Contemporary Literature* 13 (Winter 1972): esp. 487–488; Bernard Bergonzi, "In Pursuit of Doris Lessing," *The New York Review of Books*, Feb. 11, 1965, pp. 12–14; Patricia Meyer Spacks, *The Female Imagination* (New York: Alfred A. Knopf, 1975), pp. 150–158; Ellen Cronan Rose, "The Eriksonian Bildungsroman: An Approach Through Doris Lessing," *Hartford Studies in Literature* 7, no. 1 (1975): 1–17.

Ellen Cronan Rose's article is a much shortened version of her monograph *The Tree Outside the Window: Doris Lessing's* Children of Violence (Hanover, N. H.: Univ. Press of New England, 1976). I composed my own chapter before reading Rose's monograph. When I read it, I was struck by some remarkable conjunctions in our thinking about the *Children of Violence* series — most importantly, our focus on the generic question and our consequent use of Goethe, Pascal, Dilthey, and Lukács as critical touchstones. Within the confines of this focus, however, our theses, our interpretations of individual scenes, and our evaluations of the series as a whole differ markedly. Rose stresses Martha Quest's movement through stages of psychological growth, according to a pattern described by psychologist Erik Erikson. Rose argues that, in Eriksonian terms, "Martha Quest's initial encounter with the world in the person of her mother failed to establish in her that sense of trust which is fundamental to a sense of identity" (*The Tree Outside the Window*, p. 3). Interpreting Martha's reactions to world events in terms of her "unresolved infantile needs," Rose develops a thorough and brilliantly insightful reading of the *Children of Violence* as a study of Martha Quest's individual psychological development. Any student of the series will benefit by turning to Rose's study. From my own perspective, I would wish to dispute, however, both Rose's minimalization of the social theme in the series and her conclusion that *The Four-Gated City* (and thus, one must assume, *Children of Violence*) is a failed *Bildungsroman*. See my own chapter three and notes for my disagreement with Rose on the latter point.

13  Doris Lessing, "Author's Notes," *The Four-Gated City* (New York: Alfred A. Knopf, 1969), p. 655.

14  Wilhelm Dilthey, *Das Erlebnis und die Dichtung* (1906; 12th ed., Gottingen, 1921), p. 250. Quoted by G. B. Tennyson, "The Bildungsroman in Nineteenth-Century Literature," in *Medieval Epic to the "Epic Theater" of Brecht*, ed. Rosario P. Armato and John M. Spalek (Los Angeles: Univ. of Southern California Press, 1968), p. 136.

15  Granville Hicks, "All About a Modern Eve," *Saturday Review* April 2, 1966, p. 32. James Gindin, on the other hand, sees the social realism in Lessing's series as a limitation on her narrative talents. He complains about Lessing's "addiction to historical categories": "It limits the author to the view that all people are almost completely conditioned by time and place, by historical environment," and finally, in his opinion, it "limits her exploration of the depths of human perception." *Postwar British Fiction: New Accents and Attitudes* (Berkeley: Univ. of California Press, 1962), pp. 83f.

16  "Interview with Doris Lessing" by Roy Newquist, in *A Small Personal Voice*, p. 57.

17  Doris Lessing, "Afterword to *The Story of an African Farm* by Olive Schreiner," in *A Small Personal Voice*, pp. 99f. The essay originally appeared as the Afterword to a reprint of the Schreiner novel (New York: Fawcett World Library, 1968), pp. 273–290.

18  Jerome Buckley, *Season of Youth: The Bildungsroman from Dickens to Golding* (Cambridge: Harvard Univ. Press, 1974), pp. 15–16, 26.

19  G. B. Tennyson, "The Bildungsroman in Nineteenth-Century Literature," p. 136.

20  Roy Pascal, *The German Novel: Studies* (Manchester: Manchester Univ. Press, 1965), p. 11.

21  Page numbers in this chapter refer to the following edition: Doris Lessing, *Martha Quest* (New York: New American Library, 1970).

22  Georg Lukács, *The Theory of the Novel: A Historico-philosophical Essay on the Forms of Great Epic Literature*, trans. Anna Bostock (Cambridge, Mass: The M.I.T. Press, 1971; originally published in German, 1920), p. 132.

23  Johann Wolfgang von Goethe, *Wilhelm Meister's Apprenticeship*, trans. Thomas Carlyle (1824; rpt. New York: The Heritage Press, 1959), Bk. II, Ch. 2, p. 76.

24  Georg Lukács, *The Theory of the Novel*, p. 132.

25  Johann Wolfgang von Goethe, *Wilhelm Meister's Apprenticeship*, Bk. V, Ch. 3, p. 277. I amend the translation by supplanting Carlyle's "here as I am"

with the standard modern translation "entirely as I am," as does Roy Pascal, *The German Novel*, p. 8.

In *A Tree Outside the Window*, pp. 1, 3, Ellen Cronan Rose quotes this passage to make a different point from my own. She stresses the issue of individual identity-formation, whereas I use the quotation to emphasize the organicism in Goethe's view of the growth process, an organicism that Lessing develops into a theory of universal human evolution — a theory that submerges the notion of individual identity-formation under the idea of a process of constant identity-evolution in the whole human race.

26  Annis Pratt, "Women and Nature in Modern Fiction," p. 487.

27  James Gindin, *Postwar British Fiction*, pp. 83–84.

28  Johann Wolfgang von Goethe, *Wilhelm Meister's Apprenticeship*, Bk. I, Ch. 16, p. 63, and Bk. VII, Ch. 1, p. 398.

29  I draw the parallels with Jung not only because they are intriguing in themselves, but also because there is evidence that Lessing had read Jung with serious interest before writing *Martha Quest*. She quotes Jung in the series; she depicts Martha reading Jung in *The Four-Gated City*; and she uses, throughout her work, a cluster of images and concepts that seem to derive from Jung — the shadow, the trickster figure, the idea of a collective unconscious and of collective evolution, and the concept of life stages and transformations, to name just a few. In her interview with Jonah Raskin at Stony Brook she revealed that she had undergone Jungian analysis. (In *A Small Personal Voice*, p. 68.)

30  Robert K. Morris, *Continuance and Change*, pp. 6, 7.

31  Carl G. Jung, "Rebirth," *Four Archetypes*, trans. R. F. C. Hull (Princeton: Princeton Univ. Press, 1970), pp. 59–60.

32  Jolande Jacobi, *The Psychology of C. G. Jung: An Introduction with Illustrations* (New Haven: Yale Univ. Press, 1943), p. 106.

33  Ibid., p. 151.

34  Ibid., p. 150.

35  Roy Pascal, *The German Novel*, p. 77.

36  Ibid., p. 95.

37  Johann Wolfgang von Goethe, *Wilhelm Meister's Apprenticeship*, Bk. VIII, Ch. 5, p. 514.


CHAPTER THREE:  *THE FOUR-GATED CITY*

1  Dagmar Barnouw, "Disorderly Company: From *The Golden Notebook* to *The Four-Gated City*," in *Doris Lessing: Critical Studies*, ed. Annis Pratt and L. S. Dembo (Madison: Univ. of Wisconsin Press, 1974), pp. 83f.

2  Patricia Meyer Spacks, *The Female Imagination*, p. 157.

3  D. J. Enright, "Shivery Games," *The New York Review of Books*, July 31, 1969, p. 22.

4  Johann Wolfgang von Goethe, *Wilhelm Meister's Apprenticeship*, Bk. VII, Ch. 9, p. 461.

5  D. J. Enright, "Shivery Games," p. 22.
6  As is evident in the title *The Tree Outside the Window*, the image of the tree
   is central to Ellen Cronan Rose's analysis of *The Four-Gated City*. In that
   analysis, she regards Lessing as setting up an analogy: just as a tree gains its
   nutrients from the soil and returns nutrients to it, so a person gains life from a
   social context and returns life to it. Rose tests *The Four-Gated City* against
   this model and finds it wanting. "The image of the tree," she says, "makes its
   generic statement by a willful superimposition of meaning which turns Martha from the particular into the exemplary 'individual conscience in its relations with the collective.' While Lessing's use of the metaphor makes it clear
   that she does not intend her protagonist's achievement of identity to be an exercise in solipsism, it does not succeed in defining precisely the manner of
   Martha's final relation to society" (p. 57). Rose ends her discussion of *The
   Four-Gated City* by declaring that "the collective, as Lessing describes it in
   *Children of Violence*, is hostile to the individual. The logical conclusion to
   the conflict between the two occurs at the end of Part Four of *The Four-
   Gated City*. It is a bleak and pessimistic acceptance of the irreconcilability of
   the self and society" (p. 68).
     One can agree with Rose that Martha Quest's "society" is much more
   hostile to her perceptions than Wilhelm Meister's was to his—that is, if one
   defines Martha's "society" as the group of persons in power in British govern-
   ment at the time of the Catastrophe. It seems equally valid, however, to define Martha's "society" as that subgroup of persons (analogous to Wilhelm's
   Society of the Tower) who share her values and her vision of a better world.
   Since I tend to the latter view, I consider the analogy that Rose has pointed
   out to be both a valid and a consistently *successful* one, as it operates in the
   novel: Martha takes life and learning from her various societies—her parents, Solly and Josh, her political allies, the Coldridge family—and returns
   life and wisdom to the redefined society of post-Catastrophe Europe.
     Here in chapter three, written before my reading of Rose's monograph, I
   examine another side of the image of the tree—its function as a reminder of
   the organic quality of Martha's development from child of the veld to sage of
   Faris Island.
7  Johann Wolfgang von Goethe, *Wilhelm Meister's Apprenticeship*, Bk. XIII,
   Ch. 14, p. 234.
8  See *A Proper Marriage*, pp. 63, 98, 247. In notes and text, the following ab-
   breviations will be used for the volumes of *Children of Violence:*

   MQ     *Martha Quest* (1952; rpt. New York: New American Library,
          1970).
   PM     *A Proper Marriage* (1954; rpt. New York: New American Library,
          1970).
   RS     *A Ripple from the Storm* (1958; rpt. New York: New American Li-
          brary, 1970).
   L      *Landlocked* (1965; rpt. New York: New American Library, 1970).
   FGC    *The Four-Gated City* (1969; rpt. New York: Bantam Books, 1970).
9  Frederick P. W. McDowell is the most perceptive of these critics when he says

that "the fluctuating image of the great wheel at the town carnival emphasizes Martha's own restlessness and futility" ("The Fiction of Doris Lessing: An Interim View," p. 333). It is Martha's reaction to the idea of repetition that is futile, not the cycle itself. In my opinion, Robert Morris, Nancy Porter, and Lloyd Brown arrive at unnecessarily limited interpretations because they ignore the suggestion that there is saving power in the cycle of repetition. For them, the ferris wheel is simply an image of futile repetition without change. See Robert Morris, *Continuance and Change: The Contemporary British Novel Sequence*, p. 17; Nancy Porter, "Silenced History — *Children of Violence* and *The Golden Notebook*," *World Literature Written in English*, 12, no. 2 (November 1973): 165; and Lloyd Brown, "The Shape of Things: Sexual Images and the Sense of Form in Doris Lessing's Fiction," *World Literature Written in English* 14, no. 1 (April 1965): 179.

10  Several critics have noted Lessing's use of rooms, walls, and houses as symbols, most notably: Frederick Karl, "Doris Lessing in the Sixties"; Ellen Cronan Rose, *The Tree Outside the Window*, esp. pp. 49–56, 59–60, 64–65; and Claire Sprague, "'Without Contraries is no Progression': Lessing's *The Four-Gated City*," *Modern Fiction Studies* 26 (Spring 1980): 96–116.

11  Selma R. Burkom, "'Only Connect': Form and Content in the Works of Doris Lessing," p. 53.

12  Marion Vlastos, "Doris Lessing and R. D. Laing: Psychopolitics and Prophecy," *PMLA* 91, no. 2 (March 1976): 245–258. This is a beautifully crafted article explaining clearly the connections between Laing's and Lessing's theories about madness.

13  Ibid., p. 247, quoting R. D. Laing, *The Politics of Experience* (1967; rpt. New York: Ballantine Books, 1970), p. 75.

14  Sydney Janet Kaplan notes the imagery of electronics and radios and says, "It is, of course, all in keeping with the struggle to connect individual and communal consciousness — a process of *communication*" ("The Limits of Consciousness in the Novels of Doris Lessing," in *Doris Lessing: Critical Studies*, p. 127).

15  See *PM*, 220, 255, 324; *RS*, 122, 230.

16  Doris Lessing, "The Small Personal Voice," p. 4.

17  "Doris Lessing at Stony Brook: An Interview by Jonah Raskin," p. 66.

## CHAPTER FOUR: *THE GOLDEN NOTEBOOK*

1  Doris Lessing, *The Golden Notebook* (New York: Simon and Schuster, 1962). All page numbers in the chapter refer to this edition.

2  Doris Lessing, "The Small Personal Voice," p. 4.

3  See the Introduction to *The Golden Notebook*, pp. xvii, xv.

4  Since I am classing Doris Lessing with those novelists already judged to be postmodern, it may be helpful to name a few of them: John Barth, Donald Barthelme, Samuel Beckett, Robert Coover, Julio Cortázar, Alain Robbe-Grillet. For a full discussion of postmodernism, see Ihab Hassan, *Paracriti-*

*cisms: Seven Speculations of the Times* (Urbana: Univ. of Illinois Press, 1975), pp. 39–59.

5  In the Introduction to *The Golden Notebook* Lessing makes clear her intention to describe the intellectual, moral, and political "climate" or "feel" of her era. She accomplishes this task by mirroring the personal consciousness of Anna Wulf, who is a representative postmodern woman in her simultaneous recognition of the force of chaos and the need for order.

6  Annis Pratt was the first critic to explore the novel's dialectical structure in her influential article "The Contrary Structure of Doris Lessing's *The Golden Notebook*," *World Literature Written in English* 12, no. 2 (November 1973): 150–160.

7  The complete structure of *The Golden Notebook* may be represented schematically as follows:
   Section 1: "Free Women" 1, Black 1, Red 1, Yellow 1, Blue 1
   Section 2: "Free Women" 2, Black 2, Red 2, Yellow 2, Blue 2
   Section 3: "Free Women" 3, Black 3, Red 3, Yellow 3, Blue 3
   Section 4: "Free Women" 4, Black 4, Red 4, Yellow 4, Blue 4
   The Golden Notebook
   "Free Women" 5

8  Albert Camus, *The Myth of Sisyphus and Other Essays*, trans. Justin O'Brien (New York: Alfred A. Knopf, 1955), p. 10.

9  Ibid., p. 10.

10  Lessing's most obvious "homage" to Camus is her use of the Sisyphus image, which she considerably transforms, adding an incongruous touch of progressivist faith to the basically absurdist tenor of the image. (See *The Golden Notebook*, pp. 182, 529, 537.)

11  Albert Camus, *The Myth of Sisyphus and Other Essays*, p. 13.

12  Matthew Arnold, "The Scholar Gypsy," lines 201–205.

13  Friedrich Nietzsche, *The Will to Power*, trans. Walter Kaufmann and R. J. Hollingdale (New York: Vintage Books, 1968), Section 416, p. 224.

14  Albert Camus, *The Myth of Sisyphus and Other Essays*, p. 89.

15  Ibid., p. 23.

16  Percy Bysshe Shelly, "To ——: One Word Is Too Often Profaned," lines 13–14.

17  Albert Camus, *The Myth of Sisyphus and Other Essays*, p. 70.

18  Jean-Paul Sartre, *Nausea*, trans. Lloyd Alexander (New York: New Directions, 1959), p. 56.

19  Friedrich Nietzsche, *The Will to Power*, Section 417, p. 224.

20  Michael L. Magie, "Doris Lessing and Romanticism," *College English* 38 (February 1977): 537.

21  Friedrich Nietzsche, *The Will to Power*, Section 1059, p. 545.

22  It has been convincingly argued numerous times that Lessing means the reader to consider Anna Wulf the author of the notebooks, "Free Women," and the whole "macrofiction" *The Golden Notebook*. See, e.g., John L. Carey, "Art and Reality in *The Golden Notebook*," in *Doris Lessing: Critical Studies*, p. 23, and Anne M. Mulkeen, "Twentieth Century Realism: The

'Grid' Structure of *The Golden Notebook,*" *Studies in the Novel* 4 (Summer 1972): 266.

23  Albert Camus, *The Myth of Sisyphus and Other Essays,* p. 84.

## CHAPTER FIVE: *BRIEFING FOR A DESCENT INTO HELL*

1  Doris Lessing, *Briefing for a Descent into Hell* (New York: Alfred A. Knopf, 1971). Page numbers in this chapter refer to this edition.

2  Most reviews of *Briefing* were unenthusiastic, and many of the major reviews were largely condemnatory. For example, in the *Spectator,* Auberon Waugh called the novel a "wretched venture," criticizing the story of Charlie's voyage and finding of the Crystal as "completely unreadable," full of "sub-poetic ramblings" (April 17, 1971, p. 534). Joan Didion, writing for *The New York Times Book Review,* scored Lessing for "her leaden disregard for even the simplest rhythms of language," her treatment of characters as mere "markers in the presentation of an idea," and her overbearing zeal "in the service of immediate cosmic reform" (March 14, 1971, pp. 1, 39).

3  Her early interest in Sufism is recorded in her review of Shah's *The Sufis:* Doris Lessing, "An Elephant in the Dark," *Spectator,* Sept. 18, 1964, p. 373. Critics who have brought to our attention both Lessing's Sufi commitment and her use of the Sufi teaching-story as a narrative model are Dee Seligman, "The Sufi Quest," *World Literature Written in English* 12, no. 2 (November 1973): 190–206, and Nancy Shields Hardin, "Doris Lessing and the Sufi Way," in *Doris Lessing: Critical Studies,* pp. 148–165; and "The Sufi Teaching Story and Doris Lessing," *Twentieth Century Literature* 23 (1977): 314–326.

4  Idries Shah, *The Way of the Sufi* (New York: E. P. Dutton, 1970), p. 197.

5  Ibid.

6  In addition to Lessing's review of *The Sufis,* we have evidence from Lessing elicited by Roberta Rubenstein. In a letter to Rubenstein dated March 28, 1977, Lessing said: "When I read it [Shah's *The Sufis*], I found that it answered many questions that I had learned—I feel too belatedly—to ask of life. Though that book was only the beginning of a different approach." Roberta Rubenstein, *The Novelistic Vision of Doris Lessing,* p. 121.

7  Idries Shah, *The Sufis* (Garden City, N.Y.: Doubleday, 1964), p. vii.

8  Shah quotes a group recital written by Mir Yahya Kashi. *The Way of the Sufi,* p. 252.

9  Doris Lessing, "An Elephant in the Dark," p. 373.

10  See Idries Shah, *The Sufis,* pp. 10, 29, 172–205, 264.

11  Mary Ann Singleton notes that Lessing derives this list of identifications among the gods from a similar list in Idries Shah's *The Sufis,* p. 195. See Singleton's *The City and the Veld: The Fiction of Doris Lessing,* p. 153.

12  D. A. Rees, "Platonism and the Platonic Tradition," *The Encyclopedia of Philosophy,* ed. Paul Edwards, 1967 ed.; rpt. 1972.

13  Idries Shah, *The Sufis*, p. 389. This correlation is noted by Roberta Rubenstein, *The Novelistic Vision of Doris Lessing*, p. 186.

14  Idries Shah, *The Way of the Sufi*, pp. 244–245.

15  Reynold A. Nicholson, *The Mystics of Islam: An Introduction to Sufism* (1914, rpt. New York: Schocken, 1975), pp. 45–49.

16  David Richter, *Fable's End: Completeness and Closure in Rhetorical Fiction* (Chicago: Univ. of Chicago Press, 1974), pp. 17–18.

17  This theme is treated again at length in *Shikasta* (1979), where the surface elements of classical and biblical myths are de-mystified programmatically, in order to re-emphasize the core of meaning that they share.

18  Doris Lessing, "The Small Personal Voice," p. 6.

19  Ibid., p. 11.

20  Sheldon Sacks, *Fiction and the Shape of Belief: A Study of Henry Fielding with Glances at Swift, Johnson, and Richardson* (Berkeley: Univ. of California Press, 1964), pp. 8, 26, and throughout.

21  Sheldon Sacks, "Golden Birds and Dying Generations," *Comparative Literature Studies* 6 (September 1969): 276 f.

22  See Richter's *Fable's End*, especially Appendix B.

23  Sheldon Sacks, *Fiction and the Shape of Belief*, pp. 15, 57.

24  David Richter, *Fable's End*, p. 11.

25  Doris Lessing, "The Small Personal Voice," pp. 6, 11.

26  Roberta Rubenstein, *The Novelistic Vision of Doris Lessing*, p. 186.

27  Sheldon Sacks, *Fiction and the Shape of Belief*; David Richter, *Fable's End*; Robert Scholes, *Fabulation and Metafiction* (Urbana: Univ. of Illinois Press, 1979), p. 6.

28  Doris Lessing, "The Small Personal Voice," p. 7.

## CHAPTER SIX: *THE SUMMER BEFORE THE DARK*

1  Dorothy Nyren, *Library Journal*, March 15, 1973, p. 886. Emphasis mine.

2  Anon., "Middle-aged Lib," *Times Literary Supplement*, May 4, 1973, p. 484.

3  Walter Clemons, "The Invisible Woman," *Newsweek*, May 14, 1973, p. 118. In the same review Clemons both censures Lessing for her "lapses into over-explicitness" in the spirit of "lecture-hall demonstration" and admits that "we are caught up in a rush of strong feeling without being able to stand aside and see how the involvement is achieved. Lessing's Kate Brown is an intelligent woman who is made irresistibly, physically real to us, and 'The Summer Before the Dark' is uncomfortably moving."

4  R. L. Widmann, "Briefly Noted," *The New Yorker*, June 9, 1973, p. 113.

5  The Widmann review opens, "Although it is exceedingly difficult to accept the lesson of this novel. . . ." Some who have attacked that lesson are Alison Lurie, "Wise-Women," *The New York Review of Books*, June 14, 1973, pp. 18–19; Doris Grumbach, "Rite of Passage," *The New Republic*, May 12,

1973, pp. 28–29; Ellen Cronan Rose, "After Touching Rock Bottom," *The Nation*, Aug. 27, 1973, pp. 151–152; and most acidly, Elizabeth Hardwick, *The New York Times Book Review*, May 13, 1973, pp. 1–2. Among the defenders of the novel's apparent thesis are John Leonard, "More on Lessing," *The New York Times Book Review*, May 13, 1973, p. 47; Timothy Foote, "Portrait of a Lady," *Time*, May 21, 1973, p. 99; and the anonymous author of "Middle-aged Lib," *Times Literary Supplement*, noted above.

6  See Sheldon Sacks, *Fiction and the Shape of Belief.*

7  Sheldon Sacks, "Golden Birds and Dying Generations," p. 277.

8  Ibid., p. 290.

9  Ibid., p. 291. Here Sacks greatly alters the argument of his *Fiction and the Shape of Belief* (1964), in which he stressed the inherent and radical distinction between "represented action" (his term for the novel of action and character) and "apologue." In the previous chapter, I drew on Sacks's arguments in *Fiction and the Shape of Belief*, in order to illustrate how closely *Briefing* follows the pure form of the apologue. *The Summer Before the Dark*, in contrast, breaks the form of the apologue in order to join it with the form of "represented action" in a fashion not acknowledged as possible by Sacks until his article "Golden Birds and Dying Generations" (1969).

10 Ibid., p. 277.

11 Doris Lessing, *The Summer Before the Dark* (New York: Alfred A. Knopf, 1973). Page numbers in this chapter refer to this edition.

12 See pp. 39, 60, 75, 139, 140, 170.

13 Lorelei Cederstrom, "Doris Lessing's Use of Satire in *The Summer Before the Dark*," *Modern Fiction Studies* 26 (Spring 1980): 133.

14 Ibid.

15 In a strikingly similar passage, Anna Wulf realizes that her story-making "must be an evasion," that it "is simply a means of concealing something from" herself and that she must force herself to keep a diary in order to ensure that she will look squarely at herself; see Doris Lessing, *The Golden Notebook*, p. 197.

16 Tzvetan Todorov, *The Poetics of Prose*, trans. Richard Howard (Ithaca, N.Y.: Cornell Univ. Press, 1977; orig. pub. in French as *La Poétique de la prose* by Editions du Seuil, 1971), p. 129.

17 Ibid., pp. 132–133, 135.

18 The fact that the source of Kate's dilemma and thus the plot of the fiction is predicated on factors beyond individual personality does not mean that *The Summer Before the Dark* does not function at times as a psychological novel. As indicated above, the effects of the action on Kate's personal emotions and character are traced rather fully, which would be neither necessary nor proper to pure romance.

19 See Barbara F. Lefcowitz, "Dream and Action in Lessing's *The Summer Before the Dark*," *Critique* 17 (December 1975): 107–120; Roberta Rubenstein, *The Novelistic Vision of Doris Lessing*, pp. 200–219; and Ralph Berets, "A Jungian Interpretation of the Dream Sequence in Doris Lessing's *The Summer Before the Dark*," *Modern Fiction Studies* 26 (Spring 1980): 117–129.

20  Barbara F. Lefcowitz, "Dream and Action in Lessing's *The Summer Before the Dark*," p. 111.

21  Ibid., p. 117.

22  Josephine Hendin, "Doris Lessing: The Phoenix 'Midst Her Fires," *Harper's*, June 1973, p. 85. Emphasis mine.

23  Several reviewers complained about the sections of discursive commentary. The reviewer in *Choice* writes archly: "the book suffers at times from too much cud-chewing" (October 1973, p. 1195).

24  Walter Clemons, "The Invisible Woman," p. 118.

25  See Angus Fletcher, *Allegory: The Theory of a Symbolic Mode* (Ithaca, N.Y.: Cornell Univ. Press, 1964), esp. pp. 305 ff.; Sheldon Sacks, "Golden Birds and Dying Generations"; Tzvetan Todorov, *The Poetics of Prose*, p. 122; and David Richter, *Fable's End*.

26  The two interpretations converge when we recognize that Jeffrey, in his dependence on Kate, represents the demand on her to be maternal. Thus the turtle can logically represent both Kate's maternal self and Jeffrey, who calls it into being.

27  Ralph Berets, in the intelligent and balanced argument of "A Jungian Interpretation of the Dream Sequence in Doris Lessing's *The Summer Before the Dark*," p. 122, acknowledges the possibility that Kate is identified with both the seal and the observer; the Jungian system of dream analysis assumes that all figures in a dream are projections of aspects of the dreamer's psyche.

28  Roberta Rubenstein, *The Novelistic Vision of Doris Lessing*, p. 215.

29  Elizabeth Hardwick, *The New York Times Book Review*, p. 2.

30  Doris Grumbach, "Rite of Passage," p. 29.

31  Many critics interpret Kate's return as a sign of failure and regression. See Elizabeth Hardwick, *The New York Times Book Review*, p. 2; Doris Grumbach, "Rite of Passage," p. 29; Ellen Cronan Rose, "After Touching Rock Bottom," p. 151; Barbara F. Lefcowitz, "Dream and Action in Lessing's *The Summer Before the Dark*," p. 118; Alison Lurie, "Wise-Women," p. 18; and David Bromwich, "Fiction Round-Up," *Commentary* 56 (September 1973): 86.

## CHAPTER SEVEN: *THE MEMOIRS OF A SURVIVOR*

1  Michael L. Magie, "Doris Lessing and Romanticism, p. 552.

2  Nancy Shields Hardin, "The Sufi Teaching Story and Doris Lessing," pp. 324, 325.

3  Malcolm Cowley, "Future Notebook," *Saturday Review*, June 28, 1975, p. 24.

4  Erving Goffman, *Frame Analysis: An Essay on the Organization of Experience* (New York: Colophon Books, Harper & Row, 1974), p. 379.

5  Ibid., p. 25.

6  William James, *The Principles of Psychology* (1890; rpt. New York: Dover Publications, 1950), Vol. 2, Ch. XXI, p. 293. Cited by Goffman, p. 2n.

7  This and all parenthetical page references in the chapter refer to the follow-
   ing edition: Doris Lessing, *The Memoirs of a Survivor* (New York: Alfred A.
   Knopf, 1975). The novel was originally published in 1974 by The Octagon
   Press, Ltd., London.

8  Robert Scholes, *Structural Fabulation: An Essay on Fiction of the Future*
   (Notre Dame, Ind.: Univ. of Notre Dame Press, 1975), pp. 70–71.

9  Frederick Engels, *Anti-Dühring*, p. 207.

10 Aniela Jaffé, "Symbolism in the Visual Arts," *Man and His Symbols*, ed. Carl
   G. Jung (Garden City, N.Y.: Doubleday, 1964), pp. 240, 241.

11 Carl G. Jung, "Dream Analysis in Its Practical Application," *Modern Man in
   Search of a Soul* (1933; rpt. New York: Harvest Books, Harcourt Brace &
   Co., 1955), p. 6.

12 Erving Goffman, *Frame Analysis: An Essay on the Organization of Experience*, p. 28.

13 William James, *The Principles of Psychology*, p. 300.

14 Tzvetan Todorov, *The Fantastic: A Structural Approach to a Literary
   Genre*, trans. Richard Howard (Cleveland, Ohio: Case Western Reserve
   Univ. Press, 1973), pp. 68, 69.

15 Erving Goffman, *Frame Analysis: An Essay on the Organization of Experience*, pp. 378–79.

16 Nancy Shields Hardin, "The Sufi Teaching Story and Doris Lessing," p. 316.

17 My colleague Professor Eric Rothstein offers a reading based on entirely different assumptions about Lessing's intent. While he accepts the judgment
   that the world behind the wall, in both its Jungian and Freudian aspects, is a
   collection of clichés, he thinks that the world is presented in such trite fashion for a purpose—to suggest that the Freudian and Jungian and mystical
   formulas, including the benevolent vision of the One, are wholly illusory
   frames that the narrator invents in order to compensate for the sense of chaos
   she experiences in the outer world of the Catastrophe. A reader's resistance to
   the narrator's ecstatic final moment, then, is a function of that reader's negative judgment on the narrator's imaginative capacities. We are, according to
   Professor Rothstein, meant to distance ourselves from a narrator so desperate
   for belief and order that *she* will accept the world behind the wall as real and
   primary. Thus the "blame" for the stiltedness of the world behind the wall
   falls on the narrator, not on Lessing as author.

   Such a recuperative reading is consistent in itself, and it even has touch-
   points with certain aspects of *The Golden Notebook*. Anna Wulf's eagerness
   to dwell in prefabricated systems of meaning (such as Marxism or Mother
   Sugar's brand of Jungian thought) is exposed by Lessing as "nostalgic" and
   self-deceptive. However, the evidence of the novels written close in time to
   *Memoirs*— *The Four-Gated City, Briefing for a Descent into Hell, The Summer Before the Dark*, and the *Canopus* series—indicates that the later Lessing consistently valorizes the mystic and the visionary, however schematic its
   formulation. If in this novel we are meant to reject the narrator's vision as over-
   simplified, are we also meant to scorn Martha Quest's premonitions, Charles
   Watkins's fantasies, and Kate Brown's dreams as "over-simplifications"? My

reading of all the later Lessing depends on the judgment that Lessing, on the contrary, wants us to privilege her narrators' imaginary worlds as more "real" than "reality."

18  Wayne C. Booth, *The Rhetoric of Fiction* (Chicago: Univ. of Chicago Press, 1961), pp. 397–98.
19  Quoted by Idries Shah, *The Way of the Sufi*, p. 60.
20  Reynold A. Nicholson, *The Mystics of Islam*, p. 96.

## CHAPTER EIGHT:  *CANOPUS IN ARGOS*

1  *Briefing for a Descent into Hell* and *The Summer Before the Dark* are two special cases in this regard. In *Briefing*, the incongruities of the surface elements of the text, which initially seem at war, are ultimately so firmly fixed into the metaphysical scheme of the work that the narrative falls flat; the didactic force straight-jackets the fantasy, leaving the reader with a feeling of stultification rather than excitement. In *The Summer Before the Dark*, Lessing interweaves the opposing elements—quest allegory and novel of character —so carefully that the effect is one of harmony and fruitful cooperation; the novel pleases and illuminates, but it is hardly exciting.
2  Roland Barthes, *S/Z*, trans. Richard Miller (New York: Hill and Wang, 1974), pp. 160, 15, 30, 5, 263.
3  Doris Lessing, "Some Remarks," preface to *Shikasta* (New York: Alfred A. Knopf, 1979), p. ix. The full title of this first volume of the series *Canopus in Argos: Archives* is *Re: Colonised Planet 5, Shikasta; Personal, Psychological, Historical Documents Relating to Visit by Johor (George Sherban), Emissary (Grade 9), 87th of the Period of the Last Days.*
4  Doris Lessing, *The Marriages Between Zones Three, Four, and Five (As Narrated by the Chroniclers of Zone Three)* (New York: Alfred A. Knopf, 1980).
5  "A Talk with Doris Lessing," conducted by Minda Bikman, *The New York Times Book Review*, March 30, 1980, p. 24.
6  Roland Barthes, *S/Z*, pp. 5–6.
7  Ibid., pp. 4–6.
8  See the definitions of science fiction by Kingsley Amis, *New Maps of Hell: A Survey of Science Fiction* (New York: Harcourt, Brace & Co., 1960), p. 18; Darko Suvin, *Metamorphoses of Science Fiction: On the Poetics and History of a Literary Genre* (New Haven: Yale Univ. Press, 1979), pp. 4, 7–8; Donald A. Wollheim, *The Universe Makers: Science Fiction Today* (New York: Harper & Row, 1971), p. 10; Sam Moskowitz, *Explorers of the Infinite: Shapers of Science Fiction* (Westport, Conn.: Hyperion Press, 1974), p. 11; and David Ketterer, *New Worlds for Old: The Apocalyptic Imagination, Science Fiction, and American Literature* (Bloomington: Indiana Univ. Press, 1974), pp. 15–18.
9  Michel Butor, "The Crisis in the Growth of Science Fiction," trans. Richard Howard, in *Inventory: Essays by Michel Butor*, ed. Richard Howard (New

York: Simon and Schuster, 1968), p. 225. Originally published in French in *Répertoire* (Paris: Les Editions de Minuit, 1960).

10  Donald Wollheim, *The Universe Makers*, pp. 30–31.

11  Much of this developing saga was recorded in short stories in the early magazines *Weird Tales*, *Argosy*, and *Amazing Stories*, and most notably in the 1950s in *Astounding* (later titled *Analog*), *The Magazine of Fantasy and Science Fiction*, and *Galaxy Science Fiction*. Some of the major works in the Galactic Empire mode are Bradbury's *The Martian Chronicles* (1950), Isaac Asimov's *The Foundation Trilogy* (1942–1966), Robert Heinlein's *Double Star* (1956), *Starship Troopers* (1960) and *Stranger in a Strange Land* (1962), Frank Herbert's *Dune* (1966), and Ursula Le Guin's *The Left Hand of Darkness* (1970).

12  See "The Cosmogony of the Future," in Donald A. Wollheim, *The Universe Makers*, pp. 42–44.

13  In *The Manchester Guardian Weekly* (Nov. 25, 1979, p. 23), reviewer W. L. Webb notes somewhat archly the similarities of Lessing's story to the speculations of Von Däniken in *Chariots of the Gods: Unsolved Mysteries of the Past* (New York: Putnam, 1969). It is likely that some details of the SOWF theory and mechanism were suggested by Lessing's readings in quasi-science, especially those books which offer astronomical theories to explain the existence of the stone monuments and straight paths (leys) of the British Isles. For example, in *The View Over Atlantis* (London, 1969; rpt. New York: Ballantine Books, 1972), John Michell argues that these paths and monuments constitute "a great scientific instrument sprawled over the entire surface of the globe" (p. 69) for the purpose of both detecting and directing the flow of an essential life force connected with polar magnetism. "The strength and direction" of this current, he theorizes, are "influenced by many factors including the proximity and relative positions of the other spheres of the solar system, chiefly the sun and moon" (p. 70). It is through rediscovering and reestablishing the proper currents of this energy that "the Logos becomes manifest in the restoration of the Holy Spirit" (p. 201), Michell finally concludes. His theory is remarkably similar to Lessing's fictional premise in *Shikasta*. Perhaps Lessing read his book, or some work upon which he based his theory (prominently, Alfred Watkins's *The Old Straight Track*, 1925, and W. J. Perry's *Children of the Sun*, 1923). Some skeptical readers will undoubtedly experience the same rationalist recoil from Lessing's novel as they would from Michell's or Van Däniken's book. The obvious difference, of course, is that Van Däniken and Michell ask to be accepted as spokesmen of the empirical truth, whereas Lessing's claim is to metaphorical truth — the kind of truth proper to fiction. Lessing may even in a concrete way believe the theories she presents as fiction, but that would not alter the fact that in *Shikasta* her readers are asked to relate to them "only" as fiction, as metaphorical truth.

14  Darko Suvin, *Metamorphoses of Science Fiction*, pp. 7–8; emphasis mine.

15  Olaf Stapledon, *Last and First Men: A Story of the Near and Far Future* (1930; rpt. Hammondsworth, Middlesex: Penguin Books, 1963), p. 17.

16  Lessing's phrasing echoes hymns such as "Walk daily with your Savior," "Walk with the Lord along the Road," "Walking, Savior, close to thee," and "Walking with Jesus day by day." See Katharine Smith-Diehl, *Hymns and Tunes — An Index* (New York: Scarecrow Press, 1966), p. 329.

17  Annemarie Schimmel, *Mystical Dimensions of Islam* (Chapel Hill: Univ. of North Carolina Press, 1975), p. 109.

18  Ibid., pp. 109–130, chapter section titled "Stations and Stages."

19  Reynold A. Nicholson, *The Mystics of Islam*, p. 30.

20  Roland Barthes, *S/Z*, pp. 5, 12.

21  *The Sirian Experiments* (New York: Alfred A. Knopf, 1981). Lessing describes the book in her March 1980 interview with Minda Bikman for *The New York Times Book Review*, cited above.

22  Both Annis Pratt and Claire Sprague have observed the affinities of Lessing's thought with Blake's. Professor Pratt shows the relevance of Blake's *The Marriage of Heaven and Hell, Jerusalem,* and *Songs of Innocence and Experience* in her essay "The Contrary Structure of Doris Lessing's *The Golden Notebook.*" Professor Sprague has alluded to Lessing's Blakean affinities in "Without Contraries is no Vision: *The Four-Gated City* and *The Dispossessed,*" a paper delivered at the 1978 MLA Doris Lessing Special Session, and in "'Without Contraries is no Progression': Lessing's *The Four-Gated City,*" *Modern Fiction Studies*, 26 (Spring 1980), 96–116.

23  Minda Bikman, "A Talk with Doris Lessing," pp. 26, 24.

24  See Annemarie Schimmel, *Mystical Dimensions of Islam*, p. 14.

25  Ibid., p. 141, in her chapter "The Path," pp. 98–186.

26  Ibid., pp. 132ff.

27  Evelyn Underhill, *Mysticism: A Study in the Nature and Development of Man's Spiritual Consciousness*, 3d ed. (London: Methuen, 1912), p. 206.

28  Ibid., p. 206.

29  Annemarie Schimmel, *Mystical Dimensions of Islam*, p. 147, quotes the Persian proverb *hamu ust*, which Schimmel traces to the poet 'Attar.

30  Doris Lessing, *The Making of the Representative for Planet 8* (New York: Alfred A. Knopf, 1982).

31  Doris Lessing, *The Four-Gated City*, p. 591.

32  Doris Lessing, *The Golden Notebook*, p. xvii.

33  Roland Barthes, "From Work to Text," in Josué V. Harari, ed., *Textual Strategies: Perspectives in Post-Structural Criticism* (Ithaca, N.Y.: Cornell Univ. Press, 1979), p. 76.

34  Doris Lessing, *The Golden Notebook*, p. 59.

# Selected Bibliography

## NOVELS BY DORIS LESSING

*The Grass Is Singing.* London: Michael Joseph, 1950; New York: T. Y. Crowell, 1950. Rpt. New York: Popular Library, 1976.

*Martha Quest.* [*Children of Violence,* Vol. I.] London: Michael Joseph, 1952; New York: Simon and Schuster, 1964. Rpt. New York: New American Library, 1970.

*A Proper Marriage.* [*Children of Violence,* Vol. II.] London: Michael Joseph, 1954; New York: Simon and Schuster, 1964. Rpt. New York: New American Library, 1970.

*Retreat to Innocence.* London: Michael Joseph, 1956; New York: Prometheus, 1957.

*A Ripple from the Storm.* [*Children of Violence,* Vol. III.] London: Michael Joseph, 1958; New York: Simon and Schuster, 1966. Rpt. New York: New American Library, 1970.

*The Golden Notebook.* London: Michael Joseph, 1962; New York: Simon and Schuster, 1962. Rpt. New York: Ballantine Books, 1973.

*Landlocked.* [*Children of Violence,* Vol. IV.] London: MacGibbon and Kee, 1965; New York: Simon and Schuster, 1966. Rpt. New York: New American Library, 1970.

*The Four-Gated City.* [*Children of Violence,* Vol. V.] London: MacGibbon and Kee, 1969; New York: Alfred A. Knopf, 1969. Rpt. New York: Bantam Books, 1970.

*Briefing for a Descent into Hell.* London: Jonathan Cape, 1971; New York: Alfred A. Knopf, 1971. Rpt. New York: Bantam Books, 1972.

*The Summer Before the Dark.* London: Jonathan Cape, 1973; New York: Alfred A. Knopf, 1973. Rpt. New York: Bantam Books, 1974.

*The Memoirs of a Survivor.* London: The Octagon Press, 1974; New York: Alfred A. Knopf, 1975. Rpt. New York: Bantam Books, 1976.

*Re: Colonised Planet 5, Shikasta.* [*Canopus in Argos: Archives*, Vol. I.] London: Jonathan Cape, 1979. New York: Alfred A. Knopf, 1979.

*The Marriages Between Zones Three, Four, and Five.* [*Canopus in Argos: Archives*, Vol. II.] London: Jonathan Cape; New York: Alfred A. Knopf, 1980.

*The Sirian Experiments.* [*Canopus in Argos: Archives*, Vol. III.] London: Jonathan Cape; New York: Alfred A. Knopf, 1981.

*The Making of the Representative for Planet 8.* [*Canopus in Argos: Archives*, Vol. IV.] London: Jonathan Cape, 1982; New York: Alfred A. Knopf, 1982.

*The Sentimental Agents.* [*Canopus in Argos: Archives*, Vol. V.] (Projected)


## OTHER MAJOR WORKS BY LESSING

*This Was the Old Chief's Country.* Short Stories. London: Michael Joseph, 1951; New York: T. Y. Crowell, 1952.

*Five: Short Novels.* London: Michael Joseph, 1953.

*Going Home.* Autobiographical essay. London: Michael Joseph, 1957; rev. ed. New York: Ballantine Books, 1968.

*The Habit of Loving.* London: MacGibbon and Kee, 1957; New York: Ballantine Books, 1957.

*Each His Own Wilderness.* In *New English Dramatists, Three Plays.* Ed. E. Martin Browne. Harmondsworth, Middlesex: Penguin Books, 1959.

*Fourteen Poems.* Northwood, Middlesex: Scorpion Press, 1959.

*In Pursuit of the English: A Documentary.* London: MacGibbon and Kee, 1960; New York: Simon and Schuster, 1961.

*Play with a Tiger: A Play in Three Acts.* London: Michael Joseph, 1962. Also in *Plays by and About Women.* Ed. Victoria Sullivan and James Hatch. New York: Random House, 1973, pp. 201–275.

*A Man and Two Women.* London: MacGibbon and Kee, 1963; New York: Simon and Schuster, 1963.

*African Stories.* London: Michael Joseph, 1964; New York: Simon and Schuster, 1965.

*Particularly Cats.* Autobiographical essay. London: Michael Joseph, 1967; New York: Simon and Schuster, 1967.

*The Temptation of Jack Orkney.* Short Stories. London: Jonathan Cape, 1972; New York: Alfred A. Knopf, 1972.

*A Small Personal Voice.* Essays. Ed. Paul Schlueter. New York: Alfred A. Knopf, 1974.


## IMPORTANT INTERVIEWS WITH LESSING

Bannon, Barbara A. "Authors and Editors." *Publishers Weekly*, June 2, 1969, 51–54.

Bikman, Minda. "A Talk with Doris Lessing." *The New York Times Book Review*, March 30, 1980, pp. 24–27.

Driver, C. J. "Profile 8: Doris Lessing." *The New Review* 1 (November 1974): 17–23.

Howe, Florence. "A Conversation with Doris Lessing (1966)." *Contemporary Literature* 14 (Autumn 1973): 418–436. Rpt. in Paul Schlueter, ed., *A Small Personal Voice* (New York: Alfred A. Knopf, 1974), pp. 77–82.

Newquist, Roy. "Interview with Doris Lessing." In *Counterpoint*. New York: Rand McNally Co., 1964, pp. 413–424. Rpt. in Schlueter, ed., *A Small Personal Voice*, pp. 45–60.

Raskin, Jonah. "Doris Lessing at Stony Brook." *New American Review* 8. New York: New American Library, 1970, pp. 166–179. Rpt. in Schlueter, ed., *A Small Personal Voice*, pp. 61–76.

Torrents, Nissa. "Testimony to Mysticism: Interview with Doris Lessing." Trans. Paul Schlueter. *Doris Lessing Newsletter* 4 (winter 1980): 1 ff. Originally published in the Spanish journal *La Calle* 106 (April 1–7, 1980): 42–44.

## CURRENT BIBLIOGRAPHIES

King, Holly Beth. "Criticism of Doris Lessing: A Selected Checklist." *Modern Fiction Studies* 26 (Spring 1980): 167–175.

Pichanik, J., A. J. Chennells and L. B. Rix. *Rhodesian Literature in English: A Bibliography* (1890–1975). Gwelo, Rhodesia: Mambo Press, 1977. Mambo Press, Senga Road, P.O. Box 779, Gwelo, Zimbabwe.

Seligman, Dee. *Doris Lessing: An Annotated Bibliography of Criticism*. Westport, Conn.: Greenwood Press, 1981.

## SELECTED CRITICISM OF LESSING'S WORK

Allen, Walter. *The Modern Novel in Britain and the United States*. New York: E. P. Dutton, 1964, pp. 276–277.

Anon. "Middle-aged Lib." Review of *The Summer Before the Dark*. *Times Literary Supplement*, May 4, 1973, p. 484.

Anon. Review of *Martha Quest* and *A Proper Marriage*. *The New Yorker*, Jan. 30, 1965, pp. 122–123.

Anon. Review of *The Grass Is Singing*. *Times Literary Supplement*, April 14, 1950, p. 225.

Anon. Review of *The Summer Before the Dark*. *Choice*, October 1973, p. 1195.

Barkham, John. Review of *The Grass Is Singing*. *The New York Times*, Sept. 10, 1950, p. 4.

Barnouw, Dagmar. "Disorderly Company: From *The Golden Notebook* to *The Four-Gated City*." in *Doris Lessing: Critical Studies*. Ed. Annis Pratt and L. S. Dembo. Madison: Univ. of Wisconsin Press, 1974, pp. 74–97.

Berets, Ralph. "A Jungian Interpretation of the Dream Sequence in Doris Lessing's *The Summer Before the Dark*." *Modern Fiction Studies* 26 (Spring 1980): 117–129.

Bergonzi, Bernard. "In Pursuit of Doris Lessing." Review of *Children of Violence. The New York Review of Books*, Feb. 11, 1965, pp. 12–14.

Brewster, Dorothy. *Doris Lessing*. New York: Twayne, 1965.

Bromwich, David. "Fiction Round-Up." Review of *The Summer Before the Dark. Commentary* 56 (September 1973): 86.

Brown, Lloyd. "The Shape of Things: Sexual Images and the Sense of Form in Doris Lessing's Fiction." *World Literature Written in English* 14, no. 1 (April 1975): 176–186.

Burkom, Selma R. "'Only Connect': Form and Content in the Works of Doris Lessing." *Critique* 11, no. 1 (1969): 51–68.

Carey, John L. "Art and Reality in *The Golden Notebook*." In *Doris Lessing: Critical Studies*. Ed. Annis Pratt and L. S. Dembo. Madison: Univ. of Wisconsin Press, 1974, pp. 20–39.

Cederstrom, Lorelei. "Doris Lessing's Use of Satire in *The Summer Before the Dark*." *Modern Fiction Studies* 26 (Spring 1980): 131–145.

Clemons, Walter. "The Invisible Woman." Review of *The Summer Before the Dark. Newsweek*, May 14, 1973, p. 118.

Cowley, Malcolm. "Future Notebook." Review of *The Memoirs of a Survivor. Saturday Review*, June 28, 1975, p. 24.

Dalton, Elizabeth. "The Saving Graces of Prose." Review of *Children of Violence. The Kenyon Review* 17 (Summer 1965): 572–573.

Didion, Joan. Review of *Briefing for a Descent into Hell. The New York Times Book Review*, March 14, 1971, pp. 1, 39.

Enright, D. J. "Shivery Games." Review of *The Four-Gated City. The New York Review of Books*, July 31, 1969, p. 22.

Foote, Timothy. "Portrait of a Lady." Review of *The Summer Before the Dark. Time*, May 21, 1973, p. 99.

Gindin, James. *Postwar British Fiction: New Accents and Attitudes*. Berkeley: Univ. of California Press, 1962, pp. 65–86.

Grumbach, Doris. "Rite of Passage." Review of *The Summer Before the Dark. The New Republic*, May 12, 1973, pp. 28–29.

Hardwick, Elizabeth. Review of *The Summer Before the Dark. The New York Times Book Review*, May 13, 1973, pp. 1–2.

Hardin, Nancy Shields. "Doris Lessing and the Sufi Way." In *Doris Lessing: Critical Studies*. Ed. Annie Pratt and L. S. Dembo. Madison: Univ. of Wisconsin Press, 1974, pp. 20–39.

Hardin, Nancy Shields. "The Sufi Teaching Story and Doris Lessing." *Twentieth Century Literature* 23 (1977): 314–326.

Hendin, Josephine. "Doris Lessing: The Phoenix 'Midst Her Fires." Review of *The Summer Before the Dark. Harper's*, June 1973, p. 85.

Hicks, Granville. "All About a Modern Eve." Review of *A Ripple from the Storm, Landlocked*, and *The Golden Notebook*. *Saturday Review*, April 2, 1966, p. 32.

Kaplan, Sydney Janet. "The Limits of Consciousness in the Novels of Doris Lessing." In *Doris Lessing: Critical Studies*. Ed. Annis Pratt and L. S. Dembo. Madison: Univ. of Wisconsin Press, 1974, pp. 119–132.

Karl, Frederick R. "Doris Lessing in the Sixties: The New Anatomy of Melancholy." *Contemporary Literature* 13 (Winter 1972): 15–33.

Lefcowitz, Barbara F. "Dream and Action in Lessing's *The Summer Before the Dark*." *Critique* 17 (December 1975): 107–120.

Lehmann-Haupt, Christopher. Review of *The Making of the Representative for Planet 8*. *The New York Times*, Jan. 29, 1982.

Leonard, John. "More on Lessing." Review of *The Summer Before the Dark*. *The New York Times Book Review*, May 13, 1973, p. 47.

Leonard, John. "The Spacing Out of Doris Lessing." Review of *The Making of the Representative for Planet 8*. *The New York Times Book Review*, Feb. 7, 1982, pp. 1, 34f.

Lurie, Alison. "Wise-Women." Review of *The Summer Before the Dark*. *The New York Review of Books*, June 14, 1973, pp. 18–19.

Magie, Michael L. "Doris Lessing and Romanticism." *College English* 38 (1977): 531–552.

Marchino, Lois. "The Search for Self in the Novels of Doris Lessing." *Studies in the Novel* 4 (Summer 1972): 252–261.

McDowell, Frederick P. W. "The Fiction of Doris Lessing: An Interim View." *Arizona Quarterly* 21 (Winter 1965): 315–345.

Morris, Robert K. *Continuance and Change: The Contemporary British Novel Sequence*. Carbondale: Southern Illinois Univ. Press, 1972, pp. 1–27.

Mudrick, Marvin. "All That Prose!" Review of *Children of Violence* and *The Golden Notebook*. *Hudson Review* 18 (Spring 1965): 110.

Mulkeen, Anne M. "Twentieth Century Realism: The 'Grid' Structure of *The Golden Notebook*." *Studies in the Novel* 4 (Summer 1972): 262–274.

Nyren, Dorothy. Review of *The Summer Before the Dark*. *Library Journal*, March 15, 1973, p. 886.

Porter, Nancy. "Silenced History — *Children of Violence* and *The Golden Notebook*." *World Literature Written in English* 12, no. 2 (November 1973): 161–179.

Pratt, Annis. "The Contrary Structure of Doris Lessing's *The Golden Notebook*." *World Literature Written in English* 12, no. 2 (November 1973): 150–160.

Pratt, Annis. "Women and Nature in Modern Fiction." *Contemporary Literature* 13 (Winter 1972): 476–490.

Rose, Ellen Cronan. "After Touching Rock Bottom." Review of *The Summer Before the Dark*. *The Nation*, Aug. 27, 1973, pp. 151–152.

Rose, Ellen Cronan. "The Eriksonian Bildungsroman: An Approach Through Doris Lessing." *Hartford Studies in Literature* 7, no. 1 (1975): 1–17.

Rose, Ellen Cronan. *The Tree Outside the Window: Doris Lessing's Children of Violence*. Hanover, N. H.: Univ. Press of New England, 1976.

Rubenstein, Roberta. *The Novelistic Vision of Doris Lessing: Breaking the Forms of Consciousness*. Urbana: Univ. of Illinois Press, 1979.

Schlueter, Paul. *The Novels of Doris Lessing*. Carbondale: Southern Illinois Univ. Press, 1973.

Seligman, Dee. "The Four-Faced Novelist." *Modern Fiction Studies* 26 (Spring 1980): 3–16.

Seligman, Dee. "The Sufi Quest." *World Literature Written in English* 12, no. 2 (November 1973): 190–206.

Singleton, Mary Ann. *The City and the Veld: The Fiction of Doris Lessing.* Lewisburg, Pa.: Bucknell Univ. Press, 1977.

Smith, David. *Socialist Propaganda in the Twentieth Century British Novel.* New York: Macmillan Press, 1978, pp. 148–151.

Spacks, Patricia Meyer. *The Female Imagination.* New York: Alfred A. Knopf, 1975.

Spenser, Joanna. Review of *The Grass Is Singing. New York Herald Tribune Book Review*, Sept. 10, 1950, p. 8.

Sprague, Claire. "'Without Contraries is no Progression': Lessing's *The Four-Gated City.*" *Modern Fiction Studies* 26 (Spring 1980): 96–116.

Sprague, Claire. "Without Contraries is no Vision: *The Four-Gated City* and *The Dispossessed.*" Unpublished paper delivered at the 1978 MLA Doris Lessing Special Session.

Thorpe, Michael. *Doris Lessing's Africa.* London: Evans Brothers, Ltd., 1978.

Thorpe, Michael. *Doris Lessing: Writers and Their Work*, No. 230. London: Longman for British Council, 1974.

Vlastos, Marion. "Doris Lessing and R. D. Laing: Psychopolitics and Prophecy." *PMLA* 91, no. 2 (March 1976): 245–258.

Waugh, Auberon. Review of *Briefing for a Descent into Hell. Spectator*, April 17, 1971, p. 534.

Webb, W. L. Review of *Shikasta. The Manchester Guardian Weekly*, Nov. 25, 1979, p. 23.

White, Antonia. "New Novel." Review of *The Grass Is Singing. The New Statesman and Nation*, April 1, 1950, p. 378.

Widmann, R. L. "Briefly Noted." Review of *The Summer Before the Dark. The New Yorker*, June 9, 1973, p. 113.

## SELECTED RELEVANT GENERAL WORKS

Amis, Kingsley. *New Maps of Hell: A Survey of Science Fiction.* New York: Harcourt, Brace & Co., 1960.

Aristotle, *Poetics.* Trans. S. H. Butcher. New York: Hill and Wang, 1961.

Barthes, Roland. "From Work to Text." In *Textual Strategies.* Ed. Josué V. Harari. Ithaca, N.Y.: Cornell Univ. Press, 1979.

Barthes, Roland. *S/Z.* Trans. Richard Miller. New York: Hill and Wang, 1974. Orig. pub. in French as *S/Z* by Editions du Seuil, Paris, 1970.

Booth, Wayne C. *The Rhetoric of Fiction.* Chicago: Univ. of Chicago Press, 1961.

Brecht, Bertolt. *Brecht on Theatre.* Ed. John Willett. London: Methuen, 1964.

Brereton, Geoffrey. *Principles of Tragedy: A Rational Examination of the Tragic Concept in Life and Literature.* Coral Gables, Fla.: Univ. of Miami Press, 1968.

Buckley, Jerome. *Season of Youth: The Bildungsroman from Dickens to Golding.* Cambridge: Harvard Univ. Press, 1974.

Burke, Kenneth. *A Grammar of Motives.* Berkeley: Univ. of California Press, 1945.

Butor, Michel. *Inventory: Essays by Michel Butor.* Ed. Richard Howard. New York: Simon and Schuster, 1968.

Camus, Albert. *The Myth of Sisyphus and Other Essays.* Trans. Justin O'Brien. New York: Alfred A. Knopf, 1955.

Engels, Frederick. *Anti-Dühring: Herr Eugen Dühring's Revolution in Science.* 3d ed. 1894. Moscow: Foreign Languages Publishing House, 1962.

Fletcher, Angus. *Allegory: The Theory of a Symbolic Mode.* Ithaca, N.Y.: Cornell Univ. Press, 1964.

Freud, Sigmund. *Beyond the Pleasure Principle.* Trans. James Strachey. New York: Liveright, 1950. Orig. pub. in German in 1920.

Goethe, Johann Wolfgang von. *Wilhelm Meister's Apprenticeship.* Trans. Thomas Carlyle. 1824; rpt. New York: The Heritage Press, 1959.

Goffman, Erving. *Frame Analysis: An Essay on the Organization of Experience.* New York: Colophon Books, Harper & Row, 1974.

Hassan, Ihab. *Paracriticisms: Seven Speculations of the Times.* Urbana: Univ. of Illinois Press, 1975.

Heilman, Robert B. "Tragedy and Melodrama: Speculations on Generic Form." In *Tragedy: Vision and Form.* Ed. Robert W. Corrigan. San Francisco: Chandler Publishing, 1965. Orig. pub. in *The Texas Quarterly*, Summer 1960, pp. 36–50.

Jacobi, Jolande. *The Psychology of C. G. Jung: An Introduction with Illustrations.* New Haven: Yale Univ. Press, 1943.

Jaffé, Aniela. "Symbolism in the Visual Arts." *Man and His Symbols.* Ed. Carl G. Jung. Garden City, N. Y.: Doubleday, 1964, pp. 230–271.

James, William. *The Principles of Psychology.* 1890; rpt. New York: Dover Publications, 1950.

Jung, Carl G. *Four Archetypes.* Trans. R. F. C. Hull. Princeton: Princeton Univ. Press, 1970.

Jung, Carl G. *Modern Man in Search of a Soul.* 1933; rpt. New York: Harvest Books, Harcourt Brace & Co., 1955.

Ketterer, David. *New Worlds for Old: The Apocalyptic Imagination, Science Fiction, and American Literature.* Bloomington: Indiana Univ. Press, 1974.

Labriola, Antonio. *Essays on the Materialist Conception of History.* Trans. Charles H. Kerr. Chicago: C. H. Kerr & Co., 1908.

Laing, R. D. *The Politics of Experience.* 1967; rpt. New York: Ballantine Books, 1970.

Lukács, Georg. *The Theory of the Novel: A Historico-philosophical Essay on the Forms of Great Epic Literature.* Trans. Anna Bostock. Cambridge, Mass.: The M.I.T. Press, 1971. Orig. pub. in German in 1920.

Marx, Karl. *A Contribution to the Critique of Political Economy* (1859). Trans. S. W. Ryazanskaya. New York: International Publishers, 1970.

Marx, Karl. *Capital: A Critical Analysis of Capitalist Production*. Vol. I. London: S. Sonnenschein, 1889.

Michell, John. *The View Over Atlantis*. London, 1969; rpt. New York: Ballantine Books, 1972.

Moskowitz, Sam. *Explorers of the Infinite: Shapers of Science Fiction*. Westport, Conn.: Hyperion Press, 1974.

Nicholson, Reynold A. *The Mystics of Islam: An Introduction to Sufism*. 1914; rpt. New York: Schocken, 1975.

Nietzsche, Friedrich. *The Will to Power*. Trans. Walter Kaufmann and R. J. Hollingdale. New York: Vintage Books, 1968.

Pascal, Roy. *The German Novel: Studies*. Manchester: Manchester Univ. Press, 1956.

Perry, William J. *Children of the Sun*. London: Methuen, 1927.

Rees, D. A. "Platonism and the Platonic Tradition." *The Encyclopedia of Philosophy*. Ed. Paul Edwards. 1967 ed.; rpt. 1972.

Richter, David. *Fable's End: Completeness and Closure in Rhetorical Fiction*. Chicago: Univ. of Chicago Press, 1974.

Sacks, Sheldon. *Fiction and the Shape of Belief: A Study of Henry Fielding with Glances at Swift, Johnson, and Richardson*. Berkeley: Univ. of California Press, 1964.

Sacks, Sheldon. "Golden Birds and Dying Generations." *Comparative Literature Studies* 6 (September 1969): 274–291.

Sartre, Jean-Paul. *Nausea*. Trans. Lloyd Alexander. New York: New Directions, 1959.

Schimmel, Annemarie. *Mystical Dimensions of Islam*. Chapel Hill: Univ. of North Carolina Press, 1975.

Scholes, Robert. *Fabulation and Metafiction*. Urbana: Univ. of Illinois Press, 1979.

Scholes, Robert. *Structural Fabulation: An Essay on Fiction of the Future*. Notre Dame, Ind.: Univ. of Notre Dame Press, 1975.

Shah, Idries. *The Sufis*. Garden City, N. Y.: Doubleday, 1964.

Shah, Idries. *The Way of the Sufi*. New York: E. P. Dutton, 1970.

Smith-Diehl, Katharine. *Hymns and Tunes — An Index*. New York: Scarecrow Press, 1966.

Stapledon, Olaf. *Last and First Men: A Story of the Near and Far Future*. 1930; rpt. Hammondsworth, Middlesex: Penguin Books, 1963.

Suvin, Darko. *Metamorphoses of Science Fiction: On the Poetics and History of a Literary Genre*. New Haven: Yale Univ. Press, 1979.

Tennyson, G. B. "The Bildungsroman in Nineteenth-Century Literature." In *Medieval Epic to the "Epic Theater" of Brecht*. Ed. Rosario P. Armato and John M. Spalek. Los Angeles: Univ. of Southern California Press, 1968, pp. 135–146.

Todorov, Tzvetan, *The Fantastic: A Structural Approach to a Literary Genre*. Trans. Richard Howard. Cleveland, Ohio: Case Western Reserve Univ. Press, 1973. Orig. pub. in French as *Introduction à la littérature fantastique* by Editions du Seuil, Paris, 1970.

Todorov, Tzvetan. *The Poetics of Prose.* Trans. Richard Howard. Ithaca, N. Y.: Cornell Univ. Press, 1977. Orig. pub. in French as *La Poétique de la prose* by Editions du Seuil, Paris, 1971.

Underhill, Evelyn. *Mysticism: A Study in the Nature and Development of Man's Spiritual Consciousness.* 3rd ed. London: Methuen, 1912.

Von Däniken, Erich. *Chariots of the Gods: Unsolved Mysteries of the Past.* New York: Putnam, 1969.

Watkins, Alfred. *The Old Straight Track.* London: Methuen, 1925.

Williams, Raymond. *Keywords: A Vocabulary of Culture and Society.* New York: Oxford Univ. Press, 1976.

Wollheim, Donald A. *The Universe Makers: Science Fiction Today.* New York: Harper & Row, 1971.

# Index

216

Psychic abilities, 51, 64, 65, 148, 149. *See also* Extrasensory powers

Pynchon, Thomas, 106

Quest. *See* Images: Grail, quest

Racism, 3–7, 11–24, 34, 36, 38, 40–43, 73, 158, 178. *See also* Anti-Semitism

Rationalism, 132, 141, 146

Reader, 72, 87, 89, 91–93, 103–5, 112–15, 117, 123, 129, 130, 133, 139, 141–44, 146, 149, 150–52, 157, 158, 160, 161, 164, 165, 168–70, 174, 176, 179, 181–84

Realism. *See* Genres and modes: realism

Reality, material *vs.* ideal, 32, 33, 79, 80, 82. *See also* Ideal; Idealism

Rebellion, 26, 44, 47, 49, 53

Receptivity, 47, 58, 65, 94, 135. *See also* Evolution

Recognition, 6, 9, 21–25, 87, 99, 102, 103, 126, 150. *See also* Awakening

Redemption, 23, 24, 67, 77, 90, 155, 159, 177. *See also* Deliverance

Relativism, 76, 77, 85, 86, 179–81

Remembrance, Sufi concept of, 34, 60, 99–104. *See also* Forgetting, Sufi concept of

Repetition, 9, 10, 52, 53, 65, 137, 139, 196*n9*. *See also* Determinism; Will

Repression, 16, 18, 19, 59, 60, 81, 125, 126, 162. *See also* Sex

Responsibility, 6–12, 17, 23, 24, 37, 40, 85, 129, 173. *See also* Determinism; Will

Revelation, 23, 178, 181. *See also* Deliverance; Messenger

Richardson, Samuel, 108, 112

Richter, David, 103, 104, 106, 107, 109

Roles, as limiting, 10, 14, 24, 37, 41, 49, 84, 111, 126, 132. *See also* Women, role of

Romance. *See* Genres and modes: romance

Romantic(ism), 31–33, 35, 39, 47, 73, 74, 78–83, 85, 86, 132. *See also* Idealism; Platonic thought

Rose, Ellen Cronan, 192*n12*, 194*n25*, 195*n6*, 196*n10*

Rousseau, Jean Jacques, 31, 33

Rubenstein, Roberta, *xii*, 109, 129

Sacks, Sheldon, 106, 107, 109, 112

Salvation, 23, 88, 108, 117, 132, 136, 151, 155, 159. *See also* Deliverance

Sartre, Jean-Paul, 72, 73, 82

Savior, 48, 83, 109, 154. *See also* Messenger; Messiah

Schimmel, Annemarie, 164

Schlueter, Paul, *xii*

Scholes, Robert, 109, 134

Science fiction. *See* Genres and modes; science fiction

Self: inner, 111–18, 123, 124, 127; search for the, 111, 112, 120, 122, 125, 129. *See also* Individual: self-development of

Self-consciousness, 40, 72

Self-control, 83, 163

Self-deception, 27, 34, 38, 79, 116

Sex: aversion to, 9, 14–16, 18, 20; fear of, 43; obsession with, 15, 19; repression of, 15–19 *passim*; social control of, 37, 42–45. *See also* Sexual; Women, role of

Sexism, critique of, 9, 11, 22, 37, 42–44, 111–30 *passim*

Sexual: attraction, 20, 23, 97, 98, 119, 165; energy, 43, 57, 58; fantasy, 54; freedom, 43; tension, 15, 20, 170. *See also* Sex

Shabistari, Mahmoud, 92

Shah, Idries, *xiv*, 64, 65, 92–94, 101, 102, 184

Shakespeare, William, 22, 48

Shelley, Percy Bysshe, 33

Singleton, Mary Ann, *xii*

Smith, Barbara Herrnstein, 103

Socialism, 37, 51. *See also* Communism; Left, politics of the

Spacks, Patricia, 47, 67

Sprague, Claire, 196*n10*

Stapledon, Olaf, 147, 152, 154

Stendhal, 26, 31–33, 47, 70

Structure, fictional, *xiv*, 4, 7, 8, 17, 21, 23–25, 28, 42, 70–72, 88, 89, 91–95, 117, 129, 132, 133, 139, 141, 144, 150, 179, 181, 184–186, 197*nn6–7*. *See also* Form: literary; Novel within novel

Style: discontinuity of, 110, 143–45; Lessing's handling of, *xii*, *xiv*, 89–94 *passim*, 104, 110, 115, 139, 143, 144, 157, 166, 167, 170. *See also* Contradiction, of fictional elements; Incongruity; Narrative tension

Subjectivity, 30, 72, 86. *See also* Objectivity

Submission, 35, 43, 158, 159. *See also* Power